THE
BREAKFAST
BIBLE

SEB EMINA & MALCOLM EGGS

with Emily Berry, Richard Godwin, Henry Jeffreys, Peter Meanwell

B L O O M S B U R Y
LONDON • NEW DELHI • NEW YORK • SYDNEY

*To G. Muratori on Farringdon Road, which was the best greasy
spoon in London until it closed in sad circumstances early in 2012.
Thank you for providing a place to meet and compare notes over
sausage, egg and bubble.*

MENU

THE FULL ENGLISH 15

CLASSIC RECIPES 93

DRINKS 207

ESSAYS

AN INTRODUCTION

IN 2005 SOME FRIENDS AND I started a website called The London Review of Breakfasts. We loved going out for breakfast but had recently been faced with a lot of bad ones (limp bacon, lukewarm tea, apathetic egg...). Because nobody in the dinner-obsessed media was writing about the day's foremost meal, we thought it would be fun to do so ourselves. Especially if we wrote using pen names made from breakfast puns like Blake Pudding, Tina Beans and Malcolm Eggs. One morning, I went online, wrote a few words about the pleasures and pitfalls of eating out for breakfast, and the website was born.

Strange things began to happen. People I didn't know got in touch, enquiring whether they too might assume secret identities and share their morning-meal experiences. They weren't just writing from London, but from far-flung places such as Ohio, Iraq and Surbiton. Reporters started calling, asking for quotes about the decline or resurgence of the British fry-up. On planes and in pubs, everyone to whom I mentioned the subject wanted to tell me their breakfast routine ('I have this *unbelievable* poached egg method...') in meticulous detail, bordering on confessional. Increasingly it felt as though we had hit on something big: a vast, untapped reservoir of emotion, hidden in plain view, in the way we eat this bacon-and-eggy, marmaladey meal. Could it be, I wondered, that breakfast really is the most important meal of the day?

My interest in the subject began to mushroom. It was no longer enough to find excellent places that served breakfast; I wanted to understand what it meant. Have we always eaten the same thing at breakfast-time? What do they eat in India, China and the Middle East? How the hell do people make croissants? Why is the first pancake from a given batch always so unfortunately shaped? As the questions stacked up, they began to look like the contents page of a book – one that ought to have been written but somehow hadn't. A collection of facts, stories and flighty theories, but above all a practical book, one that brought together classic breakfast recipes from Britain and beyond. I discussed it with the network of contributors who now populated The London Review of Breakfasts. We agreed it would be enjoyable to create it: a handbook for the breakfast-eating community. In other words, just about everyone, with the exception of that baffling subspecies who forswear the meal.

Of course, it wouldn't be the first book to have been written on the subject, and early in the three-year research process (more than a thousand breakfasts were eaten) I was lucky to meet serial breakfaster Tim Hayward, a man who owns history's most important breakfasting books and was happy to see them used for the greater good. We arranged to have waffles in Camden Town. He handed the books over. I lugged them home. Poring through the collection I opened up *Breakfast Dishes* by M. L. Allen, a pocket-sized volume from 1884 detailing one hundred or so expansive spreads such as 'porridge, broiled partridge, Winchester cutlets, poached eggs and bacon, grated ham on toast and strawberry jam'. Then I leafed through *Fifty Breakfasts*, a vaguely famous book from 1904 by Colonel Arthur Robert Kenney-Herbert, a British soldier of the Madras cavalry who wrote under the pen name Wyvern. And there was Evelyn E. Cowie's 1958 effort *Breakfasts*, with a mission 'both to satisfy one's appetite and raise one's spirits'.

The culinary side was, naturally, interesting (broiled *partridge?*) but what I found curious was how all the authors had a problem – the same problem – with how breakfast was consumed. Allen hoped that her recipes would 'greatly facilitate a housekeeper's efforts to vary the usual monotonous routine'. This monotony, she believed, was something of which 'almost everyone complains'. Wyvern nailed it more solidly, declaring that 'the ding-dong monotony of "bacon and eggs" alternated with "eggs and bacon" of many English breakfast tables is wholly inexcusable'. As for Cowie, she made the bold prediction that 'the monotony which has marked the English breakfast for over a century is passing'. Time and time again, it seemed, the breakfast writers of the Western world had spied the windmills of ding-dong monotony, tilted their lances, and charged.

And then what? Was the tyranny of repetitious breakfasting swept away in a wave of heightened awareness, a Breakfast Spring? Look around you. Eggs and bacon. Cereal with semi-skimmed milk. Rocketing sales of porridge and yoghurt. As the centuries of sleepy mornings have mounted up, we've been deciding that, actually, we would like less choice. In 1660, the gluttonous diarist Samuel Pepys described a hungover breakfast of 'Mackrell, newly-ketched', 'cold turkey pie and a goose' and a 'coller of brawne'. Who today would whip that up before getting the train to the office, the bus to the classroom or the tractor to the field?

What if, when it comes to breakfast, monotony is a good thing? What if it gives us an opportunity – for once, in these choice-crazy times – to focus on improving what's there, rather than worrying about what might have been there instead? Here are the breakfast foods: there aren't many, but let us make them as good as we can. Let each fried breakfast be like a different performance of the same play, and every stack of pancakes arrive like a rendition of one of those blues songs so old and familiar that no one remembers who wrote them any more. When was the last time you heard someone complain about how monotonous and predictable it is when, first thing in the morning, they are greeted by a sunrise?

Winnie the Pooh knew what was what. Here's one of his conversations with Piglet:

'When you wake up in the morning, Pooh,' said Piglet at last, 'what's the first thing you say to yourself?'
'What's for breakfast?' said Pooh. 'What do you say, Piglet?'
'I say, I wonder what's going to happen exciting today?' said Piglet. Pooh nodded thoughtfully.
'It's the same thing,' he said.

* * * * *

The sun is always rising somewhere, which means breakfast is always just about to happen. Dinner time in Timbuktu is breakfast time in Brisbane. Wherever you are, whatever you are doing, there is a person in the world right now at this moment in the buffoonish zone between waking and breakfasting. Yawning. Considering a dream, then – wham! – the instinctive realisation that twelve hours have passed since food was last encountered.

This unknown breakfaster gets out of bed, performs a few hygiene- and clothing-related tasks, then eats. In the Middle East, she may enjoy piping-hot, mashed fava beans. In Hong Kong, he might sip *yuanyang*, a tea-coffee combination whose name refers to the conjugal love of Mandarin ducks. Wherever you go, the wonderful monotonies of morning food are played out in a slightly different way that reflects the idiosyncrasies of both a place and its people.

When we (fellow LRB contributors Emily Berry, Richard Godwin, Henry Jeffreys, Peter Meanwell and myself) began exploring the international breakfasting classics, we wondered whether there was a common thread to be found, some universal stamp of breakfasthood that always appears, whatever the culture. It turned out not to be eggs, toast or cereal. It is very hard to draw a straight line through congee, fried seaweed and pop tarts. In fact, the theme was a familiar one – repetition, or, as Wyvern would have complained, one thing alternating with another. But whereas the old books railed against this, the world is in favour. If we like breakfast, it's because of the way in which, in the small variations we make – banana or blueberries with our pancakes? Feta or halloumi on our *shakshuka*? – we get to quietly reveal who we are.

Abraham Lincoln, for example, had one boiled egg and a cup of coffee. Queen Elizabeth I had beer with mutton stew. Napoleon had tea or 'orange water' followed by chicken with onions. Bruce Lee had muesli. For the rich and powerful, breakfast offers a moment of peace and predictability before the ruling, warring or filming begins once more. But what important insights we could gain about their inner psyches if only we knew how they customised it: the preferred runniness of Abraham's yolk, Bruce's muesli-to-milk ratio, the specific shade of orange that Napoleon required of his orange water.

* * * * *

Today we are constantly being told that there is no free time in the morning. Modern life is just too busy: breakfast should be taken on the move or at a desk – that's the message. It means that breakfast has somehow turned into an act of defiance (admittedly one that's more pleasurable than handcuffing yourself to a government railing). We have too easily forgotten the wise advice of Henry Wheeler Shaw: 'If you have to work before breakfast, eat your breakfast first.'

He was right. There should always be time for breakfast. You have time to sit down for twenty minutes, with your family or by yourself, and enjoy bacon and eggs, biscuits and gravy, toast, kedgeree, *sucuklu yumurta* or yoghurt and granola. There needs to be time in the morning to read the paper, listen to the radio, have a conversation or just think freely. A better word for ding-dong monotony is 'ritual', and I hope this book will be helpful when it comes to the gently radical ritual of eating breakfast in the twenty-first century.

Incidentally, when did you last invite someone over for breakfast? Never forget what a powerful gesture it can be. Thomas Babington Macaulay observed that 'Dinner parties are mere rituals; but you invite a man to breakfast because you really want to see him.' People know this, which is why few things can cement a friendship or indeed a relationship more firmly than a shared breakfast. Indeed, if the invitation is delivered skilfully enough, the consequences can be profound:

Jesus said to them, 'Come and have breakfast.' Now none of the disciples dared ask him, 'Who are you?' They knew it was the Lord.

That's John 21:12. Now, come and have breakfast.

Seb Emina, London

THE
FULL ENGLISH

THE MAGIC NINE

THERE HAVE ALWAYS BEEN two kinds of breakfast: the everyday and the event. The latter tends to correspond with weekends, lottery wins, gold records and so on, but will hopefully be enjoyed whenever the mood and time present themselves. The former will have a constant base (toast, yoghurt, porridge) to which elements (Marmite, banana, walnuts) are added, most often to a formula similar to that of the day before. Both are wonderful. We don't want to make some morally underhand analogy involving the difference between a spouse and a lover – but if we did, we would.

The most iconic of all the event breakfasts is the one the international hotel chains call a 'full breakfast', that glorious imperial echo of bacon, eggs, sausages, toast plus whatever produce talks of relevant surrounding agriculture or cuisine, from cockles in sea-swept Wales to grits from the cornfields of the Deep South. There's the full English, the full Scottish, the full Welsh, the full Cornish, the Ulster fry, the American 'country breakfast' and, if we just want a 'cooked breakfast' (another hotel term), whatever mini-variation we desire.

We coined the term 'Magic Nine' in 2007 to define the cabal of ingredients that comprise the breakfast we know better than any other, the full English. It was identified, if we're honest, through decades of looking at Batman-esque 'ker-powww' shapes on the walls of greasy-spoon cafés. Many of its members are shared with the greats of other nations; the great Western cooked breakfast can't be straitjacketed by anything so simple as a recipe. It's better thought of as a sort of culinary Lego set whose satisfaction lies in the choices we make. Here are the building blocks of the full English breakfast.

EGGS
BACON
SAUSAGES
MUSHROOMS
TOMATOES
BLACK OR
WHITE
PUDDING
TOAST
BAKED BEANS
POTATOES

EGGS

IT'S HARD TO THINK of anything more original than the egg. As an ingredient, it's a category unto itself, a halfway house where the vegetarian comes a shell's breadth from the ultimate compromise. It's a miracle of nature and a pagan icon: 'this commodity,' observed Auguste Escoffier, 'which the ancients considered as a symbol of the world.' But on a Tuesday night, as the vaguely sci-fi box joins milk and spaghetti in our shopping basket, we don't really think of eggs in these terms and it's hard not to doubt whether the ancients did either as they moped around their ancient shops. 'Sure as eggs is eggs,' say our grandmothers, which is to say eggs are an everyday staple, not the basis of a new cult – unless it's a breakfast cult, because whatever they are, eggs mean breakfast. Sausage, mushrooms and eggs? Breakfast. Sausage and mushrooms? Who cares.

Whatever status they gave them, the ancients would have experienced eggs very differently to us, sourcing them from the nests of the red junglefowl, the wild predecessor of the domesticated chicken. Even the breakfast books of a century ago are filled with once everyday techniques that we've somehow forgotten, such as 'buttered eggs' (a buttery ancestor of scrambled), 'eggs in the dish' (heated between a hot plate and the flames of a grill) and 'golden eggs' (boiled and then rolled in breadcrumbs). The modern full English seems to have settled for three: fried, scrambled and poached.

Or has it? The choice-powered diners of the US cater for a mini-universe of fried-egg preference, ranging from the legendary ('sunny side up') to the niche ('over medium'). Scrambled eggs can mean anything from a creamy cascade to a fistful of boingy omelette pieces. As for poaching, it is often carried out in a way that we suspect is more accurately described as 'coddling', although this is hard to prove because nobody, when pushed, really knows what coddling is.

Then there is boiled, the egg as stand-alone breakfast and the recipe we look upon as the basic test of kitchen proficiency. Strangely for such a supposedly simple meal, it insists on keeping everything (except, annoyingly, the shell) in absolute privacy from the chef. Even a cook as resoundingly proficient as M. F. K. Fisher complained that 'there seems to be a plot against us egg boilers... The season, the weather, the hen that laid it, and even the water: they will conspire.'

One thing is certain. When a breakfast includes eggs, they need respect. Every day, somewhere in the world, a breakfast is ruined by underdone white or over-hard yolk or, on freak occasions, both. If an expensive restaurant serves your poached egg a little on the cool side, you have every right never to go back. And a pair fried and served on toast in a café beneath a station arch can feel as though they have made life worth living. Perhaps the ancients had a point.

HOW TO BUY EGGS

More often than not the tastiest eggs of all are advertised by way of a characterful scrawl – 'FReSh egGS' – on a piece of thick card at the side of a country road. These tend to be *very* recently laid, by a friendly chicken, perhaps with a first name, possibly a bank account. They are delicious. In regular shopping situations, meanwhile, the phrase 'fresh eggs' means something completely different: a stale, half-hearted spin on boxes that don't even qualify for the 'free-range' label. Their parent hens will have been stored in the cramped, industrial, hellish cages that have been so effectively documented by campaigners in recent decades.

Not all eggs are laid equal. So if ethics are a concern, by all means buy free-range but don't be under any illusions that this minimum gesture always equates to happy, frolicking poultry. Many producers will do the bare, grudging minimum to achieve free-range status. While it can mean several different things, 'organic' tends to point to a greater standard of welfare. In the UK, look for Soil Association-certified organic eggs to ensure they have been laid by hens that are allowed to be hens, with all the pecking, scratching, strutting and dust-bathing that this entails.

HOW TO STORE EGGS

The ideal spot for your eggs is a cool place away from both direct sunlight and the ambient heat of ovens and kettles. There's usually no need to chill, but if you feel your kitchen doesn't have anywhere else cool enough, store them in the fridge and remove them half an hour or so in advance of cooking; if you don't have half an hour, put them in a bowl of lukewarm water for 5 minutes.

Eggs are highly prone to infiltration from neighbouring smells. Store them away from strong odours like fish and whiffy cheese.

CHECKING FRESHNESS

Every day a tiny amount of the water contained in an egg evaporates through its porous shell, causing it to get lighter. You can check its freshness by placing it in a large bowl of salted water. The further your egg sinks, the fresher it is. If your egg floats to the top, get rid of it. It's over. On the other hand, if it sinks right to the bottom and comes to rest in a completely horizontal position it was laid only a few days ago.

HOW TO FRY EGGS

In a cooked breakfast frying an egg feels like the most correct of all the correct ways because if needs must, around campfires and in overcrowded kitchens, it can be done in a pan along with every other component. Here are four methods – two everyday and two psychotic – to achieve a classic fried egg. Most will agree that this features a firm white, a runny yolk and a complete absence of transparent gloop.

To serve one, you need a free-range egg (the fresher the better, as fresher eggs retain a firmer, perter shape in the pan).

The Café Baste

This is the method greasy-spoon cafés use to create something that the finest restaurants, in all their snootiness, will rarely match.

In a pan over a medium heat, heat 2 tablespoons of oil. Crack an egg into a cup or saucer. When the oil is hot but not quite popping, slide your egg into the pan, using a fish slice to keep the white together if necessary. Wait a minute or so until the white is firm and the egg slides easily around. Tilt the pan, creating a little pool of hot oil, then use a teaspoon to repeatedly spoon small amounts of oil on to the top of the white and yolk. As soon as a whitish-pinkish layer has encased the yolk, serve it up.

For the Distracted Cook

While the Café Baste has the benefit of tight control, there are times – for example on a weekend when all fifteen of the guest bedrooms are occupied – when it's not practical to scrutinise your eggs so closely. Here is a more hands-off method, one that's known in certain US states as 'sunny side down'. It should still ensure the top is done, but watch carefully – hard yolk is a major pitfall here.

Add a tablespoon of oil to a frying pan over a medium-high heat. When the pan is hot, crack your eggs into cups or saucers before gently sliding them in. Reduce the heat to low. Place a lid tightly over the pan. The eggs should be cooked in between 3 and 4 minutes.

Fried Eggs Point

'Butter! Give me butter! Always butter!' Such was the motto of Fernand Point (1897–1955), the Frenchman whose La Pyramide restaurant's three Michelin stars were almost certainly linked to his belief that the simplest dishes are the hardest to perfect. His stock test for potential kitchen employees was to wrong-foot them with the seemingly infantile task of frying an egg. Invariably they'd lose their way and Point would intervene angrily: 'You are making a dog's bed of it!' The only method, as far as he was concerned, involved inordinate amounts of butter and an excruciatingly low heat...

Crack your egg into a small plate or a saucer. Place a sizeable lump (around 15g) of unsalted butter in a pan over a very, very low heat and let it melt but take care not to let it crackle, foam or split. Slide your egg into the pan. Meanwhile, melt another lump of butter in another pan in the same way. When the white is just about creamy and the liquid yolk is hot, the egg is ready for finishing. Point prescribed pouring the second helping of warm butter over the egg once it's on a warm serving plate, but a marginally less heart-scaring effect can be achieved by using just one pan and lightly basting it with the existing butter in a similar way to the Café Baste method opposite.

Fried Eggs Loiseau

Bernard Loiseau was a pupil of Fernand Point and eventually became even more famous and even more of a fried-egg perfectionist (need we spell out the link?). His preferred method involved the temporary separation of yolk and white...

Pre-heat the oven to 250°C/the hottest gas. Crack the shell of your egg but let all of the white ooze out into one container before releasing the yolk into another, taking care not to let it break. Gently melt a knob of unsalted butter plus a teaspoonful of water in an ovenproof frying pan until the butter is just beginning to foam. Slide the white into the pan, then put the pan in the oven for a minute and a half. Gently place the yolk in the centre of the white and return to the oven for a further 2 minutes. Remove and season with salt and black pepper, taking care to keep the yolk entirely clear. Serve with a subtle mention of this process.

FACT: In India, fried eggs are sometimes known as 'bullseye'.

FACT: If in the UK your egg is stamped with the lion mark, subtract twenty-one days from its best-before date to calculate the exact day on which it was laid.

HOW TO SCRAMBLE EGGS

'Scrambled eggs' has commonly come to mean 'murdered eggs', a crook's gallery of rubbery yellow lumps to be wolfed down in a few seconds as a kind of desperate anti-hunger mannerism. At the other end of the spectrum, when it is realised that other ingredients such as milk or chilli can be added, they become a sort of culinary Vietnam War and the fundamental point – the peerless umami of the egg taste – is lost in a sinful quagmire of Tabasco sauce and double cream. Delicious scrambled eggs can in fact be achieved with the addition of handsome amounts of butter, plus some butter.

Classic Scrambled Eggs

Serves 2

5 large eggs

35g unsalted butter

Beat the eggs, oh-so-briefly, so that the yolks are broken and slightly mixed in with the whites, in a large bowl. Heat a non-stick (unless you really have it in for yourself) saucepan for around 30 seconds, then add 25g of the butter, turning the heat down to its lowest setting. When all the butter has melted, pour in the eggs and stir slowly. Keep stirring. When the texture has just thickened but importantly while it is still impossible to make out individual lumps with the naked eye, remove swiftly from the heat and stir in the rest of the butter. Season with salt and pepper and then serve ASAP. If the runniness is too much for you, you can extend the stirring time accordingly but really, really, beware – a few seconds make all the difference.

Effortless Genius

Serves 2

5 large eggs

2 tablespoons milk or single cream

25g unsalted butter

Break all the eggs into a large bowl but don't beat them, just add the milk or cream. Melt two-thirds of the butter in a frying pan on a very gentle heat. When the butter is all melted, pour in the eggs and stir, ensuring all the egg yolks break early in the process. Keep stirring and monitoring the mix as it thickens. When the egg whites are just about hardened, stir in the remaining butter. Serve nude, or laced with chopped flat-leaf parsley.

FACT: 'Scrambled Eggs' was the original name for The Beatles' track 'Yesterday', whose chorus ended 'Oh my baby how I love your legs', until Paul (presumably) decided that sadness and regret would sell more records than breakfast.

HOW TO POACH EGGS

Ask anybody who knows how immaculate poached eggs are made and a wicked glint appears in their eye. They will tell you it is to do with some kind of 'vortex' or sacrificing a chicken to Brigid, the patron saint of poultry farmers. But really all you need is heat, water, a little distilled vinegar and – very importantly – the freshest eggs you can find.

Impeccable Poached Eggs

Fill a pan with water to the point where it would just cover a broken egg. Stir in 2 teaspoons white wine vinegar. Bring it to the boil, then turn down to a gentle simmer. Lower your egg, still in its shell, into the water using a tablespoon. Gently and slowly turn it for around 15 seconds, then remove from the water (this controlled exposure will begin the congealing process, helping to prevent the broken egg from dispersing everywhere). Crack it into a saucer, then gently slide the egg into the pan, towards the edge. Simmer slowly until the white is set, which should take no more than 4 minutes. Remove with a slotted spoon and allow the water to drain back into the pan for a few seconds, then lightly dab the egg with kitchen paper to remove any excess liquid.

Perfectionists may also wish to trim away any ragged edges with a pair of scissors, but be quick as nobody likes cold egg more than untidy egg.

HINT: You can poach eggs before they are needed and store them in a bowl of iced water. Simply heat them up by placing them for around 15 seconds in a pan of gently simmering water.

SONGS TO BOIL AN EGG TO

Lower a large, room-temperature egg into simmering water, then a moment afterwards, start playing a song from the list of rock and pop classics below, chosen according to your specific runniness needs. Move it around a bit at the beginning of each verse. Remove when the song ends.

For a very soft egg:

The Beatles... 'Dear Prudence'
Madonna ....'Express Yourself'
Aztec Camera.................................... 'Somewhere in My Heart'

For a classic soft-boiled egg:

Kate Bush... 'Wuthering Heights'
The Rolling Stones.............. 'You Can't Always Get What You Want'
Roxette...'Listen to Your Heart'

For medium-boiled:

Bob Dylan .... 'Like a Rolling Stone'
Pulp.. 'Common People'
Queen ....'Bohemian Rhapsody'

For hard-boiled:

Pink Floyd.................................... 'Alan's Pyschedelic Breakfast'
Meatloaf.. 'I'd Do Anything for Love
(But I Won't Do That)' (album version)
The Doors .... 'The End'

HOW TO BOIL EGGS

Boiling an egg is *almost* a recipe that consists entirely of its name. Great, you think, I need to put the egg into something boiling and... Wait! An egg sets at a temperature of 71.1°C. Avoid boiling eggs in water at full boil, as it will give them a hard, rubbery texture that is less delicious and less digestible. A gentle, trembling simmer is best.

Boiling an Egg the Classic Way

Professional chefs will often specify 3 minutes for a boiled egg, or even 2 ½. This is not just kitchen machismo: a boiled egg will continue to cook even when removed from water and there will be a delay from the moment of boiling to the moment it reaches a customer's table. The times below assume a domestic setting in which an egg will be served immediately, that it will begin the process at room temperature and that it is what the supermarket will classify as 'large'.

Fill a pan with enough water to completely submerge your egg or eggs. Add a pinch of salt (this is not for flavour, it's a precaution – if your egg cracks, it will help keep the white inside the shell). Bring the water to the boil, then turn it down to a simmer. Before you lower in your egg, warm the shell in the steam for a few seconds. Depending on how soft or hard you want your egg, cook for between 4 and 12 minutes:

4 minutes .... very soft-boiled (yolk very runny, white a bit runny too)
5 minutes .... classic soft-boiled (yolk runny, white just a little runny)
6 minutes .. medium-boiled (yolk creamy with firm tinge, white not runny)
12 minutes .... hard-boiled (yolk and white not runny at all)

VARIATIONS: Size: For a medium egg, subtract a minute. For an extra large egg, add a minute.

Altitude: The higher you are above sea level, the lower the boiling point of water. Cooking time will increase accordingly. For every 1,000 metres' height, you should increase cooking time by 25 per cent. For locations below sea level, apply the same principle in reverse.

Gentlemanly Boiled Eggs

This alternative method is based on various recipes found in the great breakfasting cookbooks of the Victorian era, before rock music had been invented. It gives a gently whitened albumen and a lovely, runny yolk.

Bring a pan of water to the boil. Use the steam to warm the shell of each egg before lowering it in. Cover the pan and immediately remove it from the heat. Leave for 8 minutes (losing a minute for a medium egg and adding one extra for a large egg). Serve in an antique egg cup.

HOW TO BAKE EGGS

Being beyond the so-called 'eggs any style' of most cafés, baked eggs are useful when you need to impress difficult guests or revive a friendship, or possibly a marriage. But they are also ridiculously easy and can be spruced up by throwing in extras such as spinach or truffles, or chopped fresh herbs like flat-leaf parsley or tarragon.

One form of baked eggs is *en cocotte*, or eggs baked in individual ramekins. Preheat the oven to 200°C/gas 6. Boil the kettle. Lightly butter as many ramekins as there are eggs to be cooked, then break an egg into each. Atop the yolk, gently install a piece of butter. Season with salt and pepper. Place the ramekin/s in a baking tin and put the tin in the oven, on a central shelf. Pour boiling water into the tray so that it's about half full. Bake for 15 minutes and you'll have a clutch of individual servings. Serve as soon as you can.

You can evolve this formula to lovely effect by introducing other components to the inside of the ramekin. Try pieces of cooked black pudding or raw, chopped asparagus. Experiment with alternative toppings to butter too: cream and thick Greek yoghurt will each add a new dimension.

HOW TO CODDLE EGGS

'It's so vague and nobody really knows what it's all about,' said Father Ted. He was talking about Catholicism, but he might as well have been talking about coddled eggs. Depending on what you are reading, they are defined as everything from 'very lightly cooked eggs' to 'eggs prepared in a certain kind of container' to eggs boiled in an off-heat method. Both Cordon Bleu in the 1980s and Mrs Beeton in the 1880s concluded that whatever they are, they are 'ideal for invalids'. It's telling that Alexander Filippini's 1893 treasure trove *One Hundred Ways of Cooking Eggs* contains not a single nod to the practice; nor in fact does *Larousse Gastronomique*. We have divined the following methods.

Molly-coddled Eggs

Crack your egg into a cup or small glass. Fill a small frying pan with water, stir in a teaspoon of white wine vinegar and bring it to the boil. Turn off the heat and then slide the egg into the water, gently using a spoon to preserve the integrity of the white. Cover the pan. Leave alone for 10 minutes.

Jolly-coddled Eggs

Break the egg into a buttered ramekin or similar-sized container. Half-fill a frying pan with water, then bring it to the boil before turning down to a gentle simmer. Place the container in the water, then cover the pan. Leave for 5 minutes.

HOW TO MAKE AN OMELETTE

You know you're in a great hotel when, while scouting the breakfast buffet, you stumble across a dedicated omelette chef wedged in amongst the muffins and juice jugs. To those who claim an omelette is not a breakfast food we say: if it wasn't a breakfast food why would it be *on the payroll*?

Beyond the luxuries of international chain hotels, however, a side effect of salmonella-related runnyphobia is that we in the West tend to overdo our omelettes, wolfing down rubbery creations with little consideration for the oozy joys we are missing.

Basic Omelette Method

A proper omelette pan is preferable but you can live without one. Whatever the pan, the ideal diameter is 20–23cm in diameter. For an omelette for one, beat three eggs in a bowl with a fork, then stir in a tablespoon of water, a bold pinch of salt and a few brisk grinds from a pepper mill. Heat a pan, add 15g unsalted butter and when it starts to froth, pour in the egg. Leave alone for a minute or so, then swill the pan around a little, lifting up the edges of the omelette with a fork so that a certain amount of the runny yolk on top finds its way down to the surface of the pan. When the omelette is about three-quarters firm and one-quarter runny, fold it over, tilt the pan and gingerly shuffle it on to the plate.

Ham, mushrooms, bacon, tomatoes, sometimes spinach and occasionally onion are the core breakfast omelette ingredients and can – in conjunction with the sort of common sense that forbids 'bacon with ham' – be combined pretty much as you will. Many will fry ingredients for a while before pouring the egg over them, creating a frittata-style medley. However, for most breakfast omelettes, a better result will be had by preparing your filling elsewhere and then just folding the omelette over it at the final stage, ensuring everything is exactly right, without the eggy faction of your omelette interfering with the other lot. Notable exceptions to this rule are ham and chopped fried bacon, which are for some reason more pleasing if mixed in with the beaten egg at the very beginning.

French Omelette Method

From the grandest Parisian hotel to the lowliest lorry drivers' stop-off, the French seem to have a knack for raising the simplest of omelettes to the finest of cuisine – a fluffy, runny, cigar-shaped delicacy. Here's the trick.

For a one-person omelette, beat three eggs in a bowl with a fork. Heat a pan (20–23cm is the ideal diameter), add the butter and when it starts to froth, turn the heat up and quickly pour in the egg. Hold the pan in your left hand and a fork in your right. Use the flat of the fork to frantically stir the egg while at the same time quickly shaking the pan back and forth. After about 45 seconds, when the egg has just begun to set, turn off the heat. Lift the pan and tilt it away from yourself and use the fork to fold the near side of the omelette, but only as far as the centre. Then shake the pan slowly and steadily, shuffling the far lip of the omelette up against the rim of the pan and back in on itself. Serve with the seam facing down – a perfect yellow cylinder of delight.

A NOTE ON BRUNCH
by Poppy Tartt

Brunch is eternally conflicted. Is it breakfast, or is it lunch? Apparently coined as a portmanteau word in the UK in an 1895 *Hunter's Weekly* article by writer Guy Beringer, brunch was conceived as 'a new meal, served around noon, that starts with tea or coffee, marmalade and other breakfast fixtures before moving along to the heavier fare'. This seems fairly clear to us. But in fact, notions about brunch and what it should consist of differ considerably. The term may have originated in Britain but as a meal in its own right brunch is given a lot more time of day, in all senses, in America and Australia. These are places where the *'unch* in brunch really comes into play. We're talking about a meal that might feature *salad*, for goodness sake.

In the UK, more often than not, brunch is breakfast by any other name. Because we like breakfast so much, we don't want it ever to stop. And we definitely don't want to risk missing it, as Beringer well knew when he insisted: 'By eliminating the need to get up early on Sunday, brunch would make life brighter for Saturday night carousers.'

The best brunches encompass many of breakfast's standard-bearers – bread, eggs, meat from the pig and caffeinated drinks. OK, so the odd international breakfast ingredient might make an appearance – feta cheese, hollandaise, rösti – and the overall impression might be fancier, but this meal is not fooling anyone. It's breakfast with more time, more flexibility and a bigger table to spread the newspapers on. The *br'* in brunch is the *brooom* of a motorbike, revving us up and off, through lunch and beyond. It is our contention that brunch is a meal invented to extend and celebrate breakfast, and do away with lunch altogether.

BEYOND HENS' EGGS

Well, isn't it a wonderful coincidence that the eggs of mankind's favourite farmyard bird are also the most suited to the breakfast table. Size, flavour, texture, usability: the hen's egg gets a standing ovation in all categories. But just as the fact that you love crumpets does not mean you won't dabble in English muffins from time to time, there is pleasure to be found in other kinds of eggs.

Quails' Eggs: Quails' eggs are notable for a higher ratio of yolk vs white. They are a staple of Chinese medicine. Soft-boil quails' eggs by placing them in a pan of cold water, turning on the heat and then removing as soon as the water has boiled. Alternatively, for fun and novelty value, they can be fried or poached in much the same way as hens' eggs, obviously with a more delicate touch and a far shorter cooking time. Scrambling quails' eggs is not time well spent.

Duck Eggs: These are a meatier alternative containing indecent amounts of golden yolk. There have been much-disputed rumours that they also offer an increased salmonella risk, but a well-known private restaurant in London served duck eggs Benedict, month after month, without a single problem.

Others: Goose eggs, turkey eggs, ostrich eggs, gulls' eggs: they all have differences in size, texture, taste, but in terms of cooking method, the same principles apply as those listed above.

BACON

FOR CENTURIES, BACON has been Britain's favourite meat. It's one of the top reasons we are so fond of our homeland. The word 'bacon' originally referred to pork in general, but eventually came to refer exclusively to the back or belly of a pig when salted, smoked or both. Domestic pig-rearing was so common in early Anglo-Saxon times that bacon was used as a form of currency. In Shakespeare's *Henry IV*, peasants are referred to as 'bacon' on account of the amount they eat, while Piers Plowman in the eponymous fourteenth-century poem bewails his poverty by lamenting: 'And by my soul, I say, I have no salt bacon!'

Until the Industrial Revolution, bacon was prepared annually with the slaughter of the pigs at Martinmas (11 November), the traditional beginning of winter. The whole family would help salt the flitches (sides) and make hams, sausages, blood puddings and other delicacies from the rest of the animal. All parts were used 'save the squeak', according to a popular saying. Pigs such as the Tamworth were bred specially for their bacon, while Gloucestershire and Wiltshire became noted areas of production.

Bacon cured in those times would have contained around six times the amount of salt that we use today and been far fattier – fat meat preserves better than lean, so pigs were especially plumped up for purpose. Refrigeration and changing health concerns have reduced the salt and fat content, and pig-keeping is rare (though the government tried to revive it during the Second World War). Supermarkets are dominated by Danish brine-cured bacon, but renewed pride in our culinary heritage has ensured that quality native bacon is now readily available. An interest in heritage breeds has seen rare swine, such as the delicious Gloucester Old Spot, rescued from near extinction to bounce once again.

It is fair to assume that bacon found its way on to the breakfast plate purely because it was there hanging in the larder. So happily did it combine with the similarly available eggs – the salty meat coming on so boisterously to the blushing yolk – that the dish spread fast. In *The English Housewife* (1615), Gervase Markham gives a recipe for 'Best collops and eggs' (collop being the old word for a rasher). He advises soaking the bacon, 'for that will take away the extreme saltness', before slicing off the collops and putting them in a dry pewter dish and setting them before the fire 'so as they may toast through and through'. He recommends poaching the eggs (with vinegar) and laying them on the bacon, concluding 'and in this sort you may poach eggs when you please, for it is the best way and most wholesome'.

Bacon remains the most popular meat in Britain and North America. It is the last temptation of the vegetarian and the Jew. It is the subject of a daft craze on the internet, in which enthusiasts compete to produce the most outlandish bacon recipe, incorporating it in anything from cupcakes to chewing gum. It is worth fighting for. As J. B. Priestley put it: 'We plan, we toil, we suffer – in the hope of what? A camel load of idols' eyes? The title deeds of Radio City? The empire of Asia? A trip to the moon? No, no, no, no. Simply to wake up just in time to smell coffee and bacon and eggs.'

FACT: The phrase 'bringing home the bacon' has its origins in pig wrestling, a popular sport at country fairs. The prize for capturing a pig greased in oil is the pig itself – thus the bacon is brought home.

FACT: The Monday before Ash Wednesday is also known as 'Collop Monday'. It's a day when supplies of bacon are traditionally eaten with eggs, in preparation for Lent.

BREAKFAST PROVERBS

A sleepy fox has seldom feathered breakfasts .... Latin/Romanian

Sing before breakfast and you'll cry before supper .... English

If you pour tea on hot rice at breakfast, you will
never advance in the world .... Japanese

Dawn does not come twice to awaken a man .... Arabic

He who doesn't clean his mouth before breakfast
always complains that the food is sour .... African

If you eat a late breakfast, you will go to a closing market ...... Korean

Marriages are all happy, it's having breakfast
together that causes the trouble .... Irish

A nod frae a lord is a breakfast for a fool .... Scottish

No breakfast for the dear one, but a luncheon
for the strangers .... Kashmiri

Rails split before breakfast will season the dinner ... American Southern

If you eat it up at supper, you cannot have it at breakfast ...... Spanish

Eat breakfast alone, share lunch with a friend,
give supper to your enemy .... Russian

Though breakfast be good, dinner is better .... Chinese

The orphan does not rejoice after a heavy breakfast .... Ghanaian

If I were not even to eat breakfast I should be an infidel .... Hindustani

Who has wine for dinner, he has water for breakfast .... Bosnian

Rather go to bed supperless than
run in debt for a breakfast .... American, attrib. Benjamin Franklin

HOW TO BUY BACON

There is a great deal of nasty bacon around: squelchy, slithery, sinister rashers that have been injected with water and God knows what else and weep white discharge into the pan. The pig was made for a nobler fate. As a simple rule, the happier the pig, the happier he or she will taste. Organic or independently reared bacon is worth the extra money. Britain has relatively high standards of pig welfare and rich pork traditions, so our native bacon is preferable to most imported varieties. Once you have established a reputable pig source, there are three principal variables to choose from: the cut, the cure and the smoke.

The Cut: Bacon is made from the two flitches (sides) of the pigs, running from the back, down the sides to the belly underneath. It is sold in two cuts: the leaner back (loin) and the fat-streaked belly (known as streaky bacon). Both are common in Britain, while in the US streaky rashers are near ubiquitous but back is eaten as 'Canadian bacon', and sold without the stalk of fat. Scottish Ayrshire bacon uses the whole strip, cured off the bone and rolled up in on itself, so that each sliced rasher has a distinctive pinwheel form.

The Cure: A side of bacon can be cured in one of two ways, dry (by rubbing salt, sugar and nitrates such as saltpetre into the flesh) or wet (by soaking in brine). The dry way is more traditional, but though the latter method is more common in industrialised processes, it is not an anachronism – since the mid-nineteenth century, the famous Wiltshire cure has used brine.

Cures vary in saltiness, sweetness and aromatics, with maple, juniper berries, coriander and star anise often added for flavour. Suffolk sweet-cured bacon, prepared with brown sugar, caramelises beautifully in the pan; traditional Welsh bacon takes a heavy salting.

The Smoke: Once the flitch of bacon has been salted and hung, it can be smoked according to preference – often the farmer will just do the salting, leaving it to the wholesaler to smoke or not. Broadly speaking, we prefer a smoked, dry-cured streaky rasher.

HOW TO MAKE BACON

It is satisfying to prepare bacon at home: not only do you come into kinship with your ancestors, but you end up with loads of bacon. It is possible to make all kinds of bacon at home, but the easiest is dry-cured, unsmoked streaky. Since you're not using chemical preservatives, the finished product will be saltier than regular supermarket bacon. It will also lose its colour when cooked, but in recompense, you can moderate the flavouring to achieve your perfect cure.

500g table salt
150g soft brown sugar
1 fatty pork belly (preferably organic)

Dry aromatics
15g pink peppercorns
15g black peppercorns
15 juniper berries

Wet aromatics
Maple syrup
Treacle

Prepare the cure. In a non-metallic tub of some sort, mix the salt, sugar and dry aromatics.

Slice your belly into two or three squares for ease of handling. Now rub each piece of belly with as much cure as you can get on there, on all sides. (You will have cure left over, which you keep.) Put the belly pieces into a sealed non-metallic box in the fridge. Ensure that your fridge is not on its coldest setting and that the bacon is not in the coldest part of the fridge – or the cure won't take.

Wait. After 12 hours or so, take the bellies out. The cure will have leached out a yellowy liquid. Tip this in the sink and brush the old cure off. Now add some new cure. Repeat this process over five days, morning and night. On the last day, you might like to add some maple syrup, or perhaps a bit of treacle to the cure, to give it a nice finish. When the belly is stiff and dry, rinse off the remaining cure and pat dry with a clean tea towel.

You can keep the belly hanging in muslin if you have a cold larder, or in the fridge, wrapped in muslin or greaseproof paper. Take thin slices when you need them. It will keep for a few months, and is excellent in soups, stews and salads as well as fried with a lovely egg.

HOW TO COOK BACON

Unless you are idiotic enough to countenance a microwave, you will either use a frying pan or a grill to cook your bacon. It is very difficult to mess up, provided you keep an eye on it: when Gervase Markham mentioned bacon in his list of fricassées, he noted 'the frying whereof is so ordinary that it needeth not any relation'. To be sure, however...

Frying

Medium heat; no oil if the bacon has any fat content (only add a little vegetable oil for the leanest back). Turn when appropriate; depending on the thickness, it will be ready in 4–10 minutes. If frying with egg, the bacon should go in first, and the heat reduced when the egg joins the pan. If the bacon oozes brine, dab it away with a piece of kitchen paper and brand yourself with a hot spatula for having bought poor bacon. Don't really do this: just buy better bacon.

Grilling

Medium heat; turn halfway through (usually between 3 and 6 minutes, depending on cut and preferred crispiness). This is the healthier way, as it allows much of the fat to run away, but it will come down to taste as to which is the more delicious. In both cases, it is worth dabbing the cooked rasher with kitchen paper before serving to remove excess fat.

SAUSAGES

SAUSAGES WERE INVENTED by some far-sighted genius seeking ways of preserving meat and using up those tricky bits of offal. The word comes from the Latin *salsus*, which means salted. However, in English, sausage has come to mean meat packed into a casing that may be salted, smoked, air-dried, pre-cooked or cooked from fresh.

The pungent smokiness of the Spanish *chorizo*; the bulbous smoothness of the German *Bratwürst*; the toothsomeness of the French *toulousaine*; the Polish *kabanos*, the Moroccan *merguez*, the *lap cheong* of China, the suspicious cylinders of Russia – each is lovely in its own way, but no match at breakfast for the sausage prepared by a ruddy British butcher from pork shoulder and belly, breadcrumbs, water and herbs.

Most British regions lay claim to their own special recipes, which vary in the proportions of meats, the coarseness of the grind and the niceties of spicing. The Frenchman will claim superiority in that most French sausages are 100 per cent meat, but in fact it is the high fat content and distribution of cereal matter that ensure the succulence of the British sausage. Moreover, the contrast between that succulence and the outer crispiness is a significant factor in its primacy. We would like to make the case for an internationally recognised OCIS scale (outer crispiness/inner succulence) to measure the excellence of a sausage. With an OCIS factor of around 2.4 oinks to the squeak, for instance, the British sausage triumphed quite comfortably at a recent test held in highly rigorous scientific conditions around a North London hob.

FACT: One of the first comedy plays was *Orya*, or 'The Sausage', written by the Greek dramatist Epicharmus in around 500 BC. Even though the full text has not survived, the title by itself is funnier than most other comedy plays.

HOW TO BUY SAUSAGES

It's just not worth scrimping on sausages. The legal minimum meat content for a pork sausage is a scandalously low 42 per cent – and that 'meat' can include 30 per cent fat and 25 per cent 'connective tissue' – so less scrupulous manufacturers will pump their bangers full of sulphites and sawdust, guar gum and gizzards. The serious breakfaster shouldn't put up with economy meats, though occasional exceptions may be made for certain grades of hangover and the friendlier kind of greasy-spoon café.

When choosing your own sausages for cooking, look for a short, comprehensible list of ingredients and a high meat content (upwards of 80 per cent). However, do not assume that a sausage boasting 95 per cent meat will be superior to one containing a higher proportion of breadcrumbs or rusk, which are vital to the character and the texture of the British banger. In all cases, independent, organic producers are recommended.

There are many kinds of sausage. No one knows exactly how many, but the figure is estimated to fall between the number of B flats in Beethoven's Second Piano Concerto and the instances of the letter 'n' in Flaubert's *Madame Bovary*. It would be insane to list all known sausages here and slightly pointless too, for apple and leek, beef and ale, jalapeño and cheese – these novelties have no place on the breakfast plate. Indeed, the fried-breakfaster can narrow the field to six native varieties and two adopted foreigners.

Pork 'breakfast': Sausages sold as breakfast sausages are typically pork spiced with nutmeg, cloves and pepper, with no herbs. All good butchers will have a standard. It is a friend of ketchup and the classic sandwich banger.

Cumberland: A speciality of the north-west. Traditionally it has a very high meat content, is served in a coil rather than traditional links and is flavoured with marjoram, nutmeg and pepper, though sage often makes an appearance. The lion of the full English.

Lincolnshire: A county once overrun by pigs and amateur sausage-makers has given its name to a classic sausage made with coarse meat and flavoured with sage. It is a particular friend of brown sauce.

Gloucester: An important centre for pork for centuries, Gloucester is home to the eponymous Old Spot (a fat breed, reared on grain, whey and apples), which has lately been revived. The sausages made locally are often of exceptional quality – a superior consort in a full English.

Toulouse: From the French south-west, this is made solely of meat (no rusk), which is very coarsely chopped, resulting in a more rugged tube. Good baked with tomatoes and mushrooms.

Chorizo: The now ubiquitous paprika-seasoned Spaniard is making demands on breakfast chefs – its smoky, salty, toothsome flavour makes it a sort of easyJet take on bacon. Unsuitable for a full English, it's delicious fried with eggs, tomatoes and green peppers for a rakish Mediterranean fricassée.

Glamorgan: A meatless sausage, 'not a whit inferior to those of Epping', according to one sampler in 1862. Made with an approximate ratio of 2:1 breadcrumbs to cheese, flavoured with leek, onion, mustard powder and chives, it is a very agreeable vegetarian option.

Lorne: A Glasgow speciality and an essential component of the Scottish breakfast. Made from equal proportions of beef mince and fat (pigs being less common in Scotland), it's set in a special Lorne tin, turned out, cooled, sliced into squares and fried with eggs.

HOW TO COOK SAUSAGES

Agnes C. Maitland, in *What Shall We Have for Breakfast?* (1901), wrote: 'The ordinary English method of dressing sausages is to fry them in their own fat, or to cook them in a tin before the fire. In either of these modes of cooking they must not be considered done until they burst. They should be served on toast.'

Her prescription of toast is good, but sausages should not be allowed to burst. Sausages first became known as bangers during the Second World War, when the high water content of inferior sausages caused them to explode on the heat. The practice is not encouraged.

Should we fry, grill or bake? Each method has its advantages and drawbacks. The German method of boiling, and then finishing off in the fryer, has gained some currency recently, but while it's a sensible precaution to boil before barbecuing, it seems needlessly fiddly at breakfast. One rule holds true for all methods: never, but never, prick a sausage. See that delicious, flavoursome, juicy fat seeping out into the pan? That's the sausage crying.

Frying

The perfectionist's method – and for a fried breakfast you will surely be using a frying pan anyway. The sausage goes in a minimal coating of oil on the lowest possible heat. Aim for a 30–40-minute slow cook, depending on thickness, turning only every 10 minutes or so. If the sausage does not split – splitting is a sign of a poor sausage anyway – the fat will remain within and you will be rewarded with a sticky, juicy delight, slightly caramelised.

Grilling

The supposedly healthier method – though provided you don't prick, there is no real difference. Put the grill on a hot heat, put the sausage underneath and cook for 15–20 minutes, turning occasionally for even cooking.

Baking

The easy method – and it's useful to have the oven on if you are preparing a complicated fry-up for a lot of people. Heat the oven to 180°C/gas 4, put the sausages in a heatproof dish and cook for 30 minutes. This method can result in a dry sausage, so be careful not to overdo the little blighters.

HOW TO MAKE SAUSAGES

Is it worth making one's own sausages? We concur with the wisdom of Ma Maitland: 'It is seldom worth while to prepare sausage-meat at home, as sausages of excellent quality can be purchased almost everywhere.' That said, making sausages is an outrageously enjoyable activity if you like getting your hands on a pile of meat and intestines. There are tricky moments, but as the meat squeezes into the skins and you twist off an unending series of snags, you feel like the complete master of your own breakfast.

Having got the hang of this, you can experiment with ingredients to your heart's content. As long as you keep to the correct fat/meat ratio, you can even vary the type(s) of meat involved – a tasty sausage can be made from lamb, beef or even game. If you can mince it, you can make a sausage out of it.

Meat, Fat, Skins, Flavour

Sausage ingredients aren't hard to find, but you'll need to make a trip to the butcher: most supermarkets don't stock the skins and in any case a butcher will be able to provide you with a wider range of cuts.

The key to a good sausage is achieving the right ratio of meat to fat. You should aim for about 60 per cent of the former to 40 per cent of the latter. Buy the best meat you can afford. The right mix can be achieved in several ways, but the classic fat for sausages is back fat, quite simply the fat that comes between the skin and the meat on the back. It's the smoothest, most edible fat you can get from a pig. Mix it with some lean pork shoulder. Your butcher will likely have some of both. If you can't find back fat, try mixing equal amounts of lean shoulder and belly pork, although getting the ratio right will take a bit of experimentation.

When it comes to skins the choice is between natural casings (in other words, intestines) or artificial collagen casings, which will give your sausages a crisper outside. Unless you're super squeamish (this seems unlikely if you're making bangers from scratch), the intestines are the way to go – nature's perfect container. They come salted, so they will need soaking in fresh water. Pig intestines, or 'hog casings', make good hearty fat sausages, and are more robust. Lamb intestines make thin chipolata-type sausages (their slender nature requires a bit more care in the handling).

In terms of flavourings, the world is your proverbial oyster (in fact, Cumbrian sausages used to be made with literal oysters). A good traditional sausage has some savoury spices – white pepper, mace and sage, for example – plus a little greenery, such as fresh thyme and rosemary or a little leek.

The last thing to remember is some breadcrumbs, the secret to keeping the sausages succulent. These can be easily made from any leftover stale bread: just blitz it in a food processor or use a grater. About 10 per cent of meat weight works well.

Mince and Stuff

So far so simple, but it's what comes next that prevents many of us from becoming accomplished sausage-smiths. Getting the meat into its snug little house requires kit. At the high end, you can invest in an electric mincer/stuffer that will not only mince the meat but also push the mix straight into the skin. At £170 upwards, this is a big investment for the first-time *saucissonière*. There are also hand-cranked mincer/stuffers that will set you back about £25; or, at a stretch, you can adopt a nice voice, ask your butcher to mince the meat and fat for you, and use the DIY 'icing bag method' to push your mix. In this most manual of methods, a plastic funnel is inserted into an icing bag in place of its default star-shaped nozzle. The bag is packed with sausage filling, skin is then threaded on to the funnel, and brute force is used to transfer filling from bag into sausage skin.

Whichever kit you choose, mince your meat and fat to a coarseness of your preference, add the herbs and spices, salt the meat (around 1 teaspoon per 500g of filling), toss in the breadcrumbs, roll up your sleeves and mix well with your hands. If you're feeling particularly thorough you can then pass the mix back through the mincer. At this stage fry a little of the mix in a pan and have a taste, adjusting the seasoning if necessary.

Once your meat is ready, the challenge of the skin is all that stands between you and your golden sausages. Having soaked the salted skin overnight, run cold water through it, to check for any holes, and to give it a final wash. Like (and we apologise for this simile, but it's the best one) slippery prophylactics, it needs threading gently on to the nozzle of your stuffer. Bunch the whole length up, checking that there is no air trapped at the end, and leave some skin spare at the end to knot later. Then slowly feed in the meat mix, creating a giant 'mother sausage'. As you push it through, be careful not to over-stuff, as this can lead to splitting, but equally you don't want air pockets to form. Like all good things, the process can take a little while to get the hang of, but you soon get a feel for the right meat-pushing pace.

Knot

Stop filling the casing in time to leave a good length at the end where it meets the stuffer. Tie a strong double knot at the other end (remember that spare skin you kept back?) and work through the mother sausage back towards the stuffer, twisting it at regular intervals into your desired link lengths. It's a bit like making a balloon animal. Be extra careful not to break the skin: twist gently, letting the meat push back towards the stuffer. Once you've reached the end, double knot, and you've created your string of sausages.

A Breakfast Sausage Mix

Although striving to create your own signature banger is part of the joy of sausage-making, this recipe may prove a useful springboard for your creativity. For a fresh perky breakfast sausage, this mix is loaded with herbs, and has a beguiling lemony zing. Use hog casings, twisted off into fat little snags about 8cm long.

Makes 8 short fat sausages
500g meat (60% lean pork shoulder, 40% back fat)
50g breadcrumbs, made from any stale bread
1 teaspoon salt
½ teaspoon ground mace
½ teaspoon freshly ground white pepper
½ teaspoon ground coriander
2 teaspoons grated lemon zest
2 tablespoons chopped parsley
2 teaspoons thyme leaves
4 teaspoons chopped sage
1.2m hog casings

Sausage Patties

There is a special something about a sausage and its plump juicy goodness, but it's not always practical to spend time stuffing meat tightly into narrow skins. If you want a decent shortcut, try a sausage patty, which allows you some of the fun of creating your own, without the intestine-based hassle. Minced pork is lean, so adding the streaky bacon ups the fat content. Breadcrumbs help keep it moist, and you can vary the spices, or add more herbs to taste.

Makes 4 patties
3 rashers smoked streaky bacon
250g minced pork
20g breadcrumbs, made from any stale bread
¼ teaspoon freshly ground white pepper
¼ teaspoon ground coriander
¼ teaspoon ground mace
½ teaspoon salt
1 large handful flat-leaf parsley, finely chopped
1 tablespoon thyme leaves, finely chopped
1 tablespoon sage leaves, finely chopped
2 teaspoons olive oil

Dice the bacon rashers as finely as you can, and mix all the ingredients except the oil together in a large bowl. Combine well with your hands using a kneading motion, until everything is combined and the meat has a smooth texture.

Divide the mixture into four, and shape into circular patties of an even thickness. Heat the oil in a heavy-based frying pan, and cook the patties over a medium heat for 20 minutes, turning halfway through.

MUSHROOMS

THE CULTIVATED MUSHROOM, available at any time of year, is a relatively new phenomenon, but the mushroom as a breakfast food is not. The autumn bounty of field mushrooms has always been available to the skilled forager, and what we have gained in convenience we have sacrificed in taste.

The Chinese were the first to bend mushrooms to their will, using oak logs for shiitake cultivation as early as the thirteenth century. The French cracked the common white mushroom 300–400 years later, but their methods were kept a tight secret, and it wasn't until the late twentieth century that British mushroom farming brought the prices down to fry-up-friendly levels. Even so, the ubiquitous plastic punnet, tightly gripped in plastic film, so often contains fifty pallid ghosts of what a mushroom should be.

This is partly why the mushroom is a breakfast component that many will reject, usually lobbing around slug comparisons as they barter for extra toast – but maybe there's a deeper influence at work. Louis Krieger, a mycologist for the New York State Museum in the 1930s, described fear of mushrooms as something 'innate in all of us'. It was traceable, he suggested, to some distant ancestor, who 'coming upon these seemingly unplant-like plants called mushrooms, doubtless stopped short until through sheer curiosity, and urged by hunger, he made a meal of the first pretty cluster of mushrooms he found in the woods and – was killed'.

For all their variety, every mushroom belongs to one of two categories. There are those that are commercially cultivated and therefore widely available in all seasons: Portobello, chestnut, common mushrooms – the ones you'll normally use for your cooked breakfast. Then there are those that will only grow wild and need to be sought out in season from organic-smelling shops and soft bearded men at farmers' markets. These are the penny buns, the chanterelles and the hickory chickens – wayward, poetic cousins to the workmanlike cultivated fungus.

When it comes to the wild kind it's worth considering a bespoke approach to your Magic Nine breakfast. The bolshy flavours of pork and tomato are likely to drown out its delicate flavours – so out go bacon, sausages, black pudding, tomato and beans. Then, with only four ingredients left, a smart breakfaster considers two carbs to be one too many… Ah, having booted out potato you are left with wild mushrooms and scrambled eggs on toast, one of the best breakfasts in the world.

FACT: Mushrooms are neither plants nor animals. Fungi form a separate group, or kingdom, of organisms, which also includes yeasts and, less appetisingly, mould.

CULTIVATED MUSHROOMS

White, Common, Button (*Agaricus bisporus*): These, the most common of the commercial mushrooms, are the pale mass-produced specimens lying in their thousands in large tubs; the ones you'll find at the newsagent on a token shelf near the magazines. Sometimes they will actually taste of mushroom but more often they're present purely as a good intention. Season them heavily and serve as part of a wider breakfast.

Chestnut, Crimini, Portobello (*Agaricus bisporus*): In the same species as the mushrooms above, you will find chestnut and Portobello mushrooms – the thinking man's *Agaricus bisporus* – and crimini or 'portobellini' mushrooms. These are marked out by a juicier texture, an alluring deep brown hue and a denser, nuttier taste, and – in the case of Portobellos – excellently generous proportions. Use in omelettes, on toast, or in any combination of the Magic Nine.

Shiitake (*Lentinula edodes*): Tastewise a bit like a condensed square mile of Japanese woodland – in a good way. These slightly slippery, chewy mushrooms are intense and meaty, lifted by a good grind of salt and pepper into the heights of mushroomy (alas, no other word will suffice) bliss. The flavour and texture, not to mention the completely wrong cultural associations, make them a touch incongruous in a full cooked breakfast. A better use is in a starring role: in an omelette, on toast or in a pared-down breakfast of, for example, smoked back bacon, mushrooms and scrambled eggs.

WILD MUSHROOMS

Field or Meadow (*Agaricus campestris*): Our word 'mushroom' is derived from *mousseron*, which is French for 'field mushroom'. In the days before the mass cultivation of *Agaricus bisporus*, *A. campestris* was the mushroom of the people, collected from the open fields and then eaten immediately: field mushrooms pass their best very quickly. In flavour terms this is to the common mushroom what free-range organic chicken is to its battery-farmed equivalent. Seasonal in summer and autumn.

Penny Bun (*Boletus edulis*): Large, cartoonish mushrooms with amusingly bulbous stalks that come in about twenty edible varieties. Delicious and succulent and a prime choice for a breakfast omelette. *Ceps* in French and *porcini* ('piglets') in Italian. Seasonal in autumn.

Chanterelle (*Cantharellus cibarius*): The champagne of mushrooms: beautiful to look at, delicious to consume, impressive to own and vaguely French. These elegant bugle-shaped mushrooms need to be savoured, centre stage, or if served as part of a wider cooked breakfast, then with ingredients of a deserving quality. Cook gently so as to avoid hardness. The chanterelle season runs from late summer to late autumn.

Morel (*Morchella elata/esculenta*): Prized by mushroom-hunters, battled over by chefs, the sublime and rare morel has more names than a Dutch designer drug: morchella, dryland fish, sponge mushroom, miracle, hickory chicken. It is the state mushroom of Minnesota. The intricate honeycomb-esque caps can hold a fair bit of dirt so should be brushed carefully and, if particularly dirty, briskly washed. It's also poisonous when raw. Cook as a centrepiece, not as a side, using oil. The morel season is spring.

Truffles (*Tuber magnatum*: white, *T. melanosporum*: black): Caviar, really big wristwatches, truffles: symbols of the decadent old wealth that allows one to do one's weekly shop in the food hall at Fortnum & Mason. Both white and black truffles can transform half a dozen eggs by being placed in the box (or if they have no box, then amongst them in a covered bowl) for a day. The scent infuses the eggs. Scramble those eggs, grate a white truffle on top, and it will be obvious why the ancient Egyptians saw mushrooms as 'food from heaven'.

SOME OTHER EDIBLE MUSHROOMS

Amethyst deceiver, beefsteak, chicken of the woods, fairy ring champignon, field blewit, giant puffball, green-cracked russula, grisette, hedgehog fungus, horn of plenty, horse mushroom, Judas' ear, matsutake, oyster mushroom, pavement mushroom, pig's trotter, pom-pom, the prince, shaggy ink cap, saffron milk cap, St George's mushroom, sticky bun, umbrella mushroom, velvet shank, wood ear.

SOME POISONOUS MUSHROOMS

Death cap, destroying angel, false chanterelle, false morel, fool's mushroom, fly agaric, panther cap, red-staining inocybe, shaggy pholiota, sulphur tuft, the sickener, woolly milk cap, yellow stainer.

HOW TO STORE MUSHROOMS

When storing wild mushrooms you need to achieve a balance. Leave them exposed and they'll dry up and shrivel. Wrap them in plastic and they'll perspire and then rot. A paper bag in the fridge will work, or wrap them carefully in kitchen paper. If they dry out, they're still usable but have now passed out of the breakfast category – see other books for help with stock and flavouring uses.

Pre-packaged mushrooms can be chilled in their container. Once open, eat everything in it as soon as possible.

LAST BREAKFASTS

Oatmeal, sausage, eggs, toast, strawberries
Final breakfast of Ike Turner, 12 December 2007

Twenty-four scrambled eggs, flour tortillas, ketchup
*Last breakfast of Robert Streetman, executed
by the state of Texas on 7 January 2001*

Six large eggs cooked in butter with extra salt, one pound of bacon,
half a pound of sausages, twelve buttermilk biscuits
The daily breakfast of Elvis Presley

Oatmeal porridge with milk, smoked herrings, jacket potatoes, ham
and eggs, fresh bread and butter, marmalade, Swedish bread, tea, coffee
Third-class Breakfast Menu, RMS Titanic, 14 April 1912

Bread and cheese with water
Commoner's breakfast in the Roman city of Pompeii, AD 79

HOW TO PREPARE MUSHROOMS

Most mushrooms, especially cultivated ones, should be cleaned but not washed: use a barely damp piece of cloth or kitchen paper to remove any dirt, or just turn a blind eye. An exception is particularly earthy wild mushrooms or those whose shape may conceal dirt, such as morels: rinse, then dry with some kitchen paper.

HOW TO COOK MUSHROOMS

For a mushroom that is en route to a fried breakfast – or a slice of toast – you'll find sautéing is the best of all methods. It's fast and simple, and you'll achieve a tender, juicy, slightly buttery result. An exception is the Portobello. Its jumbo size and entertaining shape make it a real shame to chop one up. If you wanted small pieces of mushroom, why didn't you just buy some small mushrooms? Keep it whole. Use the grill.

Sautéing

First cut the mushrooms, as per your preference. Wild mushrooms are great whole if they are smaller than, say, the size of a ping-pong ball.

You should use the largest pan you have to hand: applying heat will lead to moisture being released and a bigger surface area helps evade the dreaded creep into stewing territory. Heat the pan for a minute or so over a medium heat then, for every 200g of mushrooms you are cooking, add a knob of unsalted butter and a teaspoon of olive oil, stirring until the butter's melted. Add the mushrooms and a pinch of salt. As juices begin to appear, whack up the heat and stir with not a little vigour.

When all of the liquid has evaporated or been soaked up, turn off the heat, grind on some pepper if you like, and serve.

Grilling Portobello Mushrooms

Turn the grill up to a medium-high setting. While you're waiting for it to heat up, brush the mushrooms lightly with olive oil and season with a little salt. Grill for around 5 minutes on each side.

TOMATOES

THE TOMATO IS SURELY South America's greatest gift to the world. At the very least, it would be in the quarter-finals, along with *el jogo bonito*, the potato, Che Guevara, the Incan Empire, cocaine, Jorge Luis Borges and sexy dancing. A subtropical fruit originating in Peru, the tomato was widespread in the Americas by the time Cortés invaded Mexico in the early sixteenth century. The first tomatoes brought back to the Old World resembled small yellow berries and were first viewed with suspicion, thought to be an aphrodisiac. However, they thrived in climates stretching from France to India and soon became ubiquitous. It is hard to conceive of any of the great cuisines of the world without the acid-sweet tang of the tomato, even that of England, of whose national breakfast it is a vital component.

It is a pity that this foremost of fruits should be so often sidelined on the breakfast plate, underestimated and underdone. The pork products tend to hog the attention, and too many cafés and homes settle for anaemic orbs, hard and joyless. The worst are those insipid little spheres found in the supermarket chilled counter.

However, with a little care the tomato can become, if not the star of the show, then the best supporting player. Often the discerning breakfaster will pare down her assembly to a minimalist combination of eggs, bacon and tomatoes plus toast. A tomato balances the breakfast, adding sweetness and acidity to cut through the fat elsewhere. A breakfast without one is monotonous and even on their own tomatoes truly sing. Sliced tomatoes on garlic-rubbed white toast with a drizzle of good olive oil – an informal version of the Italian *bruschetta* – is about the freshest way to commence a summer's day.

FACT: In France, because of their supposed aphrodisiac qualities, tomatoes used to be known as *pommes d'amour* or 'love apples'. The word 'tomato', meanwhile, comes from the Aztec word *xitomatl*, meaning 'plump thing with a navel'.

A NOTE ON KETCHUP

That ketchup is everywhere is testament to the tomato's innate qualities. The sauce emphasises the sweet-sour-savoury profile of the fruit. However, tomato ketchup on the side of a full English should be taken as a mark of failure. It points to one of three sins: the ingredients are poor (maybe the sausages aren't up to scratch?); the cook has committed an error (punctured the yolk?); or the breakfaster is very hungover (ketchup is quite good for hangovers).

No, in the domain of the full English, the tomato *itself* is the condiment. If it is cooked correctly, there will be no need for ketchup. In a bacon sandwich? Slather the stuff on mercilessly.

HOW TO BUY TOMATOES

When searching for breakfast tomatoes, look for fruit with natural sweetness and convenable size. For example, the beef tomato has its place in a burger, but is too humungous to cook evenly, while in ordinary circumstances, the wee cherry tomatoes are a little fiddly and have a tendency to lose their integrity when cooked. Look for tomatoes somewhere in the middle – plums, Santini and *dolce rosso* are excellent examples. You are after a deep crimson colour and a giving flesh. Once you have your tomatoes home, remove from all packaging and place them in a fruit bowl immediately. Do not on any account store them in the fridge unless you hate tomatoes and want to take some kind of sick revenge on them.

HOW TO COOK TOMATOES

Our advice, if the time and the oven are available, is to go for the roast.

The Regular Roast

Roasting tomatoes whole is the best way to make the most of the flavour. Take two medium tomatoes per person and place in a baking dish upside down. Score a deep cross into the top end and smear a little unsalted butter and some fresh thyme, basil or rosemary inside. Put them in an oven heated to around 180°C/gas 4 – approximately what you would need for sausages – and it should take 25–35 minutes to give a tomato the heat it needs.

The Slow Roast

A really outstanding result can be had if you have a lot of time available. The effect of a very slow roast is a little like those 'sun-blush' tomatoes you find in delicatessens. Slice your tomatoes in half through the middle (never the stalk), season well, including a little sugar in the mix, and lay face up in a baking tray. Scatter a few sprigs of thyme on top if you have some. Cook at 140°C/gas 1 for an hour and a half. Particularly good with salty, home-cured bacon.

The Fry

For the practically minded breakfast chef, the fry remains the most straightforward method. Slice the tomatoes in half through the middle, season with salt and pepper and cook on a medium-low heat face down for 5–7 minutes, turning halfway through so that they finish face up. Butter provides a richer flavour than olive oil. A splash of balsamic vinegar, or a pinch of sugar, will perk up a tired tomato.

The Cherry Fry

Cherry tomatoes need not be sliced for frying. Simply toss them in a little melted unsalted butter or heated oil and gently bounce them around a pan on a medium heat for about 5 minutes, until they begin to burst. Leaving them intact keeps all of the natural flavours inside and allows for an enjoyable mouth explosion.

The Grill

A larger tomato can be cooked under a grill. Slice in half through the middle and lay face up on the grill, seasoned with olive oil, salt and pepper. Cook fiercely at first, close to the heat, to caramelise the surface, then turn the heat down and lower the grill tray. The tomato is cooked when the sides are giving, maybe 20 minutes later.

Tinned Tomatoes

The plum tomato, peeled, tinned in juice and finally untinned, is a fixture of the greasy spoon, where the customer is often given the choice: 'Tomatoes or beans?' In this context the plum tomato can be a welcome addition, even if we usually answer 'Beans, please!' To cook at home, simply heat the contents of a tin of Italian tomatoes in a saucepan for 5 minutes, adding a pinch of salt and sugar and a knob of unsalted butter.

BLACK OR WHITE PUDDING

EACH YEAR AS AUTUMN RUSTLES across Europe, glorious festivals of porcine blood-letting take place as families kill their pigs in preparation for the coming year's banqueting. So that none of the precious animal goes to waste, the first act is to catch the blood, to make that most delicious of products – the *Blutwurst, morcilla, boudin noir, jelito, sângerete*, black pudding – however you call it, the blood sausage.

Today pig slaughter no longer rates as a fun family activity, but the tradition of making and eating blood or black pudding has a long lineage. From as early as 1000 BC Homer's *Odyssey* refers to a sausage made of blood and fat roasted over a fire, whilst Aristophanes' political comedy *The Knights*, some 500 years later, hinges on the antics of a blood-sausage seller of loose morals. The Greeks loved it, and the Romans too, with a recipe for blood sausage cropping up in *Apicius*, the earliest Roman collection of recipes. The Latin love of spiced blood sausages travelled with the Empire, and lingered in medieval Europe's cookery long after Rome's collapse, with recipes appearing throughout the Middle Ages and black puddings cropping up on the table of Henry VIII.

Black puddings originated as a peasant dish, borne of a wise aversion to waste. The blood of the freshly slaughtered pig is reserved and stirred vigorously to prevent coagulation, and mixed with a cereal such as oats, a good helping of fat and spices, and the resultant mixture is poured into the now-cleaned intestines of the pig. Once tied, the pudding is boiled gently and can be stored. At its best there's a crumbly velvety richness to black pudding that captures the very essence of why eating pigs is a thoroughly enjoyable activity.

Black puddings are not for everyone, though, and those possessing a squeamish aversion to eating blood are not alone. For Jews and Muslims both blood and pigs are forbidden. The Jewish Torah is fairly straight down the line ('If anyone eats blood, that person must be cut off from his people') as is the Qur'an ('He hath only forbidden you dead meat, and blood, and the flesh of swine').

For those who are anti-blood but still pro-pig, the white pudding is a reasonable alternative. It sees the intestines stuffed with varying ratios of meat, fat or offal, as well as the cereals and spices of the black version, making a paler, more reserved counterpart. At its simplest the Scots' white or mealie pudding is a hearty mix of oatmeal, onions and beef suet, lightly spiced. Travel south, and by the time you reach Devon and Cornwall, the white or hog's pudding is a much meatier affair, more akin to a highly spiced, oat-speckled sausage – the recipes for which are closely guarded by the few butchers who produce it. The Irish too are particularly fond of the delicacy, which deviates from a Scots mealie pudding with the addition of pork liver, and as James Joyce points out forms a key life-affirming part of an Irish breakfast: 'White puddings and eggs and sausages and cups of tea. How simple and beautiful was life after all!'

FACT: Every year the village of Ramsbottom near Manchester plays host to the World Black Pudding Throwing Championships. Several Yorkshire puddings are placed on a 6-metre-high ledge, and participants attempt to dislodge as many as they can with a single throw of a black pudding.

HOW TO BUY BLACK PUDDING

It's hard to get hold of the raw ingredients for black pudding as current food regulations ban the sale of fresh blood, so unless you have a pig to hand it is sensible to buy it ready made. When buying a pudding, it is preferable to go for smaller sausage-shaped links of pudding, rather than slices of larger ones, which tend towards dryness.

Black puddings have a dedicated following, and there are a range of small producers making gourmet varieties. In the UK, the black pudding tradition is strongest in the north of England and Scotland. In Lancashire it is famed. History tells of a large concentration of pork butchers in the town of Bury during the industrial nineteenth century, and the tradition of black pudding making and selling in the market persists to this day. In Stornoway on the Isle of Lewis, in the Scottish Outer Hebrides, they make the Gaelic black pudding *marag dubh*. The unique recipe draws on the mixed livestock kept by the crofters, and uses sheeps', cows' and pigs' blood, thickened with rough oatmeal. In Ireland, there is a town called Clonakilty in County Cork, where since the late nineteenth century farmhouses have supplemented their incomes by making and selling their version of the gory snack. Most of these black puddings can be bought online.

HOW TO MAKE BLACK PUDDING

If you're slaughtering your own pig, we found some handy advice in Charles Elmé Francatelli's 1852 *Plain Cookery Book for the Working Classes*: 'When a pig is killed, the blood should be caught in a pan, and a little salt must be stirred in with it while yet warm, to prevent its coagulation or thickening.'

For those of us with no pig to slaughter, the best bet is to befriend your local butcher. Back fat and sausage skins aren't always easy to come by on the high street and an amenable butcher will often sell or give you small amounts of each. New regulations mean they are no longer able to offer fresh blood, so unless you can befriend an abbatoir or get your hands on a pig, you'll need to buy dried pigs' blood online and rehydrate it.

Once you've assembled the ingredients, you'll also need the right kit. Old-fashioned cast-iron mincers can be bought relatively cheaply, or you can go the DIY route by way of a wide-mouth funnel and icing bag. As with the sausage recipes, this involves attaching the funnel to the bag instead of the star-shaped nozzle, packing it with blood mixture, attaching the casing and squeezing it all through. This method is a bit more hands on, so be sure to wear an apron and work somewhere that you can wipe clean of blood spatters. The following recipe makes a small number of puddings, but can easily be scaled up by the more ambitious. As with the sausage recipes, a little experimentation will go a long way.

Makes about 8 links of black pudding
2m large hog casings (sausage skins)
50g oatmeal (soaked weight – see method)
50g pearl barley (cooked weight)
¼ teaspoon salt
¼ onion
100g back fat
Pinch each of ground mace, cayenne pepper and ground coriander
40ml single cream
200ml fresh pigs' blood (or reconstituted dried blood)

Soak the sausage skins and, in a separate bowl, a big handful of oatmeal in cold water overnight. Before you start making the puddings, boil the pearl barley with a pinch of salt for around 45 minutes, until it is soft and cooked through.

While the barley is cooking, dice the onion and the fat. In a large pan (big enough to hold all the ingredients), sauté the onion in a quarter of the fat until it softens but does not colour. Add the rest of the fat and cook over a low heat for 5 minutes. Add the spices and, stirring, cook for another minute. Strain the oatmeal, then weigh out 50g, as it will have gained in weight during the soaking, and add it to the mix along with the cream. Cook for a couple of minutes more. The oatmeal should soak up the cream, and the mixture should thicken. Strain the blood through a sieve to remove any congealed lumps, and add to the pan with the pearl barley and cook for a further 5 minutes. Take the mixture off the heat.

You are now ready to fill the skins. Rinse the soaked skins in fresh cold water, to get rid of any final salty residue, and taking one length (usually about 1 metre), tie a double knot in one of the ends. Find the other, open end of the skin, and thread this – slowly, to avoiding splitting it – on to the tapered end of your filling apparatus. The smell of the skins is probably the least pleasant part of the whole proceedings, but you really are getting to grips with a medieval form of cookery.

Once the skin is threaded on to the funnel, with one hand hold the skin to stop it slipping off, and spoon the blood mixture into the filling apparatus. (This can be messy, not to mention slippery, so best to do this over a large bowl in the sink.) The trick is to fill the skin without letting lots of air in and you may need to use a chopstick or spoon handle to poke through any funnel blockages. Try not to over-fill the sausages, and once you have a suitable puddingy length (about 8–9cm) twist the skin and start to fill again. As you near the end of the skin, make sure you leave yourself enough room for a good double knot.

Once the skin is filled, it needs cooking. In as large a pan as you can find, bring water to a gentle boil, and carefully slide in the puddings. To avoid them bursting, pierce each pudding two or three times with a needle to let air out. They should take about 20 minutes to cook. Once they are ready, the liquid leaking out will be a dark brown colour. Carefully remove from the pan, and leave to cool, ideally hung up somewhere. Once dry, they'll keep in the fridge for three to four days.

HOW TO COOK BLACK PUDDING

Any pudding you buy in the shops will have been cooked already, so all that remains is to cut a thick slice with a hot knife, and gently fry in a little oil, in a heavy-based frying pan. Leave the slices undisturbed for a few minutes on each side until the outside has a crust, and the inside is warmed through.

HOW TO BUY WHITE PUDDING

The kind of white pudding you'll be able to buy over the counter is largely determined by where you live. Hog's pudding contains a large ratio of pork to oats and is extremely hard to buy outside the West Country. Mealie pudding, ubiquitous in Scotland, contains little or occasionally no meat at all, being made up of mostly oatmeal and suet. Some but not all butchers in England will sell commercially produced meat- or liver-based oaten white pudding that fits somewhere between the two. Most white pudding varieties can be bought online.

HOW TO MAKE WHITE PUDDING

Hog's pudding is perhaps the white pudding best suited to the breakfast table. It's shaped like a horseshoe, steamed, then sliced and fried. While modern recipes are notoriously hard to prise from the few butchers who make them, here is one based on a method from Thomas B. Finney's 1938 tome, *Handy Guide for the Use of Pork Butchers.*

Makes 2 x 50cm lengths of pudding
500g pork from a fatty part of the animal, hock or hand
(or the usual 60/40% lean meat to back fat ratio)
50g breadcrumbs, made from any stale bread
50g porridge oats
1 teaspoon salt
1 teaspoon freshly ground white pepper
¼ teaspoon ground mace
½ teaspoon cayenne pepper
¼ teaspoon grated fresh nutmeg
½ teaspoon thyme leaves
120cm hog casings

Mince the meat twice for a smooth texture. Thoroughly mix in all the other ingredients (except the casings). Having soaked the casings overnight, stuff as per the sausage recipe on p.44, but instead of creating lots of little links, twist into two long puddings, each about 50cm long, and shape each into a horseshoe. Tie a secure knot in the end of the sausage skins. Carefully place the puddings in a steamer, and steam gently for 40 minutes.

Once the puddings are cooked, plunge them into cold water to cool, give them a wipe with some kitchen paper and then leave to dry in the fridge, where they can be kept for three to four days. Slice and fry before eating.

HOW TO COOK WHITE PUDDING

White pudding is best sliced and fried for a few minutes on each side in a heavy-based pan. Mealie pudding will need warming through in hot water for about 20 minutes, and can then be released from its skin to be served in a pile alongside breakfast.

TOAST

'THERE IS ANOTHER KIND OF BREAD and butter usually eaten with tea, which is toasted by the fire and is incomparably good. This is called toast,' wrote C. P. Moritz, a Swiss pastor, recounting a holiday in England in 1782. What's surprising about the quote is that he seems to see toast as groundbreaking, when surely cooking bread until hot and crisp is blindingly obvious? Toast is one of the simple foods. This is why 'toast and cereal' are forever paired on breakfast menus in hotels, an ever-present footer with a slight air of flippancy. You can imagine a sarcastic hotelier adding, 'and the rooms will contain beds and doors and stuff'.

When making a cooked breakfast, the simplicity of grilling bread shouldn't be cause for complacence. Quite the opposite: toast can easily become an afterthought, and with grave consequences. For tragedy value, few things match the moment when toast arrives late, breathless, as the final bead of yolk is mopped up by that reluctant understudy, sausage.

Or this: you've remembered to shoo it into the toaster and have removed it before it burns. Are you in the clear? No. At the very beginning, before you'd even started on the sausages, you failed to remove the butter from the fridge. Unscheduled minutes are lost as you scrape away despairingly with a knife, wondering where it all went so wrong in the world.

Is there a right way of making toast? A wrong way? Thomas J. Murrey complained in his 1885 book *Breakfast Dainties* that 'many seem to think they have made toast when they brown the outside of a piece of bread'. His vision for the stuff (presented as a simple matter of right and wrong) was to both remove the crust and 'evaporate all moisture'. Murrey is long gone and we can afford to be frank: this was just his personal preference. Toast is an individual matter. Some feel offended by anything that goes beyond warm bread, others by that which is not only cold but also burned. Most of us like it triangular, harvest-gold, and served while the butter's still melting.

There may be no wrong way of making toast, but there are wrong breads to make it with. Sun-dried tomato bloomers and squidgy olive breads aren't right. And fancy Italian loaves – ciabatta, focaccia – have that slight reek, when served with eggs, of the pretentious airport brasserie. The best toast for a fried breakfast is made from bread that is soft (ask yourself honestly, will this mop up yolk?), dense and can be easily cut into stout slices. It's a spectrum that runs from cheap white sliced at the one end (perfectly fine with real butter – always butter) to artisan sourdough at the other.

HOW TO MAKE BREAD

Making toast is easy, but first you need bread. Bread-making is complicated. When you start, it alternates between being baffling, irritating, messy and heartbreaking. A loaf takes hours. The first good one takes weeks. Sticky goo gets everywhere. Then it dries, leaving rough concrete on your work surface, coating your mixing bowls, smeared across your face. Your fingers are impossible to clean. All for a sort of large, weird-tasting lozenge. You throw it to the birds. Even the most wretched, oily pigeon flaps off into the distance.

But slowly, your loaves improve. You learn the importance of water in the bottom of the oven. Remember to slash the tops. Knead properly. Mind your heat. Eventually it happens: something you are willing to share. Someone says, 'This is nice,' and it has all been worth it.

The next stage is addiction, which goes in two directions at once: experimentation and refinement. Your friends see less of you, but they like you more. Every day, your house has a different aroma. If you are happy, you bake to express it. If you are sad, you bake to escape it. If you are on a deadline, you bake to avoid it. You'll never achieve that perfect loaf, because your standards go up quicker than your expertise. You log on to a baking forum. You have joined the fellowship.

An Everyday Loaf

From a basic formula the bread-baker can achieve an infinity of results. Flour, water, salt, yeast and sometimes fat are mixed to a golden ratio. It's the basis for something delicious or inedible: which depends on luck (when you're a beginner) and experience (when you're a veteran).

Here is the basic formula for a well-proportioned batch of dough. For example, it would make two average-sized loaves, or one of elephantine proportions. Fat in the form of butter or oil aids bread's longevity, so add this if you need the loaf to last for longer than a day or so.

1kg strong white bread flour
20g salt
20g soft unsalted butter or vegetable oil (optional)
10g dried instant yeast
600ml lukewarm water

Remember this number: 1216. 1kg flour, 20g salt, 10g yeast and 600ml water. 1216 helps you remember the basic proportions for a loaf of bread.

For any given batch just adjust the amounts proportionally. A decent, honest loaf can be simply generated by halving all the amounts listed above. For many of the alternative breakfast breads listed on the following pages, the method will be the same until the kneading stage is done.

Measure all your ingredients and arrange them so that they are no further from you than the length of a baguette. In a large bowl, mix the salt into the flour. Integrate the fat if you're using it (butter will take a while to rub into the mix thoroughly). Add the yeast, then quickly pour on the water. Mix the lot with a wooden spoon, or any tough, long, inanimate implement, until it's all the same ominous-looking whole.

Sprinkle a little flour on to your work surface to prevent sticking, then tip out the dough and knead. A good method is to plunge your fingers into the dough, stretch it towards you until it begins to break up and then fold it forward over itself. Now grab the side nearest you and flip the dough upside down in a hard slapping action. Turn it by 90 degrees and repeat. If your hands get too sticky, use flour to clean them. Occasionally switch to briskly massaging the dough with the ball of your hand. This will help create a consistent, airy dough. You're looking for the wonderful moment when the chaotic wilderness in your hands becomes silky and pliant. Kneading will normally take around 10 minutes: the dough should be elastic, pinging straight back into its original shape when you prod it with a finger.

Now, shape the dough into a round (flatten it with your fists, fold the sides in, flip over, coax). Coat it with a little oil and then place in a clean, large bowl covered with a plastic bag or a damp tea towel. Leave this in a warm place. If you have nowhere warm, you can use the oven: heat it to its lowest temperature (normally 50–60°C/lowest possible gas), then turn it off and leave the door open for around 30 seconds to cool it down a little, before introducing the bowl with the dough (don't use plastic if doing it this way).

When the dough has doubled in size, usually after around an hour (warning: beware of wishful thinking – it will be obvious), it's time to shape. If you're using a loaf tin, see opposite. Otherwise: flatten the dough heavily with your fists. Roll it towards you, tightly, creating a shape a little like a rolled-up newspaper. Gently seal the seam with your fingers. Use your fists to flatten it into a thin rectangle, then stretch it to twice its original length. Fold the rightmost third into the centre, then the leftmost third over on top of that. Flatten it all for a final time, this time into a square. Now, roll it towards you tightly, seal the seam with your fingertips and gently roll it back and forth to smooth it all out. The dough should be in the shape of a slightly squashed, over-sized cigar. Coat its outside if you so wish: you can dust it with some wholegrain or rye flour, or roll it in a bowl of milk and then a bowl of seeds or grains.

Dust a baking sheet with some flour, place the dough on it and cover it once again until it has doubled in size. While this is happening, pre-heat the oven to as hot as it will go and place a small baking tray in the very bottom. Boil the kettle. When the dough has risen, use a large knife to slash long, diagonal lines right across its top. Fill a cup with boiled water, open the oven and slug it into the baking tray at the bottom, closing the door immediately afterwards. Fetch the dough on its baking sheet and place it on the most central shelf that will still give it enough space to rise. Have a wire rack ready nearby, as this is where the bread will cool.

After 10 minutes, check how the bread is colouring. If you're using a fan-assisted oven and it's browning very quickly (i.e. it is looking dark brown), reduce the heat to 170°C/gas 3. If it's browning openly but not over-dramatically (a more golden shade), go for 180°C/gas 4. If it's still pale and pasty, turn it to 200°C/gas 6. If your oven isn't fan-assisted, the same principles apply: just increase all these heats by 20°C.

A loaf (or a batch of loaves) can take anything from 20 to 50 minutes to bake, depending on size and oven. You'll know it's done when it's risen, has a crust that's golden brown and – most importantly – you hear a hollow knocking sound when you tap the base with a knuckle. Keep checking until all these boxes are ticked, then place the loaf on the wire rack to cool.

Using a Loaf Tin

If using a loaf tin, introduce it at the shaping stage (the tin will do the shaping part for you), but make sure you grease it thoroughly and then dust with flour before introducing the dough: few things are more frustrating than having to brutally hack away the nether regions of a perfect loaf to free it from an unprepared tin. If you want to coat the top with seeds or grains, you can use a basting brush to lightly apply some milk, before sprinkling them liberally on. Slash the top and use water in the bottom of the oven as per the everyday loaf method.

Frying Bread?

The fried slice is declining – health concerns about bread that is sodden with grease to the point where it is shiny seem to be having this effect. That said, there are still those who believe the bread element in a full English should never be cooked in the toaster. Occasionally they also claim the health effect can be limited by using a little fresh oil instead of the traditional method of using the same pan as the other ingredients. This seems a little pointless – it's still less healthy than toast and misses the whole point, which is to capture flavours and fats that would otherwise be wasted.

Serves 2
1 tablespoon sunflower oil
2 slices bread

If you've been cooking sausages, bacon, black pudding, etc. in a frying pan, remove these items and store them somewhere warm. Turn up the heat and throw in the oil, combining it with the fats and juices in the pan. Add the bread and cook for 2–3 minutes on each side or until it turns golden and crispy. You can add more oil if the pan becomes dry. Serve with the rest of the fried breakfast.

An Amazing Toast

Take a piece of rye bread, the dense Prussian kind that comes in those cuboid packets. Cut it in half and put it in the toaster, on its highest setting. You may have wondered why the toaster goes up to 6 when anything above 3 burns conventional toast: the answer is rye bread. That stuff is so dense!

Meanwhile, heat a combination of almonds and sunflower, sesame and pumpkin seeds in a dry pan, removing from the heat when the seeds start to pop. When the toast springs up, spread it with unsalted butter and peanut butter (crunchy) leavened with a little honey. Sprinkle with the nuts and seeds and consume immediately. You will have no need to eat until lunch.

Soda Bread

If you urgently need a homemade loaf this is where you come, the substitution of yeast with baking powder removing the need for hours of proving, shaping and re-proving. This Irish staple is thus perfect for the breakfaster who lives in the moment: you can go from decision to digestion within the hour. Better still, it does not immediately mark you out as a corner-cutter because the dense, crumbly texture and intensity of flavour are distinct enough that you can credibly claim to prefer it. Maybe you do.

Makes 1 loaf
300g plain flour
7g salt
3 teaspoons baking powder
190ml thin natural yoghurt (or a 50/50 mix of
thick yoghurt and semi-skimmed milk)

Pre-heat the oven to 200°C/gas 6. Mix the flour, salt and baking powder in a bowl, then pour in the liquid and stir/coax it until it's a consistent mass of dough. Knead it for a minute or so, but don't worry about getting it to the silky state you'd expect from a yeast bread.

Shape into a round, then flatten it a little before using a knife to cut a deep cross in the top of the loaf. Give the top of the loaf a gentle all-over stabbing, then dust with a little flour – rye is nice but white will do – and place on a floured baking sheet. Place in the oven for around 25 minutes, or whenever a tap on the base makes a hollow knocking sound. Cool on a wire rack if you like, but warm is best.

Soda Farls

If even soda bread is too long-winded for your deadline, the final resort is soda farls. Free of the need for either proving or baking, these are dead easy to make. Their sturdy texture, taste, shape and portability make them ideal to take the bread role in a cooked breakfast. They freeze well. They can be toasted. Why the hell aren't more people making soda farls?

Makes 4 farls
200g plain flour
1 teaspoon bicarbonate of soda
½ teaspoon salt
160ml buttermilk (if you can't find buttermilk,
use a 50/50 mix of natural yoghurt and semi-skimmed milk)

Stir the dry ingredients together in a mixing bowl. Add the buttermilk bit by bit, stirring constantly with a wooden spoon until it's all more or less combined into a dough. Knead for a minute or so, shape into a ball and then roll it out into a rough circular shape no more than a centimetre thick. Cut this circle into four quarters.

Heat your largest, heaviest-based frying pan and chuck in a small handful of flour (rye, if available, would be a nice touch). Place the farls in the pan and cook for between 7 and 10 minutes on either side, or until golden brown and nicely risen. Serve while still warm, or cool on a wire rack and then toast as required.

Potato Farls

The word 'farl' has nothing to do with what a farl contains and everything to do with its shape. It derives from an Old English word, *feorth-dœl*, meaning 'fourth part'. The potato farl (or cake, if you form it into fried-egg-sized patties) is a formidable foil for egg yolk. This method is an adaptation of an adaptation, emanating from the wise kitchen of Dan Lepard before passing through the hands of the brilliant South London-based food writer Helen Graves. Don't despair if your breakfast party does not divide into four, as farls can be stored in the fridge or freezer and heated up later.

Makes 4 farls
125g plain flour
1 teaspoon salt
½ teaspoon baking powder
60g unsalted butter, at room temperature and cut into small pieces
250g mashed potatoes
1 large egg, beaten
1 small onion, finely chopped
100ml warm milk
2 tablespoons chopped flat-leaf parsley

In a large bowl, stir together the flour, salt and baking powder. Add the butter to this mixture, combining it with your fingers until smooth. In a separate bowl, use a wooden spoon to mix together the mashed potato, egg, onion, milk and parsley. Tip all this into a bowl with the flour mixture and combine all together to form a lovely potatoey dough. Roll this out into a circle around the same size as your frying pan of choice, ideally around 5mm thick.

Dust your frying pan with a little flour (rye would be great, white will do fine) and heat it on medium. Add the potato dough (a 'bannock', as it's called in its full rounded form) and leave to cook for around 5 minutes or until there's goldness and crispness. Turn it over and cook the other side for about the same length of time.

Cut into four and serve, either amongst a classic fry-up or with a poached duck egg, three rashers of streaky bacon and a Portobello mushroom cut into four equivalent 'farls'.

Cornbread

Who remembers the first time they tried corn? It's hardly up there with getting on a plane or seeing our parents kiss. For America's original European settlers, it *was* memorable – a completely new thing! And they weren't keen. Corn was too heavy for their wheat-reared sensibilities, and way too coarse. But the American wilderness was neither the time nor the place to be fussy and the maize plant soon became the staple of the frontiersman, who picked up cookery techniques from the indigenous peoples whose corn gods were scattered across the continent. One trick he liked the look of was the turning of corn into something not a million miles away from bread, a practice that ranged from the Senecan *naktsi* ('buried-in-the-ashes-and-baked corn bread') to the Cherokee *di-ga-nu-li* ('doghcads' – a loaf with the shape of a canine's skull).

Fast forward a handful of centuries and cornbread is a traditional staple of Deep South breakfasting. It deserves a wider audience. Real Southerners don't use sugar, and use coarse ground cornmeal for some or all of the recipe, which gives it a crunchy gritty texture. This recipe offers a result that is rich and crispy on the outside and moist on the inside.

Note: A well-seasoned 25cm Appalachian cast-iron skillet would be the authentic route here, but alternatively you can use a heavy-based shallow pan that will go in the oven.

Makes 1 loaf
420ml buttermilk (or milk plus fresh lemon juice – see method)
140g fine cornmeal*
70g coarse cornmeal*
60g plain flour
1 teaspoon salt
½ teaspoon bicarbonate of soda
¾ teaspoon baking powder
1 medium egg
50g unsalted butter

*Cornmeal can be hard to find in the UK, though some supermarkets sell it in their Afro-Caribbean specialist food sections. You can also use fine and coarse-ground polenta.

Pre-heat the oven to 250°C/the highest your oven will go. If not using buttermilk, put the juice of a lemon in a measuring jug and top up to 420ml with milk. Leave for 10 minutes to thicken to 'soured milk'.

Mix the dry ingredients in a bowl. Beat the egg with the buttermilk or soured milk. Put the butter in the pan, then put that in the oven for a couple of minutes to melt. Whilst the butter is melting, mix the egg and buttermilk or soured milk together with the dry ingredients and stir well, leaving the batter a bit lumpy.

Take the pan from the oven, and carefully swirl the hot fat around a bit so that the sides are coated. Pour the hot fat from the pan into the batter and mix well. Pour the batter back into the hot pan and return the pan to the oven. Bake for 20–25 minutes and then serve immediately.

Bagels

The origins of the bagel are mysterious. The siege of Vienna has tried to take the credit, naturally (see croissants, p.179), but the story of it being produced in 1683 as a thank-you gift for the King of Poland is far-fetched ('Oh great,' you imagine him saying, having saved the city from a huge Turkish invasion, 'a bagel.'). Yiddish paperwork preceding the siege by a good seventy years has been unearthed in Kraków, offering evidence of an already thriving bagel scene.

Today, Jewish New York is the hometown of the delectable hoop. To order one like a true New Yorker, you need to master an intricate bagel vocabulary based around a huge number of varieties (cinnamon? pumpernickel? 'everything'?) and different kinds of cream cheese. Some have gone so far as to claim that if you're anywhere else in the world it's in fact impossible to do the bagel justice. Being unfiltered, goes the theory, the Big Apple's water system contains a mysterious mineral balance, one both miraculously bagel-friendly and unavailable elsewhere. It all seemed a bit convenient, so we put it to the test and made two experimental batches: in each set we used a different city's tap water, New York in one (smuggled over by a friendly courier) and London in the other. We ended up with two identical bunches of bagels. NYC will have to settle for merely being very good at them.

For many reasons the bagel is not a fry-up-friendly bread, but it is superb toasted at breakfast and is worth learning to make from scratch.

Homemade bagels are amazing. They show you how important and enjoyable are the time-honoured techniques of rolling, boiling and glazing. And they leave you with little time for unscrupulous bakers who skip the last two stages, the result being the dreaded 'fool's bagel', a plain bread roll shaped like a ring. Even the siege of Vienna isn't interested in such nonsense.

Makes 10 sizeable bagels
500g strong white bread flour
5g dried instant yeast
10g salt
20g caster sugar
250ml warm water
55ml sunflower oil, plus extra for coating the bagels
1 large egg
Sesame, poppy or pumpkin seeds

Mix the dry ingredients (apart from the seeds) together in a bowl, then add the water and oil. Mix together, then knead the dough until silky. Shape into a round, coat with some oil, cover and then leave to rise until it's twice the size, usually after around an hour.

Flatten the dough, and roll it into a long sausage shape. Cut this into ten pieces. Roll each piece in turn, lightly with the heels of your hands, into a sausage as long as it can be, then wet the ends and press together, forming a ring. Leave to rise on a delicately oiled hard surface or board. If you're looking for something to do in the meantime, beating the egg in a bowl will use up a minute or so.

Pre-heat the oven to 200°C/gas 6. When the bagels have doubled in size, boil a pan of water and lay a tea towel out on a hard surface. Reduce the pan to a gently simmering state, then slide as many bagels as you can without touching (too much), one by one, into the water. Cook for about a minute and a half on each side, then remove them with a slotted spoon and place on the tea towel.

Once all the bagels are poached and drained, lay them on as many baking sheets as you need and brush them with the beaten egg. Sprinkle with the seeds and place in the oven. They need around a quarter of an hour before they turn golden brown, when you can remove them and shuffle them carefully on to a wire rack to cool.

Crumpets

Crumpets make a wonderful breakfast. Not as a full English component, but as a buttery foundation for marmalade, Marmite, jam, or just about any breakfast spread you can think of. Is it worth making your own crumpets? The ones you buy in the supermarket are actually very nice, while making them is difficult, long-winded and hard to justify. 'Why did I bother?' you ask, chewing on a hockey puck whose gummy insides taste like a real ale brewery. 'These are not supposed to be attempted by the non-industrial amateur.' Even the Wolseley's baking staff (these people make croissants daily) have lamented their inability to turn out a suitably airy disc.

Really it comes down to two pitfalls, both of which take place once the item is in the pan. First, can you keep the bubbles coming through the batter, even as the mix begins to set? Second, is it possible to use a stainless-steel ring to keep the circular shape without the crumpet becoming terminally stuck? The answer is yes; this recipe will work. If you don't want to bother, that's fine. Very few people have been judged lacking for not hand-making crumpets.

Makes around 10 crumpets
750ml milk
425g plain flour
10g salt
10g caster sugar
5g dried instant yeast
2 teaspoons bicarbonate of soda
1 teaspoon white wine vinegar

Heat the milk in a saucepan on an especially low heat. Be careful not to let the milk overheat – it just needs to be a bit warm: think blood temperature. Sift the flour into a large bowl and mix in the salt and the sugar. Next, add the yeast and bicarbonate of soda, followed by the warm milk and the vinegar. Whisk together until you have a creamy, lump-free batter. Cover with plastic film and leave alone in a warm place for at least an hour, but as long as 3 hours if necessary: you want the batter to be utterly packed full of bubbles.

To get a perfectly circular crumpet, many will use egg rings or specialist crumpet rings. Be careful, as if the rings aren't non-stick you can get into a stuck-crumpet situation, no matter how carefully you grease. If you're unfussy about shape and depth, you can tip the batter into the pan with no ring at all (some may accuse you of having made a pikelet). Whatever your method, you need to use something like kitchen paper to liberally grease every inch of surface that will come into contact with the batter.

Use a heavy-based pan, and simultaneously cook as many crumpets as you can fit in (without them touching each other, if you're not using rings). Heat the pan on medium, then tip in about a ladleful of batter. Almost immediately, bubbles should start to rise to the top of the mixture. Stay aware of the heat. Check the bottom of the crumpet occasionally: if it's starting to turn very dark, turn the heat down, but not too low as the heat creates the bubbles.

After a couple of minutes the batter will have solidified to the point where it no longer needs the support of the ring: use a pair of tongs to pick up the ring so that the crumpet itself slips out (otherwise, the heat of the ring may give your crumpet a crunchy perimeter). If it won't slip easily, use a small knife to tease it out.

When the top of the crumpet is cooked, flip it over for 5–10 seconds. Place on a wire rack to cool. A single crumpet will take around 10 minutes, but this will depend on thickness (i.e. the dimensions of your rings). Keep practising.

English Muffins

There are very few bread types that the great contemporary baker Dan Lepard has not explored – he's a man who knows his *pain de mie* from his *pain beaucaire*. But at the breakfast table he favours the English muffin above all: a freshly baked specimen, served with egg and bacon. That comforting blast of bacon's salty umami plus the sweetness of the world's favourite toasted disc is what the McDonald's marketing team exploited when creating the Egg McMuffin (see p.103). This association has, however, made us treat the muffin as a cheap, commercial bread. This is unfair. It's time to rehabilitate the muffin.

Makes 8 muffins
500g strong white bread flour
5g dried instant yeast
10g salt
1 ½ teaspoons caster sugar
300ml warm water
2 teaspoons sunflower oil
Semolina flour, for dusting

Mix the dry ingredients together in a bowl, then add the warm water and oil. Mix the dough well, then knead until silky. Shape the dough into a round, then cover and leave to rise until doubled in size.

Flatten the lot and then, using a sharp knife, divide the dough into eight pieces. Shape them into mini-rounds, rolling each in semolina flour and then pushing them down until they're about 2.5cm high. Place the muffins on tea towels, cover, and leave until they've once again doubled in size.

Place your wire rack in a receptive position. Heat the biggest, heaviest-based frying pan you can find, on a medium heat at first, and put into it as many muffins as will fit without touching one another. After about 7 minutes start checking the base of the muffins. When they've turned a golden-brown colour, turn them over and turn the heat right down. They should be rising nicely by now.

After another 7 minutes or so, check again. If they are now golden brown on both sides and feel quite light, you can eat them while warm, or cool for toasting on demand.

BAKED BEANS

NOWHERE IS THE PHRASE 'divided by a common language' more fitting of the so-called special relationship than in our understanding of the term 'baked beans'. The orange cascade so precious to the English breakfast is but a niche item across the pond where baked beans originated and are now sold on specialist shelves under the label 'Heinz Premium Vegetarian Beans'. The name is exactly right for something with such a utilitarian, unspecial taste. Tinned beans are popular in America, but they are of the Boston style – a tasty pork and molasses-based concoction adapted from a Native American dish of beans stewed in bear fat with maple syrup. These are not for breakfast.

Heinz introduced their tinned beans to Britain at the end of the nineteenth century, initially as an exotic item sold through Fortnum & Mason's luxury food hall (where they are still available at the time of writing for a surprisingly reasonable 55p). Just a decade later, Captain Scott would pose with a giant tin early in his doomed attempt to reach the South Pole. By the Second World War they were so fundamental to the British larder that for rationing purposes the government classed them as an 'essential food'. They continue to have a place in just about every cupboard in the land. Hugh Grant allegedly made use of a family-sized tub when assaulting a photographer; the Queen attended the fiftieth anniversary of the Heinz factory in Wigan.

Baked beans get an entry pass to the Magic Nine for three reasons, which in declining order of priority are the lubricating qualities of their sauce, their status as a vegetable and their taste. They are a minor player, but a controversial one. Struck by the thought of bean juice mingling with their egg yolk, many will turn a conspicuous shade of green. Really this is unnecessary, given that an old-fashioned sausage bulwark (or, as Alan Partridge once had it, 'breakwater') offers a simple solution. The real danger is insufficient stewing time plus lazy quantity control giving rise to an out-of-control baked bean militia. If they are not kept in check, beans will overrun your breakfast plate; your bacon, mushrooms and toast will be engulfed like victims in a disaster movie about jungle ants. Discipline your beans. Give them a good stew.

FACT: Since 1986, the world record for the longest baked bean bath has been held by 'Captain Beany from Planet Beanus', who spent 100 hours in a bean-filled tub.

FACT: 'Bean' is the UK's most common vegetable-based surname. It is held by more than 8,200 people.

HOW TO BUY BAKED BEANS

Heinz have fared rather badly in several 'blind taste tests' over the years. It's possible they have been resting on their laurels as younger, brighter brandz dive into the market with tangier formulas at cheaper prices. Or it might be a case of familiarity breeding contempt, with participants equating the exoticism of an unfamiliar tomato sauce with 'tastes nice'. But it's the tin, stupid. That world-famous '57 varieties' cylinder is so beautiful it makes the beans actually taste better. A blind taste test is missing the point.

However, there is something to be said for a little experimentation. Recipes are constantly shifting; supermarket varieties come and go; today's Heinz obsessive is tomorrow's own-brand ideologue. What we need is a way of looking at *any* tin of beans and deducing something of what lies within.

Let's assume the quality of beans comes from a combination of flavour and texture, with a good texture being one that is not insipid and watery. On this basis there is a trinity of measures with which we can best deduce tinned bean quality:

1. Bean percentage
2. Tomato percentage
3. Purity

The first two we can glean easily: they are standard information on the table of ingredients. A tin of Heinz beans, for instance, is 49 per cent beans and 27 per cent tomatoes.

Purity is gauged by looking out for items that are obviously synthetic, and also suspicious-sounding versions of natural ingredients such as 'reconstituted tomato paste'. In Heinz beans, we might knock marks off the purity-feelgood rating for the inclusion of glucose-fructose syrup and 'modified' cornflour.

With these three factors in mind, the bean seeker enables himself to make a slightly better-informed decision. Of course even bearing this in mind, the beans might taste like sweetened cardboard.

Ingredients of a tin of Heinz beans:
Beans (49%)
Tomatoes (27%)
Water
Sugar
Glucose-fructose syrup
Modified cornflour
Spirit vinegar
Spice extracts
Herb extract

HOW TO MAKE BAKED BEANS

Anyone who's been served 'homemade beans' in a restaurant knows that making baked beans can be about as worthwhile as making your own light bulb (pointlessly time-consuming when a perfectly good version is cheaply available). The trick is not to try to imitate tinned beans but to try to outdo them. Here's a recipe that borrows much from Boston's traditional Saturday night bean, but is similar enough to the Heinz version to fit in at the breakfast table. It takes a lot of soaking and stewing time, so you should prepare a large batch and reheat as required.

Makes about 8 helpings
400g dried haricot beans
Olive oil
150g smoked streaky bacon, chopped
2 medium onions, chopped
4 tablespoons maple syrup
1 x 400g tin tomatoes
3 tablespoons cider vinegar
500ml water

Soak the beans in water overday (if you want to have them ready for the following morning, best to soak in the day and cook in the evening).

Drain the beans and put them in a large pot, then cover with plenty of water. Bring to the boil and then simmer for 45 minutes, checking regularly and topping up the water if necessary. When the beans are tender, drain and set them aside.

Now heat some olive oil in a large saucepan and add the chopped bacon and onion, cooking until softened. Introduce the maple syrup, tomatoes, vinegar and beans, plus water. Bring to the boil, then turn the heat right down. Leave to stew for around 2 hours, stirring occasionally and adding more water if everything begins to get a bit dry.

The sauce should end up heavy and the beans on the point of disintegrating. Serve with your cooked breakfast or a fried egg and a slice of toast.

HOW TO COOK BAKED BEANS

Put your beans into a pan. Heat gently until at preferred consistency.

POTATOES

IN BREAKFASTING CIRCLES there is little more controversial than the role of the potato. Some argue that potato is an abomination and the only starch on the table should be bread, whereas others embrace the hash brown or the potato scone.

In our opinion, the measure of any breakfast starch is how well it mops up the various liquids created by a proper fry-up – egg yolk, baked bean juice, fat and sauces such as ketchup, HP and mustard. You don't want your potato to bring too much more fat or liquid to the table; its job is to absorb what is already there. Which is why French fries, so perfect with a steak or a hamburger, become a fatty thing too far when paired with a proper cooked breakfast.

Many, however, disagree forcefully about exactly which of the potato-based foods are the most suitable ones. Often a quiet meal or indeed marriage has been broken up by debates such as this and it's a little-known fact that a disagreement over this very issue between Russia and the Ottoman Empire triggered the bloody Crimean war. Passions are raised whenever the word 'potato' is heard at the breakfast table. To bring a little peace and harmony back to mornings, here is a scientific scale of absorption, 10 being the most absorbent and 1 being the least. This way readers who find themselves in disagreement can point to the numbers and find their case proven once and for all. You can't argue with the numbers.

Potato Bread/Farls – 10/10: There is almost nothing that cannot be mopped up by this starchy hybrid. It is currently being tested as a sustainable way to deal with oil spills.

Bubble and Squeak – 8/10: Almost as absorbent as potato bread but more delicious, making this the connoisseur's choice.

Home Fries – 7/10: Cubed potatoes fried in a haphazard manner, often with onions and sweet peppers, and served in an American diner with almost everything. They are often superfluous but come into their own when confronted with an excess yolk situation.

Hash Browns – 5/10: Almost a meal on their own. They need to be matched carefully at the breakfast table because of their oily nature.

Chips – 4/10: This would be the score for a fatter British-style chip, the perfect chip to turn to for that anytime classic 'egg and chips'.

French Fries – 2/10: Very thin-cut chips in the American and Continental manner. Not very absorbent and therefore ill suited to breakfast.

There, that should settle all arguments once and for all. Now here are the recipes.

Bubble and Squeak

It is not really in the spirit of the dish to include a recipe for bubble and squeak. Bubble should be made of whatever leftover vegetables you have to hand. To cook ingredients especially for it would be like deliberately creating waste to make compost: very, very tasty compost.

Bubble is a Trojan horse in which cabbage or other worthy vegetables can be smuggled into a breakfast under the cover of potatoes and fat. One could go further and say that in making this dish a sort of alchemy occurs where the base metals of cabbage and potatoes are turned into pure gold through the application of heat and fat (heady stuff at breakfast time). For this reason bubble is the king of breakfasting potato-based dishes. The potatoes can be mashed, boiled or even leftover roast. The fat should ideally be bacon dripping but a mixture of butter and oil will do. Cabbage is also essential but you can add other vegetables such as carrots, broccoli or onion. Under *no circumstances* should you use garlic. (Regarding garlic at breakfast: how many recipes in this book contain garlic? Count them.)

Don't worry if the mixture sticks to the pan – you are aiming for a hash rather than a patty. There should be bits of crusty fried potato within the mash. Improvisation is the point here, but if you're forcing us to give you a recipe, here is a version from scratch.

Serves 4–6
750g King Edward potatoes
1 knob unsalted butter
100ml milk
Salt and pepper
250g Savoy cabbage
3 tablespoons bacon fat, or a mixture of vegetable oil
and unsalted butter

Peel and cut the potatoes into small pieces, then boil in salted water until tender. Drain them and mash (don't worry about lumps, this is meant to be a rough dish). Add a knob of butter, the milk, mash further and season. Leave the potatoes to cool for as long as you can wait.

Roughly chop the cabbage into strips, place it into a saucepan with 1cm of salted water and cook over a high heat for 4 minutes. Add cold water to the now-cooked cabbage to cool it, drain thoroughly and then mix with the potato.

In a large saucepan melt the bacon fat (or oil and butter) until it bubbles. Add the potato and cabbage and form into a large rough pancake. Fry on a medium-high heat for 5 minutes or until a crust starts to form on the bottom. When the crust has formed, turn over the mixture in batches so that you have a hash (i.e. don't try and turn over the whole pancake at once – perfection is not the name of the game here).

Pat the mixture down into a big pancake shape and cook until a crust forms on the bottom. Add more fat if it looks as though it is drying out. You can keep turning, depending on how crispy you like it. Remove and serve with poached eggs and bacon.

Hash Browns

British readers will probably have only tried these in their bastardised mass-produced, frozen and then deep-fried incarnation. The main flavours in these tend to be salt and stale oil. Making them from scratch offers a much more delicious experience. There are a few things to remember in order to make a good hash brown: first, remove as much water as possible from the potato before frying; second, remember that the onion is there for flavour – you do not need much; third, don't grate your potato too finely or the potato will turn into a kind of dough when you squeeze the water out, which will give you something closer to a latke. Some recipes call for egg to bind the mixture but it isn't necessary. As long as you get the uncooked hash brown pancake into the hot oil in one piece, it will stay together.

Makes 2 hash browns, enough for 4 people
400g waxy potatoes
½ onion, finely chopped
Salt and pepper
3 tablespoons sunflower, groundnut or light olive oil (not extra virgin)

Peel the potatoes, then grate coarsely. Place the grated potato in a tea towel, wrap the towel around it to form a ball and squeeze hard so that most of the water comes out. Thoroughly mix the potato with the chopped onion and season well. Form into two square pancakes approximately 7 x 7 x 1.5cm high and with a large kitchen knife squash and trim the pancakes.

Heat the oil on a medium to high heat in a frying pan, preferably non-stick, and then very carefully lift the pancakes with a spatula into the hot oil. After 6 minutes flip the pancakes; don't let them get too dark – you are aiming for a golden-brown colour. Cook for another 6 minutes. Take out, pat with kitchen paper to remove excess oil and serve.

Jewish Latkes

Were a hash brown to mate with a pancake, a latke would be the progeny. Since it is probably a sin for inanimate foodstuffs to mate, the latke is made by frying a batter of grated potato, flour and egg into flat pancakes. Yiddish in origin, the dish is consumed in many variations across Eastern Europe and America. The pancakes may be served with a variety of condiments: soured cream (*smetana*) is the favoured condiment in Russia and Belarus; apple sauce in Germany; bacon in Sweden. Fried eggs, sausages and black pudding are excellent too.

The latke's strong cultural resonance is celebrated at the University of Chicago each year, where academics gather annually for the Latke vs Hamantaschen debate, an attempt to decide which of the Jewish delicacies is superior (hamantaschen are the sweet triangular pastries of Ashkenazi tradition). It has been contended that latke molecules facilitate alkene bonding and that the latke is a source of light; like the latke itself, these contentions should be taken with a pinch of salt.

Serves 2
500g floury potatoes, peeled
1 small onion
1 medium egg
2 tablespoons plain flour
Salt and pepper
Pinch of ground turmeric (optional)
1 tablespoon vegetable oil

Grate the potatoes into the centre of a tea towel. Chop the onion very finely and lob that in too. Gather the ends of the tea towel and – standing over a sink – twist the potato mix into a ball, as tightly as you can. You are doing this in order to squeeze as much water as you can from the potato; the more water you remove, the crisper your latkes will be. (It is amazing how much water can be extracted from a potato.)

Beat the egg in a bowl, and sieve the flour in, mixing them to form a batter. Combine the potato with the batter and season extremely well. At this point you can add the turmeric, which will add a faint fragrance and turn the latkes a more appetising yellow colour.

On a relatively high heat, warm the oil in a large frying pan. Place a tablespoon of the potato batter into the pan at a time, flattening each dollop with the back of the spoon to form a thin round. (There should be enough batter for four latkes.) After 5 minutes, turn the latkes over. After 5 more minutes, remove from the pan, drain on kitchen paper, and consume immediately.

Swiss Röstis

The rösti is a substantial, versatile, rich and moreish potato cake – a Swiss invention that some have said goes part of the way to atoning for muesli. Often, in Swiss cafés, a rösti will do for chips; sometimes, in posh restaurants, a rösti will accompany a fine cut of meat. Traditionally, however, it is a humble farmer's breakfast, consumed plain with a cup of milky coffee before heading out on to the Alps with an alphorn.

The rösti varies from canton to canton. It can be made with either raw or cooked potato. Cheese, bacon, onions and rosemary can variously be layered among its folds. A popular variation calls for a cup of coffee to be poured over the thing. The version we give here is a standard boiled-potato version, which you can customise to your heart's content.

Serves 2
400g potatoes, boiled in their skins
Salt and pepper
40g unsalted butter
75g Emmental cheese (optional)

Peel the potatoes, which you will have boiled the night before. (The Swiss insist that you should not peel before boiling; it does make a difference to the flavour.) Grate the potatoes into a bowl using a coarse grater. Season extremely well.

Put half of the butter into a medium to large frying pan on a low heat. Swirl it around so that it coats the sides and, once it is bubbling, transfer the potato to the pan, spreading it evenly and pressing it down to form a cake. Once the cake is formed, try to leave it be.

After approximately 15 minutes, flip the rösti: hold a plate on top of the pan with one hand and the pan handle in the other; in one deft action, turn both over so that the rösti is upside down on the plate. Now put the remaining butter in the pan, put the pan back on the heat and slide the rösti into the pan.

After another 15 minutes, the rösti will be ready to serve. (You may choose to grate some cheese on to it for the last 5 minutes, using the plate as a lid to encourage it to melt.) Sausages and fried eggs are excellent accompaniments.

Breakfast Chips

It all used to be so easy. Chips were bits of potato cut up and then deep-fried in oil or fat. And then the scientists got involved. Now the right sort of potato has to be used, cut to an exact thickness, blanched and then cooked twice in horse fat. All very well if you live in Belgium or Sicily. The food writer Jeffrey Steingarten wrote an essay about the difficulty of obtaining horse fat in New York City; it's equally difficult in London.

Many chip recipes require the potatoes to be parboiled and then cooled. No one is going to do this for breakfast. So what is required is a recipe for a fatter chip, that doesn't require blanching, freezing, triple cooking or horse fat. Enter the classic British chip.

This recipe mimics the double cooking by starting the chips on a lower temperature and then raising it for a final blitz. It is worth investing in a food thermometer in order to get this right.

Serves 4
750g mealy potatoes (Idaho or Russet)
250ml groundnut oil or beef dripping
Salt to taste

Peel the potatoes and cut into little planks about 2 x 1 x 5cm (you can leave the skins on for added rusticity). Wash briefly in cold water and dry thoroughly with a tea towel.

Put the cut potatoes in a saucepan at least 25cm in diameter with sides at least 15cm high. Cover with the oil or fat. Place on the highest heat on the hob and bring the temperature of the fat to approximately 140°C. Adjust the heat on the hob so as to maintain this temperature for 10 minutes. Now raise the temperature to 185°C and cook for 3–4 minutes until golden.

Remove the chips with a slotted spoon and put in a bowl lined with copious amounts of kitchen paper. Salt and serve with fried eggs and ketchup.

A GUIDE TO CLASS AT THE BREAKFAST TABLE
by Blake Pudding

Visitors to British shores are normally surprised that class is still a major factor in our daily lives despite the official end of the class war announced by Tony Blair in 1999 with his famous 'We are all middle class now' speech. The middle and upper classes may have adapted their accents and professed a liking for association football but they cannot shake off their backgrounds that easily. Nowhere is this division more apparent than in what we eat.

It is commonly thought that this class divide in food started with the Normans introducing French words to the table, so that an animal would be two different things, one in the field and the other on the table of the grasping, blood-sucking baron: sheep and mutton, ox and beef, deer and venison, for example. I would argue, however, that the division goes back even further. In Roman times the conquering powers and the Romanised Briton would have eaten anchovies and olives whereas the peasantry would have eaten the ancient equivalent of turkey twizzlers. This is the origin of the equation of Italian food with the on-the-make middle classes: witness such phrases as 'polenta-eating class' and the scorn with which some pronounce the words 'sun-dried tomatoes' or 'balsamic vinegar'.

Amongst all this, breakfast appears the most egalitarian of meals. Whereas the other meals of the day have different names depending on who is eating them and at what time (for the working classes a lunch is a dinner, a dinner is a tea and a supper is a secretive alcoholic), breakfast is breakfast across the social classes. Traditionally they all eat something similar based on pork products with eggs. But these similarities flatter to deceive: the class distinctions are still there, they are just more subtle. All the better, in fact, to trip up unwary social climbers or slummers.

When staying with someone you don't know well, breakfast offers a useful way to deduce where they stand in the social hierarchy. A house may be beautifully decorated but such taste can be bought. If the next morning they serve you unsmoked back bacon as opposed to smoked streaky it's is a clear sign that they are from the lower orders. Are the sauce bottles permanently on the table? Is everything a little too perfect? That's also a sign of lack of class.

In order to determine why these divisions exist, we must look at British breakfast's origins. For much of British history neither class would have bothered with breakfast. They may have had some leftover pheasant or gruel in the mornings but not a separate meal. The British breakfast as we know it has its origins in the great country house breakfasts of the Victorian era. These would be eaten before or/and after some form of manly field sports such as fox hunting or grouse shooting. Previous to Victorian times it would have been considered common to eat in the mornings at all as it suggested that one had to work. With Victoria's ascent to the throne such louche attitudes were gradually replaced with a muscular morality.

The other meals in these country houses were French or French-influenced, as was the case with the ruling classes throughout Europe. Breakfast, largely overlooked by the French, was thus the only available repository for British values of plainness and common sense. This common sense extended only as far as the dishes themselves and not the gargantuan quantities in which they were served. A normal morning buffet might consist of eggs, bacon, sausage, devilled kidneys, kedgeree, cold meats, meat pies, bread, pastries, kippers, Arbroath smokies and so on.

Breakfast was the only meal of the day at which guests would help themselves. The servants' job was merely to replenish the spread. The full English breakfast as we know it is an imitation of this traditional feast with the crucial difference that it is served up on one plate, as it was for middle-class businessmen at Edwardian hotels. This leads to the startling conclusion that the full English is irredeemably common. You can always tell members of the aristocracy because they put imaginary quotation marks around the words 'full English'. In fact, all 'made' breakfast dishes such as eggs Benedict or Florentine are common, as are omelettes. The general rule is that if it would not work on a buffet and therefore has to be especially prepared and brought to you, then it is common.

The issue can be complicated so I have come up with some hard and fast rules so that the class detective can uncover social standing at the breakfast table. The most obvious giveaways of commonness are daintiness and fuss and anything that could be thought of as Continental. Decoration, garnish and herbs have no place in the mornings of the upper classes.

Bread: White sliced bread, as in the cheapest sort, is a good giveaway. Anything with fruit or olives in is a no-no. Bread should be fresh, unsliced and crusty. However, foreigners take note, it is quite difficult to get hold of really good bread in Britain outside the bigger cities, so don't be too disappointed. A true gentleman will not eat anything sweeter than a very bitter Seville marmalade at breakfast; hence you will never see croissants or pastries on his breakfast table.

Eggs: Fried, poached, scrambled or boiled, preferably from the host's own hens. Omelettes are not acceptable for the reasons already outlined. The lowest of the low is egg-white omelettes. These should not be offered and you should not ask for them unless you want to be ostracised.

Bacon: Should be smoked and streaky. It should be served crisp but not American diner brittle. Back bacon is common.

Tea: Should be a robust blend such as English breakfast or, if you want to be really proper, Scottish breakfast. The rich malty Scottish blend is in fact the origin of the traditional breakfast blend. The biggest tea *faux pas* is to use Earl Grey, which should only be served in the afternoon if at all. Commercial blends such as Yorkshire Tea are acceptable across the social classes.

Cereals: Only porridge, served slightly salted, with some syrup or sugar available for non-Scots.

Coffee: Some of the oldest families in Britain still think that Nescafé is acceptable. The best thing to do when staying with them is to develop a taste for tea. If your host serves you some excellent coffee and then proceeds to tell you exactly where in Sumatra it was grown then he is an *arriviste* and should be tastefully shunned in future.

Sausages: A cheap sausage is an obvious sign that your hosts are not completely pukka but an unnecessarily fancy one is also undesirable. A plain gutsy butcher's pork sausage is best.

Sauces: HP sauce, ketchup and mustard are acceptable at the breakfast table but they should be kept in the cupboard, not permanently stationed on the table.

Jams and Preserves: Good homemade marmalade is wonderful, Robinson's Golden Shred less so. Marmite is rather working class but acceptable.

Butter: Never margarine. Should be served in a block on a butter dish and not cut into slices or, even worse, sculpted into balls and iced!

Smoked Fish: A good kedgeree, kipper or Arbroath smokie can melt the heart of the crustiest colonel or most disapproving maiden aunt.

Cold Meats and Pies: These disappeared from the breakfast table after the war but are now making a comeback.

By memorising all of the above you should be able to place even the best-disguised interloper. So towards a general rule of class at the breakfast table: food should be as plain as possible, ingredients should be of the best possible quality but not ostentatiously so, it should be British in origin or more specifically Scottish, and Frenchness is to be avoided at all costs. (If you follow these principles, you should be able to pass as at the very least upper middle middle class if not actually upper middle class.)

A word of warning, however: some of the British upper classes follow the rule of plainness so fundamentally that it negates all the other rules. This is because they have been educated at expensive schools where terrible food is a badge of honour. Many of the country's best families actually like diabolical food. Sometimes when you are eating with such people the breakfast will be far worse than at the worst transport caff. Families like these consider it decadent and un-British to care about what one eats. The only hard and fast rule, therefore, is if the food is truly inedible then you are breakfasting with some very old money indeed. I'm all for social climbing but really! Such people are best avoided.

CLASSIC RECIPES

FROM BENEDICT
TO *BAOZI*

TODAY, THE FULL, COOKED, Magic Nine-based breakfast means many things to many people. Most see it as an occasional treat. Some eat it every day, often at the crack of dawn before going to jobs that involve building things or knocking them down. Others claim eating eggs, three kinds of meat, four kinds of vegetable and bread in the morning is a bizarre anachronism. Handily for all, breakfast is a broad church, in which we find the cooked and the uncooked, the healthy and the unhealthy, the simple and the weepingly complicated. There are blueberry pancakes, porridge with whisky-soaked raisins, croissants dipped in black coffee... Each is a daily routine for a far-flung army of the tired-eyed, forever refining their chosen dish, approaching but never quite reaching the moment when it is completely and unquestionably perfect.

Introducing his *Breakfast Book* (1980), David St John Thomas described breakfast as 'the meal closest to the character, the meal over which we can perhaps have the greatest control if we choose to exercise it'. Breakfast is the most personal meal of the day, despite or perhaps because of the way we customise it within strictly defined boundaries (in this it has a strange affinity with dinner dress or mobile phone covers). What these boundaries are is easy to spot and hard to define. A menu offering creamy chicken penne or pan-fried sea bass is a sure sign that breakfast has been and gone: do we each have inside ourselves a 'breakfaster's compass', telling us that the moment we pour cream over our fruit salad it has made the one-way trip to dessertville? There will always be those who boast of a 9 a.m. Easter egg, cold pizza in front of *This Morning* or chicken *dhansak* in a cereal bowl. Psychologists tell us boasting is a symptom of insecurity: as you congratulate these people on their individuality, note the deadness that appears momentarily in their eyes.

Having said that, what we think of as a breakfast food now may well find itself beyond the pale twenty, forty or a hundred years from now. How many today have even heard of the medieval wheat breakfast of frumenty, let alone tried it? M. L. Allen's *Breakfast Dishes* (1884) offered methods for cooking reindeer tongues and stewing ducks' giblets, while Evelyn E. Cowie's *Breakfasts* (1958) suggested creamed sweetbreads or fried brains in breadcrumbs. Today in the greasy spoons of London we see lamb chops slowly giving way to halloumi cheese, while in America the breakfast burrito, a relatively recent innovation from New Mexico, has been embraced by mega-chains Taco Bell and McDonald's.

Breakfast is changing, but at least it's changing at a dignified pace. Innovation at dinner and lunch can leave us breathless and inspired. But more often than not, a 'daring' breakfast (think rocket leaves, chicken sausage, cream cheese blinis) leaves us longing for good, simple fare: porridge, bacon and eggs, or a mushroom omelette. Breakfast is not about faddishness and fuss. It's about variations and refinements on simple themes. Just like music in fact. Or sport, film, art, literature, gardening... Is this turning into a list of the best things life has to offer?

ALTER EGGOS
A FEW GREAT FISH
OLD FAITHFULS
GRAINS OF TRUTH
PANCAKES & OVENBAKED
YOGHURT & FRUIT
FOUR MARMALADES & A JAM
CONTINENTAL

ILLUMINATIONS

WHAT WE TALK ABOUT
WHEN WE TALK
ABOUT BREAKFAST

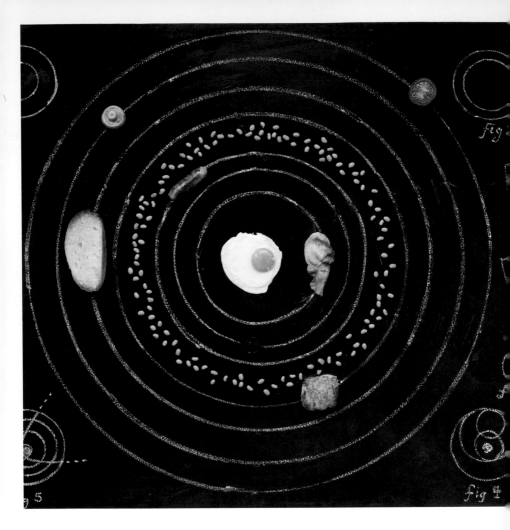

BREAKFAST SOLAR SYSTEM

If breakfast were a solar system, an egg would be the Sun. In the case of the full English and its magic nine ingredients (pp.15–91), this suggests enjoyable debates about the nature of the planets (carb giants? a bean belt?). Some claim that the egg's precedence is unfair seeing as how in breakfast, as the old saying goes, the chicken is involved but the pig is committed. But them's the breaks. Pig is a Western breakfast, while eggs are a favourite everywhere from Turkey (p.109) to Japan (p.144).

BAKED BEAN MILITIA

It has been said (at least once before) that beans are to the cooked breakfast as the Dutch Mercenary Forces were to the Royal Netherlands Indies Army. Keep them in check and they will perform unglamorous but vital tasks within the empire of the fry-up: sweetening sausage, lubricating toast, communing with chips, etc. Exert insufficient discipline upon them, however, and they will soon exhibit their mania for chaos (p.76). They teem. They flood. They carouse like drunken navvies.

COOKED BREAKFAST

England, Wales, Scotland, the Irelands: each with its own traditional cooked breakfast, as distinctive and patriotically important as its respective flag design (as in, each uses similar ingredients slightly differently and then gets very proud about it). Here we see a Welsh fry-up in which bacon, eggs and mushrooms are accompanied by laverbread (p.128) and cockles (p.113). The world is full of time-honoured cooked breakfasts. We call them the Old Faithfuls (pp.127–45). They range from the biscuits and gravy of the American Deep South (p.130) to the 'barbarian's head' buns of the Far East (p.141).

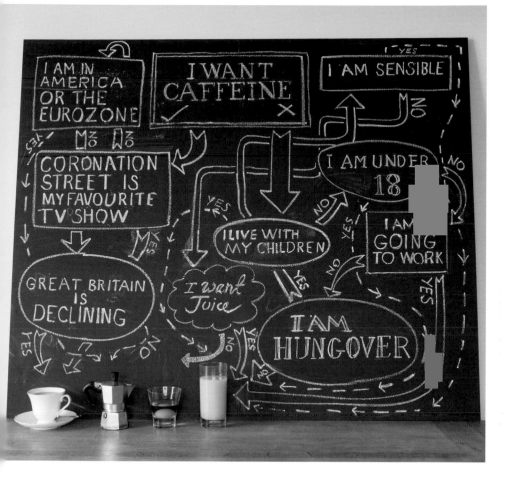

WHAT SHOULD I DRINK WITH MY BREAKFAST?

At breakfast you are allowed to do certain things that you are not allowed to do at other meals. You can read the paper. You can eat in bed (although see p.124). And, most importantly, you can drink a hot drink while you eat. But which will you have? Dependable yet elegant tea (p.211) or poetic yet business-like coffee (p.219)? Your decision says a lot about who (and where) you are. Choosing to turn your back on caffeine and go for booze rather than even, say, juice (p.229) should not be done lightly, or regularly, or without the proper recipes (pp.207–38).

COFFEE ART

You order a flat white or latte (p.227). The barista makes a heart shape in the froth. You go back, eagerly, but this time s/he just offers a regular leaf-like pattern. Is your love affair over? Did it ever begin? What if the froth contains the shape of a bear or the face of the Virgin Mary? Also see the soothsaying qualities of used tealeaves (p.214), keen to warn many of us that we'll be sent to India because of an encounter with an untrustworthy widow.

ASSORTED TOASTS

The most popular breakfast machine (p.132) ever invented? That would be the humble kitchen toaster. In goes something that isn't breakfast (mere bread) and out pops something that is (hot toast). From top left to bottom right, these slices are spread with: butter; Marmite; peanut butter; strawberry jam; set honey; a poached egg; mashed banana with crushed bran flakes, raisins, blueberries and ground linseed; *labneh* (Middle Eastern strained yoghurt) with olive oil; chocolate spread with toasted hazelnuts; marmalade; mashed avocado with salt, pepper, chilli flakes and lemon; and *muhumarra* (a spicy Arabic spread) with walnuts and pomegranates.

EMPIRE STATE PANCAKES

'Freedom is a breakfast food,' said the poet e.e. cummings. He was almost definitely thinking about American-style pancakes (pp.63–4). If pancakes symbolise America and America symbolises freedom, then, yes, freedom is a breakfast food – because it is pancakes. But have you ever noticed how the first pancake always ends up unshapely and unappealing? It's a problem that crossed the Atlantic with the Pilgrim Fathers (pp.163–4).

ALTER EGGOS

WHERE THERE IS A BREAKFAST MENU, it must include eggs – not just as a component or ingredient, as with cakes, say, or egg noodles, but as the subject of an unapologetic, egg-loving focus. Eggs celebrated in this way can of course be spotted occasionally in lunch-town or dinner-county, in a tortilla or a pizza *fiorentina*, but breakfast is their homeland, the meal that really gets them.

It's not just a Western thing. Egg dishes make an appearance on breakfast tables across the world, whether in Turkey with its *menemen* and *sucuklu yumurta*, or in China with its fascinatingly named century eggs (sadly these are not really centenarian, with all the considerable forward planning that would imply).

The purest of all egg dishes is found in Albert Camus' great eggsistentialist novel *The Stranger*. '*Je me suis fait cuire des œufs et je les ai mangés à même le plat*,' recounts our doomed narrator, Mersault: 'I cooked some eggs and ate them out of the pan.' He also eats them standing up ('*j'ai fait ma cuisine et j'ai mangé debout*'). It is clear that this is either a man in touch with the vital essence of egg-based breakfasting, or someone who doesn't have any recipes. Here are some recipes.

EGGS BENEDICT

The origins of eggs Benedict are confused. Some suggest it's a variation of French dishes named Benedictine, which indicates being cooked with salt cod; others attribute it to a stroke of genius on the part of the hungover New York stockbroker Lemuel Benedict at the Waldorf Hotel in 1894; numerous other hotels claim the inspiration was all theirs. At any rate, it seems safe to say the dish is American, as only such a wish-fulfilling platter could be. It's a dish at once restrained and indulgent. Restrained in that it makes use only of the two essential breakfast ingredients, eggs and bacon; indulgent in that it takes the scarce amber nectar that is egg yolk and transforms it into an abundant swamp. How many times, faced with the conventional fry-up, have you wished the yolk was more than a mere condiment? Benedict grants that wish and then some.

When it comes to the making, the cook's principal worry is the hollandaise, a sauce which, while it does not deserve its formidable reputation, does monopolise concentration in a dish which demands a degree of simultaneity. The inexperienced cook should ensure he fulfils the subsidiary breakfast chores of laying the table, ironing the paper, making the coffee, waking the spouse and so on before tackling this part of the recipe.

Serves 2
4–8 rashers bacon (the round Canadian sort is the ideal,
back preferable, pancetta affected)
2 teaspoons white wine vinegar
4 large eggs
2 English muffins, split (see p.75)
Unsalted butter
A snip of chives (optional, but pretty)
A slice of black truffle (optional, but expensive)

Hollandaise
2 large egg yolks
125g cold unsalted butter
A squirt of fresh lemon juice
Double cream (optional)

Bring a large pan of water to the boil for the purpose of poaching the eggs later. You are reminded to do this first, for while you will poach the eggs last, it is well to be prepared in advance.

Place a separate pan containing 2.5cm water on a low heat; insert into it a slightly larger heatproof bowl to make a bain-marie. Start to heat the water to a simmer.

Place the bacon in a pan and begin frying it.

To make the hollandaise, drop the yolks into the bain-marie and whisk as you gradually add the butter, one little knife curl at a time. Patience. Do not let the mixture overheat or you will have scrambled eggs (dismantle the bain-marie and continue whisking off the heat, returning once it has cooled if necessary; if it is splitting, throw in an ice cube to cool it down, fishing it out before it melts entirely).

Once all the butter has been added and the sauce has thickened to the consistency of a light custard, squeeze in a spritz of fresh lemon and admire the alchemy: the mixture will have turned from translucent amber to a pastel yellow. Turn off the heat and cover. Some add a lug of double cream at this point to make a demi-hollandaise; up to you.

Bring your large pan of water back to the boil, then turn down to a gentle simmer. Stir in the white wine vinegar. Lower each egg in turn, still in its shell, into the water using a tablespoon and gently and slowly turn around for 15 seconds. Crack each into a saucer, then gently slide into the pan, towards the edge. Put the muffins in the toaster. Simmer the eggs slowly until the whites have set, which should take no more than 4 minutes. Remove each with a slotted spoon and allow the water to drain back into the pan for a few seconds, then lightly dab with kitchen paper to remove any excess liquid. Trim away any ragged edges with a pair of scissors.

Assemble the dish by buttering the muffins and placing on a warmed plate; laying the bacon upon them; plopping the eggs on that; and ladling the hollandaise over the whole thing. Some snipped chives and/or cracked black pepper are desirable garniture. If you are obscene, you will add a slice of truffle.

EGGS FLORENTINE

To cook *alla fiorentina* is to cook with spinach. Of green vegetables, spinach is the most sympathetic to the breakfast palate and a dainty partner for an egg. A version of eggs Florentine may be made by following the instructions for eggs Benedict on p.98, only instead of frying the bacon, slowly sauté 500g of baby leaf spinach in butter; fresh, snipped tarragon is a pleasing garnish. For a truer Florentine, however, mornay sauce should be brought to bear, as follows.

Serves 2
500g baby leaf spinach
Unsalted butter
2 English muffins, split
2 teaspoons white wine vinegar
4 large eggs
Pinch of grated fresh nutmeg (optional)

Mornay sauce
25g unsalted butter
25g plain flour
300ml milk* plus 1 tablespoon
50g Gruyère cheese or, at a push, Cheddar, grated
2 large egg yolks
2 tablespoons double cream

*For authenticity, the milk should be infused with mace and bay leaf; bit of a waste of time, though.

Put a pan full of water (or a kettle) on to boil so that it is ready for poaching the eggs later.

Put the butter for the sauce into a saucepan and melt on a low heat; add the flour and, with a wooden spoon, encourage them to combine together to form a roux. Do not allow this to colour. Now begin to add the milk, a bit at a time, stirring all the while to prevent lumps forming. Allow it to simmer for 3 minutes or so, thickening as it does so. This is a basic béchamel sauce. If it is lumpy, pass it through a sieve and return to the pan.

Turn the béchamel into mornay sauce. Add the grated Gruyère to the pan, stirring until it is melted. Now add the egg yolks, still stirring heartily. Remove from the heat and add the cream.

Sauté the spinach in a little butter and drain well. Toast the muffins.

Bring your pan of water back to the boil, then turn down to a gentle simmer. Stir in the white wine vinegar. Lower each egg in turn, still in its shell, into the water using a tablespoon and gently and slowly turn around for 15 seconds. Crack each into a saucer, then gently slide into the pan, towards the edge.

Simmer the eggs slowly until the whites are set, which should take no more than 4 minutes. Remove each with a slotted spoon and allow the water to drain back into the pan for a few seconds, then lightly dab with kitchen paper to remove any excess liquid. Trim away any ragged edges with a pair of scissors.

Assemble the dish by buttering the muffins and placing on a warmed plate; laying the spinach upon them; plopping the eggs on that; and ladling the mornay sauce over the whole thing. A little grated nutmeg is a very nice garnish.

BENEDICT VARIATIONS

'Benedict or Florentine?' was once a common refrain around English universities, the identification with one or the other taken as an instinctive marker of a fellow's character. But the Benedict formula is ripe for further experimentation, each item, save the egg, capable of being switched. 'There is not a celebrity, a marshal, a composer, or an opera singer who has not given his name to a method of preparing eggs,' observed the French gourmand James de Coquet.

Here are some popular and/or interesting variations.

Eggs Beauregard: This Deep South term originally referred to a dish of hard-boiled eggs served with cream sauce, but has drifted and now describes biscuits and gravy (see p.130) with sausage patties (see p.46) and fried egg (see p.21). To add to the confusion this dish is also sometimes known as Country Benedict.

Eggs Benedict XVI: A dish made in honour of Joseph Aloisius Ratzinger, aka Pope Benedict XVI. Powerful, Germanic variation in which dark rye bread and *Weisswurst* sausage take the place of muffin and bacon respectively.

Eggs Benedictine: The bacon or ham of Benedict *and* the spinach of Florentine.

Eggs Blackstone: A minor (albeit tasty) version comprising eggs Benedict with a tomato slice.

Eggs Chesapeake: Variation named after the Chesapeake Bay estuary, swapping the bacon or ham of normal Benedict for crispy crab cakes.

Eggs Hussarde: A creation of Brennan's restaurant in New Orleans. The muffin halves are replaced with crisp Holland rusks and the hollandaise is supplemented by white-wine-based marchand de vin sauce.

Eggs Pontchartrain: Another New Orleans dish, named after nearby Lake Pontchartrain. What it should actually be is disputed: generally muffin halves, grits, biscuits or hash browns topped with mountain trout, fried oysters or crab cakes in either a hollandaise or a béarnaise sauce.

Eggs Royale: An Antipodean favourite replacing bacon with smoked salmon. Should be garnished with capers and finely chopped red onion. Aliases include eggs Copenhagen, eggs Madison and eggs Hemingway.

Eggs Sardou: Invented by Antoine's restaurant in New Orleans in honour of a visit by French dramatist Victorien Sardou: Benedict with steamed artichoke bottoms instead of muffins.

Alternatively, you could invent your own – chorizo for bacon? Béarnaise for hollandaise? Pumpernickel bagel for muffin? Name it after your favourite uncle.

BENEDICT FOR THE MASSES?
by H. P. Seuss

The Egg McMuffin was invented in 1972 – not by a chef but by a Chicago adman, Herb Peterson, who made the leap to McDonald's during a major period of expansion and coined the phrase 'Where Quality Starts Fresh Every Day'. A fan of eggs Benedict, he took it as inspiration for a breakfast-based departure from the usual burger sandwich, substituting muffin for the standard McDonald's bun, Teflon-poached egg for beef patty and a round of Canadian bacon for iceberg lettuce. The one ingredient it had in common with the cheeseburger was the chrome square of cheese, which here became a tiny nod to hollandaise. A shameful pleasure for many, it proves that the combination of egg and salted meat is resilient to almost any horror in the cooking and exploiting. Peterson's legacy was profound: reports estimate that breakfast food now brings in almost 50 per cent of McDonald's profits.

HUEVOS RANCHEROS

Yeee haa. Cowboy food. Occasionally this dish can just mean spicy sauce with eggs, but in this version the eggs play an integral role. Try closing your eyes and imagining making this on a fire just after doing some honest-to-God cattle rustling (and just before the farting contest). As with most things involving (a) eggs and (b) spicy things, the addition of a little chorizo would be a good idea.

Serves 2
1 tablespoon olive oil
½ small onion, chopped
1 garlic clove, finely chopped
1 Scotch bonnet chilli, deseeded and chopped,
or leave the seeds in if you like it hot
1 teaspoon tomato paste
½ teaspoon ground cumin
1 x 400g tin tomatoes
4 eggs, any size
2 tortillas
2 tablespoons soured cream

In a medium saucepan heat the oil. Add the onion and cook on a low heat for 5 minutes. After 5 minutes add the garlic and chilli. When these are nicely soft, but before colouring, turn the heat up a little and add the tomato paste and cumin. Let the mixture bubble for a minute. Add the tin of tomatoes, using a wooden spoon to break the tomato pieces up. Cook on a medium heat for 20 minutes. If it begins to dry out, add a little water.

When the sauce has reduced, make four holes in it and break the eggs into them. Let the eggs fry, occasionally basting the tops with the hot tomato sauce. Meanwhile in another frying pan warm the tortillas and place them on two warmed plates.

When the eggs are done, spoon two on to each tortilla and share the sauce between them. Serve with a dollop of soured cream on each.

···················· **HUEVOS FANTASTICOS** ····················

This recipe comes from Latin America via Los Angeles. Many well-heeled Anglo-Angelino kids spend more time with their Latin American nannies than they do with their actual mothers, imbuing them with a taste for spicy versions of conventional breakfasts. We have dubbed this dish *huevos fantasticos*. It is worth using a nice mature Cheddar, as the flavour really comes through. The marriage of the fattiness of the cheese and eggs with the heat and fruit of the chilli is magical, and somehow the dish tastes a lot healthier than it really is. Add some chorizo or bacon at the beginning if you're feeling greedy.

Serves 2
Knob of unsalted butter
1 Scotch bonnet chilli, deseeded and finely chopped
5 eggs, any size, lightly beaten
Handful of grated mature Cheddar cheese
2 slices bread, toasted
Hot sauce, preferably Cholula or Red Rooster

In a non-stick saucepan melt the butter, and soften the chilli over a medium heat. Turn the heat down to low and add the beaten eggs.

Using a wooden spoon, keep stirring the cooked egg from the bottom of the pan until you have small lumps of cooked egg suspended in partially cooked egg. You should be aiming for softly scrambled eggs. This will take 5–10 minutes. When they are still slightly runny add the grated cheese and stir until it melts in. Spoon on to a slice of toast and serve with hot sauce on the side.

SHAKSHUKA

A crimson swamp peppered with eggs resembling crash-landed UFOs, *shakshuka* has much in common with *menemen* from Turkey. It is popular in Israel, but its exact history is gloopy – Morocco, Libya, Egypt and Yemen have all claimed to be *shakshuka*'s birthplace. There are countless different formulae but important constants are the kick of hot spice, the soft sweetness of tomato sauce and of course the egginess of the eggs. Tasty flourishes include crumbled feta or grilled halloumi scattered on top of each serving.

Serves 3–4
½ teaspoon cumin seeds
80ml olive oil
2 medium onions, finely chopped
1 green chilli pepper, deseeded and finely chopped
1 red sweet pepper, deseeded and finely chopped
2 teaspoons muscovado sugar
1 tablespoon chopped thyme leaves
3 tablespoons chopped coriander leaves
2 tablespoons chopped flat-leaf parsley
1 x 400g tin chopped tomatoes
½ teaspoon cayenne pepper
Salt and pepper
6 medium eggs
Soft white bread, to sop

Heat a large frying pan over a medium-high heat. Add the cumin seeds and dry-fry for 2 minutes. Add the olive oil and allow it to heat up, then add the onion and green chilli and cook for around 2 minutes.

Throw in the red pepper, sugar, thyme and all but 1 tablespoon each of the coriander and parsley. Cook on a medium-low heat for a further 5 minutes. Add the tomatoes and cayenne, then season, and turn the heat down. Leave for 15 minutes, but keep checking on it – if it's getting dry, add a little water.

Now break the eggs into the mix so that they are more or less evenly spaced. Cover the pan and leave gently cooking for 5 minutes, or until the white has cooked but the yolk still has a bit of run to it. Sprinkle on the rest of the parsley and coriander, and serve with some bread close to hand.

MATZA BREI

Pronounced '*mut-sah bry*' this is a traditional Jewish Passover breakfast. It's a simple dish made with *matza* – the unleavened bread that was eaten during the Exodus (there was no time to wait for dough to rise). The *matza* is fried with eggs, and is good for mopping up hangovers. It can and should be eaten by anyone, whatever the time of year.

Our Jewish correspondent says: 'There are many different ways to make it. The only proper way, of course, is the way my mother and grandmother make it and this is how. I suppose you could serve it with fruit and maple syrup if you wanted. Or with cucumber and smoked salmon and a spoonful of crème fraîche. But don't do that. Just put it on a plate and eat it.'

Serves 2
4 medium eggs
Large splash of milk (about 125ml)
Pinch of salt
8 matza sheets
1 tablespoon bland oil such as sunflower

Break the eggs into a large bowl. Check to make sure there are no large blood spots and remove if necessary. If they are not detachable without breaking the yolk, discard that egg. This is how you make sure an egg is kosher. Add the milk and whisk briefly with a fork until it's just become a homogenous mixture. Add a pinch of salt.

Break the *matza* sheets into small pieces – don't worry about getting them the same size, just crumble with your fingers into the bowl. Mix them into the egg until they are covered. Leave for 10–20 minutes, until they have soaked up much of the egg.

Heat the oil on a high heat in a large wide frying pan. Pour in the egg and *matza* mixture. Stir regularly, preferably with an old half-melted plastic spatula your grandmother used to use. You want a consistency that's a bit crunchy and a bit soft – don't allow the whole thing to cook together into one cake, but don't break it apart too much either. You want pieces the size of cereal clusters, but with a hot, oily, salty, moist crunchiness. When it's reached that blessed consistency, tip at once on to a plate and eat with a fork. Here is the taste of Jewish authenticity.

MENEMEN

This dish falls somewhere between ratatouille and scrambled eggs, is nothing to do with *The Muppets* and was possibly born in the Turkish town of Menemen, site of a bloody Greek invasion in the 1920s and a failed Sufi rebellion in the 1930s. It's the epitome of home cooking. Descriptions of what it actually is tend to be fairly sketchy, but that's the joy: you can make it up as you go along. Ask any terse elderly Turkish gentleman about *menemen* and he will grow wistful, think fondly of his wife or mother, and smile at the prospect of this homely Anatolian food. Here's a recipe, from which you can legitimately adjust the proportions of the ingredients to taste.

Serves 2
50g unsalted butter
½ onion, diced
2 large ripe tomatoes
2 long thin sweet green peppers, or 1 ordinary sweet pepper
½ teaspoon paprika
Salt and pepper
4 large eggs
Handful of flat-leaf parsley, chopped

Melt the butter in a heavy-based pan. Cook the onion in the butter until it turns translucent.

Place the tomatoes in boiling water for 30 seconds, then remove the skins and dice. Slice the peppers thinly, removing the seeds.

Add the peppers and tomatoes to the softened onion and cook for 3 more minutes. The mixture should now be quite wet, so add the paprika and season well.

Crack the eggs into a bowl, and beat well, then add them to the pan. Keep stirring the mix until the eggs have set, bearing in mind that because of the other ingredients in the pan they'll be runnier than normal scrambled eggs, but they should not be jelly-like.

Serve straight from the pan, with fresh bread and sprinkled with chopped flat-leaf parsley.

SUCUKLU YUMURTA

You are on the phone. The line is terrible. A man with an unfamiliar accent is insulting your mother. This is the scene all too commonly brought to mind when the words '*sucuklu yumurta*' are uttered. Actually, all it means is 'sausage and eggs': you are about to receive eggs laced with the spicy beef sausage made throughout Turkey and nearby Muslim countries like Kosovo, Bosnia and Cyprus's relevant half.

Looks-wise, *sucuklu yumurta* is a dead ringer for something a repentant and hungry drunk might make in a pan at 4 a.m. if he discovered three eggs and began to cook them but was torn between scrambled, fried and omelette, and halfway through discovered some questionable Continental meat product at the back of the cupboard and lobbed that in too. The exoticism of its name has legitimised what others would write off as a weird mess. In the Turkish-owned breakfast houses of East London they will, if they know what they are about, serve it in the very copper pot in which it was cooked, if cooked is not too grand a word. It is delicious.

The following recipe uses scrambled eggs, but an authentic fried egg version can be had simply by frying some eggs amongst the sausage slices in the same pan, adding the eggs when the slices are turned.

Serves 2
4 large eggs
Unsalted butter
1 sucuklu sausage, chopped into thin (but not too thin) slices
Salt and pepper

Beat the eggs in a large bowl. Melt a knob of butter in a frying pan on a medium heat and chuck in the slices of sausage. After about a minute, turn the sausage slices. Melt a knob of butter in a separate small frying pan on a medium heat, and pour in the beaten eggs. Keep stirring the eggs until they are half done, at which point turn them off and add another knob of butter. Mix in the sausage with the eggs, add salt and pepper to taste, and serve.

If you have a red pepper, you can dice it and throw it in with the slices of sausage at the very beginning and it'll certainly be tasty. Chopping a bit of flat-leaf parsley and mixing it in at the end is also worth doing, if you have some to hand.

BREAKFAST BURRITO

To the newcomer, the breakfast burrito may ring the same novelty-edition alarm bells as 'breakfast pizza', 'breakfast vindaloo' and all the other staples of the student union and bored flight-side airport diner. But when prepared correctly this meeting of tortilla and cooked breakfast is a fully grown-up, accomplished dish. The breakfast burrito was invented in Santa Fe. Some would say this is ample justification for Santa Fe being granted UNESCO Creative City status.

Makes 4–6 burritos
250g peeled and diced potatoes
2 tablespoons vegetable oil
100g chorizo, diced
1 green sweet pepper, chopped
1 garlic clove, minced
2 spring onions, chopped
4 large eggs
Salt and pepper
200g Cheddar cheese, grated
4–6 tortillas
1 ripe avocado, peeled, halved, pitted and sliced
4 tablespoons chopped coriander leaves
Hot sauce, preferably Cholula or Red Rooster

Cook the potato in a saucepan of salted boiling water until just tender (about 5 minutes). Drain and set aside. Heat 1 tablespoon of oil in a heavy-based pan. Cook the chorizo over a medium heat for 2–3 minutes, then add the green pepper. Stir frequently until the chorizo is beginning to brown and the pepper softens. Add the potato. Stir the mixture occasionally until tender and browned. Add the garlic and spring onions, cook for 1 more minute, then remove the potato mixture from the pan and set aside.

Whisk together the eggs and season with salt and pepper. Heat the remaining oil in the same pan, add the egg mixture and cook, stirring to scramble until just heated through. Remove from the heat. Add the cheese to the egg so that it melts nicely.

In another pan, heat a tortilla for approximately 1 minute each side to soften. Spoon into horizontal rows in the low centre of the tortilla some of the potato mixture, egg, sliced avocado and chopped coriander. Add the hot sauce at this stage if you want it, though for guests it may be best to let them add it themselves. Fold the outer edges of tortilla in about 5cm, hold in place and roll up from the bottom to securely enclose the burrito. Repeat with the other tortillas.

PERSIAN EGGS WITH HALLOUMI

Cheese at breakfast needs to be treated with care. Context is everything. Sliced cheese in Germany, for instance, is OK. Sliced cheese in Cardiff is not. Sliced cheese in an Egg McMuffin is OK. Sliced cheese in a bacon sandwich is not. Camembert, Stilton and Parmesan are never OK. Then there's halloumi, which is the cheese with the Breks Factor. This is mainly due to the qualities it shares – saltiness, moreishness, hotness, slicedness – with bacon. Halloumi plus a lot of good olive oil, a pinch of sumac and a dash of tomato sweetness give your eggs an out-of-character quality: romance.

Serves 2
Extra virgin olive oil
1 block halloumi cheese, diced
8 cherry tomatoes, halved
4 large eggs
2 teaspoons sumac (turmeric will also work if you can't find sumac)
Soft Middle Eastern- or Turkish-style bread

Add the olive oil to a frying pan until about 1mm deep then turn on the heat to medium. Throw in the halloumi and tomatoes and cook until the cheese cubes soften and begin to darken slightly. Create small clearings in the pan into which to break the eggs, then break the eggs into them. Sprinkle with the sumac (or turmeric, if using).

When the white is cooked and the yolk is still runny, serve on plates (you should include the oil, which will have picked up the flavour of the spice) with the bread.

CHANGUA

If you've never been told that you make a man want to speak Spanish, it could be your diet. The remedy is surely *changua*, a traditional breakfast soup from Colombia's central Andes region, combining eggs, milk, spring onions and coriander. There's always the possibility that Gabriel García Márquez was eating *changua* when he heard he'd won the Nobel Prize, or that Shakira's notorious hips were fattened on the stuff. Pure speculation of course, but what we do know is that *changua* is the chicken soup of the international breakfast table, yearned for all over the internet by the homesick Colombian diaspora. It even has its own Facebook page.

Changua is made by poaching eggs in milk – that's about it. Some recipes call for frying the spring onions first, others just throw them in with the milk, and taste-wise the difference between the two methods is negligible. The eggs and milk combination isn't very British and might raise a few eyebrows but an egg poached in milk is a classy specimen: the white plump and gleaming, its yolk reminiscent of a closed eye in sunlight. It's a controversial cow-meets-hen love story and how it ends depends on you.

Serves 2
2 spring onions, chopped
Unsalted butter
240ml milk
720ml water
Salt and pepper
4 medium eggs
100g feta or similar cheese (optional)
4 teaspoons chopped coriander leaves

Sauté the spring onions in a little butter for a few minutes, then add the milk, water and seasoning and bring to a rolling boil, before turning down to a gentle, trembling simmer. Crack the eggs and add them to the 'soup', taking care not to break the yolks. Cover and simmer for a further 2–3 minutes (or longer, if you prefer more well-done eggs).

If adding cheese, crumble it in equal portions into two bowls. Pour the soup over the cheese, allowing two eggs per person. Garnish liberally with coriander and serve with hard bread or toast for dipping.

COCKLES AND EGGS

In Dublin's fair city
Where the girls are so pretty
I first set my eyes on sweet Molly Malone
As she wheel'd her wheel barrow
Through streets broad and narrow
Crying 'Cockles and mussels alive, alive o!'

What better dish to conjure up the spirit of sweet Molly Malone, plying her mollusc-based trade around the streets of Dublin, than a plate of cockles for breakfast? Today, the jarred, vinegar-soused cockles Molly sold in the 1880s are more likely to be found in an East End pub. Regardless, the cockle, a hinged heart-shaped clam, is a neglected British delicacy, and also forms a key part of the Welsh national breakfast. It is debatable whether Norfolk's Stiffkey Blues or the Gower Peninsula's Penclawdd cockles are the finest, but safe to say cockles taste better freshly steamed open and served with bacon than cold and drenched in vinegar.

Buy cockles fresh from your fishmonger and use immediately. To lose the grit, soak in a bowl of salt water for a couple of hours before cooking. Discard any open cockles at this stage. To cook, steam in a pan with a splash of fresh water for a few minutes until the shells open, and discard any that don't open. Serve in the shells with bacon and laverbread (see p.128), or pick the meat out of the shells and use in the classic Welsh dish of *cocos ac wyau*.

Per person
100g cockles (minus their shells)
1–2 tablespoons bacon fat
2 medium eggs
Black pepper

Prepare the cockles as above (or if using frozen ones, defrost at room temperature, rinse thoroughly and drain of excess moisture). In a frying pan, heat the bacon fat (or fry off a couple of rashers of streaky if you have any), then add the cockles, turning them in the fat until they are warmed through. Beat the eggs, add to the pan, season with black pepper and mix well, until the eggs are cooked through but not dry. Serve with bread and butter.

CHINESE CENTURY EGG

A Chinese hundred-year egg is possibly less exciting than it sounds, but belongs to that pantheon of delicacies, such as the Icelandic rotten shark meat dish *hákarl*, that see taste and decency in the kitchen pushed to their limits. Find yourself with a surplus of eggs on a Sunday afternoon and you too may choose to preserve rather than waste them, as was the impetus for creating this reeking, gelatinous, brown and green ovum.

Traditionally the eggs are caked in alkaline clay, or a mixture of quicklime, wood ash, sea salt and tea, wrapped in cloth and snuck away for three years. The result? They look and smell as if they've been ignored for a century, with the yolk turning dark green and the white to a transparent brown jelly with more than the faintest whiff of ammonia. Not for nothing were they nicknamed horse-urine eggs. No good for a quick snack, then, but they are considered a delicacy.

Today, not everyone waits three years for century eggs: technological advances have accelerated the age-old process, which we divulge below in a recipe borrowed with thanks from the Taiwan Livestock Research Institute.Once you've made a few century eggs, you could opt for a bowl of them with *char siu* congee (see opposite) for a traditional start to the day. (Alternatively Chinese supermarkets sell century eggs in cartons.)

1 litre cold water
72g salt (NaCl, sodium chloride)
42g food-grade lye (NaOH, sodium hydroxide)*
Around 6 large eggs
PVA**

* Lye has been used in food preparation for centuries, for hominy grits, pretzels and lutfisk, but it's an extremely corrosive alkali, traditionally made by leaching water through wood ash, so can also be used to clean drains. You should source food-grade lye (sodium hydroxide) online, and follow the safety instructions when handling it because it can cause severe burns to exposed flesh and shouldn't be ingested. Make sure that you wear gloves and goggles. Lye also reacts violently with aluminium so do not use any aluminium utensils.

** PVA glue is the white glue that you used to use at school and it can be bought in craft shops. The point of the glue is to seal off the egg from all contact with the air, so coat thoroughly.

Put the cold water in a large non-aluminium pan. Wearing the safety gear, weigh out the salt and lye, and gently dissolve in the cold water. Slowly bring to the boil, then allow to cool.

Add the raw eggs to a large sealable glass jar, and pour over the cool saline solution until the eggs are fully submerged, and store at 15–20°C for ten days. Check that the eggs stay submerged.

After 10 days, pour away the liquid and, wearing gloves, gently remove the eggs, rinse them, then allow to dry naturally. Seal the shells with PVA and leave in a dry place to age for two weeks. Once aged, crack the eggs lightly and carefully remove the shell. The white of the eggs will have a greyish, translucent colour, and a gelatinous texture. The yolk, when sliced, will be a greyish-green colour.

Lean Pork Congee (to Accompany Century Eggs)

At breakfast the classic companion for century egg is *char siu* or lean pork congee. Congee is one of those catch-all dishes that might ungenerously be termed breakfast-mush. Rice is cooked in lots of water, for a long time, until it becomes a gelatinous soup that can be flavoured to taste. If you're making it from scratch it can take ages, as you slowly break down the rice. For a swifter morning treat, use leftover rice and it'll take around an hour.

Serves 2
1 teaspoon bouillon powder
750ml freshly boiled water
150g Chinese roast pork (char siu), diced
3 spring onions, diced, green and white separate
250g leftover cooked rice
2 century eggs (see opposite)
Salt and white pepper

Dissolve the bouillon powder in the boiled water. Put the *char siu*, diced white ends of the spring onions and cooked rice in a heavy-based saucepan, then pour on the bouillon and bring back to the boil. Simmer for 1 hour, stirring frequently to help break down the rice, and stop it sticking. Add more water as you go along if it looks as if it's getting a little thick.

Towards the end of the cooking time, slice and add the century eggs to the pan, along with the rest of the chopped green spring onions, and season to taste. Stir gently so as not to destroy the eggs and keep cooking until everything is just warmed through. Alternatively, slice the eggs and arrange them in a fancy pattern on top of the congee.

A FEW
GREAT FISH

IF BACON AND EGGS are the bride and groom of the breakfast table then smoked fish are undoubtedly the bridesmaids. Not because of their fishy smell but because they are unfairly overlooked. This was not always the case: no Edwardian country house breakfast would have been complete without a huge bowl of steaming kedgeree. Smoking, once a way of preserving fish, is now carried out mainly to impart flavour. There are two ways of smoking fish: hot, where the heat from the smoke cooks the fish, and cold, where it remains raw.

TYPES OF SMOKED FISH

The main types of smoked fish that you'll encounter at breakfast are herring, haddock, salmon and mackerel.

Kippers: The herring is the basis for this most famous of all the breakfast fish. To turn it into a kipper it is split along its backbone, opened out and then cold-smoked and salted.

Despite being uncooked, kippers need very little cooking. The traditional way to prepare them is to immerse them tail up in a jug of boiling water for 5–10 minutes (jugging) but you can also grill or poach them, although you should be prepared for long-lasting aromatic implications. Like Arbroath smokies (see below) they are best served on their own with a little butter, lemon and brown bread.

Haddock: Avoid the lurid yellow fillets and ask for undyed ones. They should be a creamy-white colour and have a subtle smoky flavour. Most haddock is cold-smoked so will need cooking. Smoked haddock is a vital part of kedgeree (see p.120) and the most important ingredient in omelette Arnold Bennett (see p.122). It's also very good with a poached egg, a hash brown or potato pancake and a splash of hollandaise.

There is a kind of smoked haddock called an Arbroath smokie. This, like champagne or Roquefort, can only come from a designated area – in this case around the Scottish town of Arbroath. Arbroath smokies are hot-smoked over wood through hessian and so require no further cooking. Serve warmed with butter, lemon and lots of brown toast.

Salmon: The most widely available of all the smoked fish and sadly one of the most abused. Most smoked salmon available in the shops will be from farmed salmon dyed an artificial pink by coloured additives and then industrially cold-smoked in vast quantities. It is worth seeking out the (necessarily expensive) stuff produced by small artisan smokers who work in the traditional ways. Hot-smoked salmon is less common but worth trying as it combines the flaky texture of grilled salmon with a smoky taste.

Smoked salmon works very well in scrambled eggs. Try adding while the eggs are still scrambling so that it gets cooked in the process. Voila! Hot smoked salmon.

Mackerel: Another oily fish, not dissimilar to herring, with a gutsy flavour. Mackerel is generally hot-smoked and as such requires no further cooking. It has the further benefit of being abundant – at least in British waters – so breakfasters can consume it without the pangs of conscience that can arise with salmon, haddock and even the humble herring. Serve with a poached egg and some sautéed spinach for a healthy breakfast.

FREUD'S BREAKFAST DREAM
by Poppy Tartt

In *The Interpretation of Dreams*, Freud recounts several dreams of his own, one of which is almost definitely known in psychoanalytic circles as 'The Breakfast Dream'. This initially frightening dream, involving a beseiged castle, gives way to a final scene which finds Freud standing at a window with his brother, scrutinising passing ships. One of these ships is particularly alarming, but as it draws closer the brothers are delighted: 'We call out as with one voice: "That is the breakfast ship."'

Of its meaning, Freud observes: 'But the only thing about this breakfast ship which has been newly created by the dream is its name. The thing existed in reality, and recalls to me one of the merriest moments of my last journey. As we distrusted the fare in Aquileia, we took some food with us from Goerz, and bought a bottle of the excellent Istrian wine in Aquileia; and while the little mail-steamer slowly travelled through the *canale delle Mee* and into the lonely expanse of lagoon in the direction of Grado, we had breakfast on deck in the highest spirits – we were the only passengers – and it tasted to us as few breakfasts have ever tasted. This, then, was the "breakfast ship", and it is behind this very recollection of the gayest *joie de vivre* that the dream hides the saddest thoughts of an unknown and mysterious future.'

Though Freud sadly did not make the first meal of the day his life's work, as this dream shows he was profoundly aware, at least subconsciously, that there is one thing driving us all, and that is breakfast.

A RECIPE FOR KEDGEREE

How many recipes are there for kedgeree? More than there are stars in the sky or gods in the Hindu pantheon. More, even, than there are spellings for the various Indian dishes that claim parentage (*kitchari? kitcheri? khichdi? khichri?*). Kedgeree as we know it (kidgeree? kedagree? cutcharee?) originated in the days of the Raj. It was the first breakfast to be served in the popular TV show *Downton Abbey* – set on an English country estate during Edwardian times, where the emergence of curried rice dishes was as far as it went in terms of colonial blowback. The dish persists in certain clubs in London where India is called 'Inja' and there are huge paintings on the walls with titles such as *The Tiger Hunt, Lahore* (1857).

Some recipes call for pre-cooked rice which is then incorporated into a sauce, but it seems a shame not to make use of that lovely fishy milk. Use a large saucepan (30cm diameter approximately) with a tight-fitting lid. If you use a small one, the rice will cook unevenly. Cast iron is ideal as it holds the heat in. The smoked haddock may provide enough salt for the whole dish or you can add a little more at the end.

Serves 6
500g smoked haddock
6 black peppercorns
1 bay leaf
500ml whole milk
20g unsalted butter
1 teaspoon each of coriander and cumin seeds, roughly ground
½ teaspoon ground turmeric
1 large onion, finely chopped
200g basmati rice
100ml water
4 large eggs
Juice of 1 lemon
Handful of flat-leaf parsley, roughly chopped
1 teaspoon garam masala
Salt and pepper

Put the fish, peppercorns, bay leaf and milk into a saucepan, and bring gently to the boil. Take off the heat and set aside for 3 minutes. Drain the fish, preserving the milk. Discard the skin and bones, gently flake the fish flesh and set aside.

Heat the butter in a large saucepan (see opposite). Add the coriander, cumin seeds and turmeric, sizzle for a minute, then add the onion and soften for about 10 minutes – do not let it colour. Now add the rice and coat in the spices, onion and butter before adding the saved milk and the water. Gently bring to the boil, then turn the heat right down to the lowest and cover. *Do not touch* for 13 minutes.

Meanwhile boil the eggs until almost hard (8–9 minutes – see p.27 for general principles), peel and quarter. After 13 minutes take the rice off the heat, fluff it up, put the lid back on and leave for 10 minutes.

Uncover the rice, and stir in the smoked fish and boiled eggs. Finally, add the lemon juice, chopped parsley, garam masala, salt if needed and black pepper, and serve with an anecdote about the Rajmata of Dhrangadhra-Halvad.

Note: If you're out of basmati but sitting on a stockpile of risotto rice such as Arborio, you can make a version of kedgeree that we'd call 'kedgerotto' if only it sounded nice. Here, rather than adding all the milk and water to the rice at once, you should – as with any risotto – introduce it in instalments, adding a ladleful and waiting until it has been absorbed before adding the next. Stir in the other ingredients when the rice is as firm as you want it to be (it's hard to say what is 'correct' when it comes to Indian-Italian-British cuisine).

OMELETTE ARNOLD BENNETT

It's not clear how Arnold Bennett managed to produce such a prodigious amount of work whilst subsisting on the dish named after him. Try writing a series of critically acclaimed bestsellers set in Stoke-on-Trent after eating this omelette. Impossible, isn't it? Mr Bennett was clearly a man apart. Fortunately he had the staff at the Savoy to prepare it for him or he would never have got anything done.

It's a complicated process. Some recipes leave out the béchamel sauce base and just put cheese in but that's not what Arnold would have wanted, so please, for Arnold Bennett's sake, make it properly and take the rest of the morning to sleep it off.

Serves 2
200ml whole milk
1 bay leaf
1 teaspoon black peppercorns
Grated fresh nutmeg
250g smoked haddock (undyed)
30g unsalted butter
2 tablespoons plain flour
100g Gruyère cheese, grated
50ml single cream
3 tablespoons hollandaise (see p.98)
5 large eggs
Black pepper

Put the milk, bay leaf, peppercorns, a grate of nutmeg and haddock in a saucepan. Gently bring to the boil and then take off the heat and leave for 5 minutes. Take the fish out, remove its skin and gently flake the flesh. Strain the milk and set aside.

Now for the béchamel sauce base. Melt half the butter in a saucepan. Add the flour and mix well to form a roux. When it starts to smell biscuity, add a little of the warm, strained milk and mix thoroughly, avoiding lumps. Gradually add all the milk. When it is all integrated, add half the cheese. Cook the mixture for about 4 minutes, stirring frequently. Add the cream.

Now it all comes together. Turn the grill on to its highest setting. Mix the haddock, cheesey béchamel and the hollandaise together. Whisk up the eggs. Melt the remaining butter in a medium, heavy-based frying pan. When it is bubbling, add the eggs so that they coat the inside of the pan, stirring the mixture gently to keep it light. When it is set around the edges and base but still runny on top, add the fish mixture and a little pepper. You probably won't need any salt because the fish is salty enough already.

Sprinkle the rest of the cheese on top, then put the pan under the grill until it colours and bubbles. The inside should be delightfully gooey. Cut in half and then serve.

OMELETTE ARNIE BENNETT

For those with things to do or without staff, this is a cheat's recipe called omelette Arnie Bennett. It's not terribly Edwardian and Arnold himself would doubtless disapprove.

Serves 2
250g smoked haddock (undyed)
200ml whole milk
1 bay leaf
1 teaspoon black peppercorns
Grated fresh nutmeg
50ml double cream
Salt and black pepper
5 large eggs
15g unsalted butter
100g Gruyère cheese, grated

Cook the haddock as per the recipe opposite but discard the milk. Add the cream to the flaked fish and season.

Turn on the grill and beat the eggs. Melt the butter in a medium, heavy-based frying pan. When it is bubbling, add the eggs so that they coat the inside of the pan, stirring gently to keep the omelette light.

When the egg is set around the edges and base but still runny on top add the fish 'custard' and a little black pepper. Sprinkle with the cheese and place under the grill until golden.

BREAKFAST IN BED
by Malcolm Eggs

Breakfast in bed seems simple. You are in bed, eating breakfast. This is luxurious. What else could it be? But be honest – is it really such a treat? There is a tray on your lap. There is crumb-fear in your mind. Are you feeling decadent and pampered, or imprisoned and a little squalid? Does some part of you long to be sitting at a table?

The dirty secret of the in-bed breakfaster is that much of the time they are not enjoying the meal at all. This staple of birthday and romance is merely being *put up with* so that later it can be boasted that *it was done.* Nothing says 'our relationship is going well' more succinctly than 'we had breakfast in bed'. (It seems significant, meanwhile, that it's hard to say 'don't lend me money' more directly than 'I had lunch in bed').

So if people don't actually like it, should it be done away with altogether? This would seem over the top. For all its drawbacks, breakfast in bed is a beautiful gesture and the joy of what it means is more than enough to carry you through the ordeal of receiving it.

In any case, it's almost inevitable that at some point, whether because of expectation or expedience, you will need to make it for someone else. The key to breakfast success in the bedroom is realising that just putting some breakfast on a tray and taking it to a sleepy recipient is not enough. Breakfast in bed should be presented with ceremony. The small details are important. Try to do it in a way that combines the best bits of the breakfast table (space, freedom, options) with those of the bed (comfort, horizontality). Here are some of the key principles.

The Pillows: Hugely important. Don't try to serve breakfast in bed if the recipient only has two thin old feather pillows and a sofa cushion. You'll need enough pillows to create a triangle with a wide enough base and a tall enough peak to support both back and head while they are sitting upright.

The Tray: Use a large tray that gives you space to present the breakfast in style. If you have a tray-cloth then use it. It will look better and stop everything from sliding around treacherously.

The Small Touches: Add these to the tray before the food, so you're ready to transport it as soon as it's ready. Put some butter in a small dish and on to the tray (yes, strictly speaking it is part of 'The Food' – but it's the letting it soften that's a small touch). A small vase with one or two wild flowers is a classic (and occasionally classy) touch, as is a newspaper, a well-chosen soundtrack and cutlery wrapped in conical napkins. (Note: Remember to remove the flower vase at the moment of serving to avoid spilling water.)

The Food: Whatever you're cooking, try to time it so that breakfast is served no later than when the breakfaster would naturally get up. This avoids the nagging sense of being imprisoned by kindness. Spoon all the various condiments and sauces into small, attractive dishes and place them around the tray, leaving space to then add any main plates or dishes. Toast should be added, in a rack or small wicker basket, at the very last moment.

The Drinks: Serve on a smaller tray, separate from the food. Leave by the side of the bed to avoid spillage, but still within easy reach on a surface at least as high as the base of the mattress.

The breakfaster must now throw aside concerns about crumbs and just go with it. Enjoy the moment. Eat with gusto. Pretend you are in a hotel. Remember the adage 'dance as if no one's watching'? Breakfast in bed as if someone else will change the sheets, even if it will actually be you.

OLD FAITHFULS

WHAT IS A 'COOKED BREAKFAST'? It depends where you are. In South Wales and Cornwall the bounty of the sea gets a place at the table, often in the surprisingly delectable form of seaweed. In the American South the dishes that were once the food of the rural poor – grits, and biscuits and gravy – are now rightfully celebrated traditions. And in England it's not just about the full English. A renewed interest in old-fashioned meaty cooking, usually served in masculine, wood-panelled rooms, has revived simple but satisfying dishes such as devilled kidneys on toast. It should really do the same for the long-underrated corned beef hash, or perhaps just the hash in general – surely a fashionable chain restaurant (Hash Den?) waiting to happen.

At breakfast time in China – and in Chinatowns internationally – you'll encounter shopfront displays of *baozi* buns filled with a panoply of favourite ingredients (though perhaps not the mini full English we propose shortly); in the Balkans you'll spot intricate, pastry-based borek; and in a Japanese café at the crack of dawn, you may be offered the simple, widespread and comforting 'morning set'. All of these are the real deal, and if you're utterly bored of your Bran Flakes they each offer a way of making breakfast new again.

LAVERBREAD AND BACON

When swimming off the British Isles it is not uncommon to feel the silken yet slimy embrace of some horrifying under-sea behemoth around your thighs, prompting unseemly amounts of panicking until the revelation dawns that it was just a bit of seaweed.

Laverbread (*bara lawr* in Welsh) is its edible incarnation in which the seaweed, *Porphyra umbilicalis,* is boiled for hours to achieve a unique consistency. It has nothing to do with bread. Popular once in South Wales, and parts of Cornwall, it is too mucus-like to be served much these days, but mixed with a little fine oatmeal and fried off in bacon fat, it can be rather delicious if texturally challenging, tasting like a fragrant day at the seaside. For the brave, and the Cornish, add a dash of vinegar and serve cold.

Laverbread is available to buy in small tins, or fresh from some markets.

Per person
100g laverbread
30g medium oatmeal
4 rashers streaky bacon

Mix the laverbread with the oatmeal and form four small cakes about 1cm thick. Fry the bacon, remove and cook the cakes in the hot bacon fat. They may need a bit of attention to stop them sticking on the bottom. Fry for 2–3 minutes on each side until golden. They should be slightly crunchy on the outside and soft in the middle.

Serve with the bacon, and some mushrooms, cockles and a fried egg.

DEVILLED KIDNEYS ON TOAST

Devilled kidneys crop up regularly on the breakfast tables of nineteenth-century literature, both in gentlemens' clubs, where they breakfasted on 'pale ale and devilled kidneys at three o'clock' (in William Thackeray's *The Book of Snobs*), and in the homes of the well-to-do, where 'there were eggs in napkins, and crispy bits of bacon under silver covers; and there were little fishes in a little box, and devilled kidneys frizzling on a hot-water dish' (in Anthony Trollope's *The Warden*). The practice of devilling food refers primarily to the adding of spices, something of which Dr Johnson's biographer James Boswell was fond. With kidneys the adding of cayenne, English mustard and Worcestershire sauce goes some way to hiding the 'fine tang of faintly scented urine' which Leopold Bloom, protagonist of James Joyce's *Ulysses*, so adored.

To avoid this uric bouquet, buy your lambs' kidneys as fresh and as close to the moment of cooking as possible. They should be a deep glossy purple, with a little of their own blood. If you buy them the day before, be sure to leave them in the fridge, but out of their sealed butcher's bag, or they will start to sweat and become unpleasant. To prepare, slice in half lengthways, peel away any membrane from the outside of the kidney, and using a pair of scissors snip the hard white suet from the middle.

Serves 2
2 tablespoons plain flour
1 teaspoon cayenne pepper
1 teaspoon mustard powder
Knob of unsalted butter
4 lambs' kidneys, prepared as above
Good glug of Worcestershire sauce
50ml chicken stock
2 slices granary toast
Fresh lemon juice
Salt and pepper

Mix the flour, cayenne pepper and mustard powder together in a bowl and season well. Heat the butter in a frying pan until it begins to foam. Whilst the butter is melting, roll the kidney halves around in the spiced flour. Cook the kidneys in the butter for 2 minutes on each side, until browned, then add the Worcestershire sauce and chicken stock and cook for a further minute.

Remove the kidneys to the just-popped-up toast, and reduce the gravy a little in the pan. Pour gravy over the kidneys, top with a little squeeze of lemon and season.

BISCUITS AND GRAVY

'Biscuits and gravy' as a breakfast combo makes absolutely no sense on Her Majesty's side of the great transatlantic linguistic divide. But protest as we might, it's probably our fault: the wheat-and-pig cuisine that spawned this Deep South dish of savoury scones covered in sausage-flecked sauce was one that crossed the pond with the Pilgrim Fathers in the early seventeenth century. Born of necessity's invention and popularised in the lean years following the War of Independence, biscuits are one of the quick-bread staples of Deep South cooking, in part because the soft winter wheat grown in the South is better suited to raising with soda than yeast.

Sawmill gravy is probably only one step up from licking the skillet, a simple white sauce made by adding flour to the fat from cooking sausages, and then turned into a sauce, including all the flavoursome gritty bits from the bottom of the frying pan. Fresh from the oven, the biscuits are split and smothered in the peppery meaty gravy for a rib-sticking breakfast. The key is that the biscuits are hot and fluffy – as one nineteenth-century cookbook puts it: 'On the lightness depends the goodness of the biscuit.' Add a fried egg and some will say you are eating eggs Beauregard (see p.101).

Serves 4
For the biscuits (makes 8)
200ml buttermilk (or milk plus fresh lemon juice – see method)
300g plain flour
1 ½ teaspoons baking powder
½ teaspoon bicarbonate of soda
½ teaspoon salt
50g unsalted butter, plus extra, melted
(True Southerners don't use sugar in their biscuits)

For the sawmill gravy
8 sausages or sausage patties
80g unsalted butter, plus some for melting
2 tablespoons plain flour
800ml milk
Salt and pepper

Pre-heat the oven to 220°C/gas 7. If you can't get hold of buttermilk, squeeze the juice of ½ lemon into a measuring jug and top up to 200ml with milk, then leave for 10 minutes until it thickens to 'soured milk'.

Mix together the dry biscuit ingredients in a bowl, and rub in the butter with your fingertips until the mixture resembles breadcrumbs (this can also be done in a blender). Make a well in the centre and mix in the buttermilk or soured milk until it forms a wet dough.

At this stage start cooking the sausages or patties over a medium heat in a heavy-based frying pan (see p.42 or 46).

Tip the dough on to a floured surface and knead briefly until the ingredients are just combined. Roll the dough out until it is 2–3cm thick and then, using a scone cutter or a small glass, cut as many biscuits from the dough as you can. Try to avoid twisting the cutter too much as you cut, as it will seal the dough on the sides of the biscuits, which stops them rising properly. Arrange the biscuits on a baking tray (it's fine if the sides touch) and brush the tops with a little melted butter.

Place in the hot oven. It will take 10–12 minutes for them to puff up and turn golden (at which point leave them on a wire rack to cool for a few minutes before eating).

Whilst the biscuits are cooling check that the sausages are cooked through, remove from the pan and reserve on a plate. In the same frying pan add the butter to the oil that has come from the sausages, making sure to scrape any bits stuck to the bottom of the pan into the mix. Once the butter has melted, take off the heat, and stir in the flour. (Different sausages will give off different amounts of oil. You're looking for an equal amount of fat to flour, so if the sausages are especially greasy, add less butter.) When the flour and butter have combined into a thick paste, put the pan back over a low heat and cook for 1 minute, until the paste starts to turn golden. Little by little add the milk, stirring vigorously to avoid lumps forming, until it is all combined. If the gravy is too thick (and it should be a loose sauce) stir in a little more milk. Once the sauce is made, crumble in the meat from the sausages or patties, so the gravy is studded with little bits of sausagemeat. Season well with a little salt and a lot of pepper.

To serve, split the biscuits in half, and pour over a generous amount of gravy.

BREAKFAST MACHINES IN THE MOVIES
1968–97
by Poppy Tartt

Caractacus Potts's machine in Chitty Chitty Bang Bang
(1968, d. Ken Hughes)

Resembling a vintage fairground ride, this machine's stand-out component is the Ferris wheel for eggs, complete with bent-spoon seats. A string of sausages circles another wheel like a pork tyre and a miniature train arrives to the sound of a bell bearing a cargo of plates. Eggs are carried from one place to another by whisk-like pincers and cracked open by a tiny brass axe. The food is then heated in its ceramic plate over an elevated hob, finally being delivered to the breakfast table via a drawbridge.

Sam Lowry's machine in Brazil
(1985, d. Terry Gilliam)

Sam Lowry is a government employee struggling in a society over-dependent on machines and bureaucracy, and the contraption which is supposed to prepare his toast and coffee is malfunctioning. Its sleek metal and dimpled glass components are handsomely modernist, but the spout dispensing coffee misses the Pyrex cup and saucer and douses the toast instead. Lowry takes a gulp from a cup containing nothing but sugar and struggles to get the floppy slice of toast into his mouth.

Doc Brown's machine in Back to the Future
(1985, d. Robert Zemeckis)

Comprising a coffee machine, a toaster, a metal arm, a metal chute and a load of wires, Doc Brown's contraption is seemingly powered by a vast array of clocks. The menu is ascetic, offering just toast, coffee and dog food. Left to its own devices during the Doc's absence, the machine continues to operate but ineffectively, pouring hot water into empty space, toasting the same pieces of bread over and over and emptying tins of dog food into an already overflowing bowl. (A more successful breakfast machine, involving a live hen and a cuckoo clock, appears in *Back to the Future III*.)

Pee-wee Herman's machine in Pee-wee Herman's Big Adventure
(1985, d. Tim Burton)

This colourful machine is powered by a series of plastic windmills and a candle. It features a plastic dinosaur juicing oranges between its jaws, a 'dipping bird' toy repeatedly pecking an egg, and a life-size Abraham Lincoln figure flipping pancakes, which end up on the ceiling. Breakfast is served as a smiley face with bacon for lips and eggs for eyes, which Pee-wee greets enthusiastically with the words 'Gooood mooorning, Mr Breakfast!'

Professor Brainard's machine in Flubber
(1997, d. Les Mayfield)

This would not look out of place behind the counter of a smart diner: chrome gadgets are confined within a relatively efficient space above a cooker and the machine is controlled by a primitive-looking computer. Coffee beans are ground one by one by a metal pounder, while eggs are sliced open using a laser cutter. Serving two fried eggs with perfect yolks plus American pancakes and bacon, this is one of the few machines that appears to create a genuinely good breakfast.

GRITS

Grits hold a morbid fascination for non-Americans. Why is a popular food named after gravel? What *are* they? Something no one seems to ask is 'Where can I try some?' There is a general assumption that they are not nice. Which is wrong. They're very nice.

A savoury porridge made from cornmeal, grits are a deeply comforting breakfast food. Their contemporary heartland is the Deep South, where some will insist you must use meal that is coarse and stone ground (hence the grittiness of the name). As well as regular corn grits (which is what we mean when we just say 'grits') you may have heard of hominy grits, in which the corn kernels are first treated with slaked lime.

Best served with butter plus salt and pepper, grits can be liquid and untidy or tame and firm. Either way they play the carb role well in a trio alongside bacon and fried eggs. If eating them solo, you can't with good Southern conscience add sugar, but if you find them too bland then grated mild cheese is an endorsed embellishment.

Stone-ground cornmeal (sometimes just labelled 'grits') is tricky to find in the UK, so stock up when you can. Sachets of instant grits are sometimes found in specialist shops, though to this suggestion some will respond with a quote from the movie *My Cousin Vinny*: 'No self-respectin' Southerner uses instant grits. I take pride in my grits' (they may want to watch the rest of that scene, as the man who said that was lying).

Per person
250ml water
Salt and pepper
50g grits (i.e. coarse stone-ground cornmeal)
Knob of unsalted butter

Bring the water to the boil with ¼ teaspoon salt in a heavy-based saucepan. Add the grits, and lower the heat, stirring gently until the mixture starts to thicken. Then cover and stir occasionally, until the grits have softened and the mixture is creamy. If the mixture gets too dry add more water. Different grits cook for different times (from 5 minutes to 90) so check the packet. When happy with the texture, serve in a bowl with the knob of butter sitting on top, and season well. Mix well before eating.

CORNED BEEF HASH

There is a now-discredited school of thought that believes the name 'hash' is a corruption of Ash Wednesday. In fact the word comes from the French *hacher*, meaning 'to chop up'. *Hacher* also gives us 'steak haché' – the upmarket term for a hamburger. But despite its name the corned beef hash is a resolutely Anglo-Saxon dish.

This version leans more to the American diner than some British recipes, which can be a little too close to cottage pie for a breakfast table. It's also just a touch fancy, in that all the ingredients are cooked separately and then amalgamated into hash form. The potatoes get really crisp and the onions sweet, so it's worth the effort. Instead of the corned beef you can substitute ham, chorizo or leftover meats, though mutton is best avoided. Sweet peppers make a good addition but, as with bubble and squeak, under no circumstances should you use garlic. The traditional diner accompaniments are fried eggs (perfect), lots of ketchup (essential) and home fries (totally superfluous).

Serves 4 ordinary people or 2 who are greedy
250g corned beef
1 heaped tablespoon Dijon mustard
Salt and pepper
2 medium onions
Vegetable oil
500g old potatoes (any variety), washed but unpeeled

Cut the corned beef into 2cm cubes, mix well with the mustard, season well and put to one side. Slice the onions, add to a large frying pan and over a medium heat soften in a tablespoon of vegetable oil. Don't let them burn or colour too much. After the onions have softened and coloured a little – about 10 minutes – remove them from the frying pan.

Meanwhile, cut the unpeeled potatoes into 1cm cubes and boil for 8–10 minutes. When just about still undercooked, drain and pat dry.

Add 2–3 tablespoons of oil to the frying pan, and over a medium to high heat brown the potato cubes in batches. When they're all browned set them to one side. Add another tablespoon of oil to the pan and over a medium heat brown the corned beef. After about 5 minutes add the potato and onion to the beef and mix well. Pat the mixture into a pancake and cook over a medium heat for 5 minutes or until a crust forms on the bottom. Break up the crust and mix it back in, then form it all into another pancake and cook for another 5 minutes.

Season and serve with a fried egg, tomato ketchup and a hot sauce such as Cholula, Tabasco or Red Rooster.

CHORIZO HASH

This dish is traditionally served in bars in Madrid. It's filling and cheap and great when you're a little bit drunk. The Madrileños would be shocked to see it served as a breakfast dish as they tend to consume only caffeine and sugar in the morning, but on a rainy day in London it makes perfect sense. You could add some *morcilla* (Spanish black pudding) at the same time as the chorizo, or some red peppers with the onions; and this is one of the few times when adding garlic to a breakfast dish would not be a heresy. Serve with a fried egg for each person.

Serves 4
200g uncooked chorizo
500g potatoes (any kind), washed but unpeeled
2 medium onions
Salt and pepper

Cut the chorizo into bite-sized slices. In a frying pan cook the chorizo slices over a medium heat for about 5 minutes on each side. The chorizo is done when the pan is swimming with melted fat and the slices are crisped a little on each side. Meanwhile cut the unpeeled potatoes into 1cm cubes and parboil for 8–10 minutes until just underdone.

With a slotted spoon remove the chorizo and drain most of the fat into a container for use later. Slice the onions, and add to the fat remaining in the pan. Let the onion cook for about 10 minutes or until it is lightly browned. Remove from the pan with a slotted spoon. Add some more of the saved chorizo fat to the pan and over a medium-high heat brown the potato cubes in batches. When they are all browned return the onion and chorizo to the pan and heat through for 5 minutes. Season with salt and pepper.

FUUL

Across the Middle East, the *futuur* ('breakfast') is *fuul*, which our correspondent in Sudan describes as 'the best breakfast ever'. Also known as *fuul medames*, it's simple really – a plate or bowl piled high with hot, mashed *fuul* (fava beans) and herbs, doused in oil and 'with a doughy feta-like cheese sprinkled on the top'. Versions of this breakfast are as widespread as the Arab Spring. Elements will change according to local preference, but the inner principle of mashed bean, herb and oil – more often than not served at thermo-nuclear heat from street-side pans – remains constant, whether you take your *fuul* with Syrian sesame dip or spongy Somalian *laxoox* bread.

An ultra-simple *fuul* can be made by heating a tin of the beans in a pan and mashing them against the side as they cook, seasoning to taste and finishing it all off with a drizzle of olive oil and generous squeeze of lemon juice. *Fuul* is always excellent served with oven-warm flatbread and can be topped with a fried egg. This version sticks closely to the dish's Egyptian origins.

Serves 2
250g dried fava beans
1 fresh tomato, finely chopped
1 small onion, finely chopped
1 garlic clove, finely chopped
1 tablespoon chopped flat-leaf parsley
1 teaspoon salt
1 pinch cayenne pepper
2 tablespoons olive oil
2 tablespoons fresh lemon juice

Soak the beans overnight in a saucepan. As soon as you get up in the morning, drain and cover with fresh water. Cover the pan and cook over a medium heat until the beans are tender – this may take up to an hour. Keep an eye on the water level, adding more if you need to. In the meantime, mix the tomato, onion, garlic and flat-leaf parsley together in a bowl.

When the beans are done, drain them, add the salt, cayenne pepper, 1 tablespoon each of the olive oil and lemon juice and mix roughly, semi-crushing the beans in the process. Transfer to bowls to serve, topped with the medley of other ingredients plus the remaining oil and lemon juice.

························· **BOREK** ·························

The first step in this recipe should really read 'be born into a large Croatian family' because filo pastry is one of those things that takes a lot of practice to get right and it helps if you have a grandmother who has been making it for years to show you how. It was either that or include a recipe that readers wouldn't have a hope in hell of making. Luckily, after consultation with the publisher – 'only a fool or a madman would make filo pastry from scratch' were his words – this recipe uses shop-bought pastry.

Borek is a kind of filled pastry that is endemic across the former Ottoman Empire in many forms, including sweet ones, but it is in Albania and parts of the former Yugoslavia that it is often eaten for breakfast. It is delicious at any time of the day or night. It is one of those dishes that improves with a little ageing.

If you can't find any ripe fresh tomatoes then use tinned, rather than those tasteless ones that will only add water and skin to the filling rather than tomato flavour. Another good filling would be feta and spinach.

Serves 5
3 tablespoons olive oil
2 large eggs
50ml milk
Pinch of salt
200g filo pastry

For the filling
2 tablespoons olive oil
1 large onion, chopped
1 garlic clove, chopped
½ teaspoon cumin seeds
1 teaspoon tomato paste
250g minced beef
1 small red sweet pepper, cut into thin strips
1 small red chilli pepper, chopped
2 ripe tomatoes, chopped, or 200g tinned tomatoes
Salt and pepper
Small handful of chopped flat-leaf parsley

Pre-heat the oven to 180°C/gas 4.

For the filling, add the olive oil to a saucepan and gently soften the onion and garlic for about 10 minutes. Turn the heat up a little and add the cumin and tomato paste. Fry for 1 minute. Now add the beef and brown all over. Add the peppers, sweet and hot, then the tomatoes. Cook for approximately 20 minutes, or longer if there is still a lot of liquid. Season and add the parsley.

Grease a square Pyrex or earthenware dish – one that measures about 25 x 25 x 5cm – with a little olive oil. Thoroughly whisk together the eggs, the remaining olive oil and the milk. Add a little salt. Cover the bottom of the dish with one layer of pastry so that the sheets overlap at the edges and flop over the side of the dish – you will probably use two to three sheets. With a brush, thinly apply the egg mixture to the top of the filo pastry.

Add another layer of filo but this time only on the bottom of the dish, without the side-flopping of the first layer. Brush with the egg mixture. Add another layer of filo. Brush with the egg mixture and then layer the meat thinly on top so that it is about 1 or 2cm high. Add another layer of filo, and brush with egg mixture. Add another layer of filo, and brush with egg mixture. Now fold over the overlapping filo from the bottom layer. Pour over the remaining egg mixture.

Place the dish in the oven for 20 minutes, before turning the heat down to 150°C/gas 2 and cooking for another 40 minutes.

Serve with thick Greek yoghurt.

CHANNA MASALA AND POORI

Around a billion breakfasts are eaten every day in India and, as you'd expect, depending on where you are, they tend to be quite different. In Mumbai the street vendors do a roaring trade in simple, carb-laden *waada pavs* (potato fritters in bread rolls) while in Kerala you may mark the morning with a *paal-appam* pancake made from rice flour fermented in wine and served with a meat or vegetable stew, or perhaps just a fried egg.

This breakfast comes from the Punjab via chef and food blogger Sanjana Modha. You'll be making little deep-fried breads and serving them with chickpeas in tomato sauce. The sauce is a hero – subtly complex, perfectly balanced and with a graceful kick. Chai is your tea of choice here.

Serves 2–4
For the poori (little fried breads)
400g chapatti flour
2 tablespoons fine semolina
½ teaspoon salt
¼ teaspoon ground turmeric
¼ teaspoon chilli powder (or to taste)
1 tablespoon softened ghee or sunflower oil
Around 175ml boiled water
Sunflower oil, for deep-frying

For the channa masala
400ml tomato passata
3 tablespoons concentrated tomato purée
200ml milk
1 garlic clove, crushed (½ teaspoon)
2 teaspoons grated fresh root ginger
½ teaspoon red chilli powder (or to taste)
2 teaspoons ground coriander
½ teaspoon ground cumin
1 teaspoon ground fennel seeds
1 ½ teaspoons caster sugar
1 teaspoon salt
240g tinned chickpeas, rinsed and drained
2 tablespoons thick Greek yoghurt
3 tablespoons freshly chopped coriander

To make the *poori*, first boil the kettle. Mix together all the dry ingredients and make a well in the centre. Add the ghee or sunflower oil and gradually incorporate the water, combining with a spoon until the mixture comes together into a firm but pliable dough. When cool enough to handle, bring together with your hands and knead for 5 minutes until stickiness has given way to firmness. Cover and allow to rest for 10 minutes. Now's a good time to mix the *channa masala* and put it on the heat (see opposite).

Knead the dough again and divide into ping-pong-sized balls. Roll each ball on a very lightly oiled surface to a disc around 10cm in diameter.

Heat enough oil to deep-fry the *pooris* (a wok can be useful here) to about 180°C, but as always when dealing with a lot of hot oil, be careful and don't fill your pan or wok to more than a third of the way up.

Add two or three *pooris* to the oil at a time, gently agitating them with a slotted spoon until golden on both sides. Remove with a slotted spoon and drain on kitchen paper. Repeat for the remaining *pooris* and keep hot.

For the *channa masala,* in a large bowl whisk together everything but the chickpeas, yoghurt and coriander. Pour into a wide saucepan and bring the sauce to a boil. Cover and simmer on a medium-low heat for 10 minutes. Uncover and stir periodically to ensure it doesn't stick. Add the chickpeas, cover again and simmer for a further 5 minutes. Uncover and allow to cool for 5 minutes. Finally, quickly whisk in the yoghurt and chopped coriander.

Remember to be swift – the yoghurt should not split in the curry. Serve the hot *pooris* with the *channa masala* and chai.

BAOZI

The Chinese warlord Zhuge Liang is tramping with his army through the mountains, somewhere in the third century AD. Having just conquered all of Sichuan, they reach a torrid-looking river when suddenly the wind whips up, the rain pours and the sky darkens. The river demon, say the locals, is causing havoc and the sacrifice of a human head will be required to find a way across. Zhuge, tired of all the head-rolling he has already done to subdue Sichuan, settles on a culinary solution. He creates a head-shaped dough bun that, thrown into the river, somehow mollifies the fiend. Implausibly, the 'barbarian's head' or *mantou* bun is born and subsequently becomes very popular. The idea of popping a filling in the middle catches on, and the name *baozi* is coined – *bao* means 'to wrap'.

Ubiquitous across Asia, *baozi* (China), *mandu* (Korea), *nikuman* (Japan), *bánh bao* (Vietnam) or *siopao* (Philippines) can have as many fillings as there are names, from minced pork and *char siu* (see p.115) to sweet azuki bean or lotus paste. Some are even filled with a steaming hot soup that must be sucked from a small hole bitten into the top.

They are surprisingly easy to make, giving you maximum control over how you fill your 'barbarian's head'. Use a bamboo steamer if you have one.

Makes 8
For the dough
300g strong white bread flour
1 teaspoon dried instant yeast
Pinch of salt
1 ½ tablespoons caster sugar
180ml warm water
1 tablespoon vegetable oil
Filling of choice (see opposite)

Sieve the flour into a bowl, and add the dried yeast and salt. Dissolve the sugar in the warm water, and stir in the oil. Make a well in the centre of the flour, and mix in the sugary, oily water. It should come together into a sticky dough.

Turn the dough out on to an oiled work surface and knead until smooth and elastic; this should take 10–15 minutes. Roll out the dough into a sausage shape about 5cm in diameter, and cut into eight rounds. Sit the little loaves on a sheet of baking paper (not on the cut sides) and leave to prove for about 20 minutes. They'll puff up slightly, and air bubbles should be visible on the cut sides. You can then either steam them as they are, for fluffy slightly sweet rolls, or add a filling.

To fill, roll each piece of dough into a round about 15cm in diameter. Make a circle with the index finger and thumb of one of your hands and lay the dough on top. Create an indent in the round's centre, pushing it down gently through the circle, being careful not to stretch the dough too much. You should now have an upside-down bowler hat in your open fist. Into the indent add a dessertspoon of your filling, then bring the edges up around the filling to wrap the contents and twist the edges together to seal.

Sit each filled bun on its own lightly oiled square of baking paper, and leave for 20 minutes. Arrange your bamboo steamer over a rapidly boiling pot of water, and add the buns on their squares of paper. Try not to overcrowd the steamer – they will nearly double in size. Steam for 15 minutes, remove and eat hot.

If you have leftover dough, it will keep overnight in a sealed container in the fridge. You'll need to knock it back, roll out and leave to prove again. Fillings can be made in advance and kept chilled.

Three Fillings (each makes 4)

The joy of the homemade *baozi* is that you can fill it with whatever takes your fancy. Here are a few, traditional and otherwise, but experiment.

The classic *baozi* has a minced-pork-based filling, but the vegetable version is delicious too. In the spirit of cultural closeness we have devised an elaborate full English *baozi*, a recipe we believe has never been tried on the streets of China or anywhere else for that matter.

Spiced pork
100g minced pork
1 large mushroom (preferably shiitake)
2 spring onions
1 garlic clove
1 walnut-sized piece of fresh root ginger, grated
1 teaspoon sesame oil
Dash of mirin (or sherry)
1 tablespoon soy sauce

Finely chop the mushrooms, onions and garlic, and mix with the ginger and the minced pork. Add the oil, mirin and soy sauce and leave for at least an hour to marinate. When adding to the dough take care not to add too much liquid with the filling.

Vegetable
100g firm tofu
Handful of washed spinach
Handful of beansprouts
½ large mushroom (preferably shiitake)
2 spring onions
1 garlic clove
1 walnut-sized piece of fresh root ginger, grated
1 teaspoon sesame oil
Dash of mirin (or sherry)
1 tablespoon soy sauce

Roughly chop the first six ingredients, and add the ginger and liquids. Combine well and leave at least an hour to marinate.

Full English
Meat from 2 sausages
4 rashers streaky bacon, chopped
1 flat mushroom, diced
1 slice black pudding, diced
2 spring onions, chopped
2 teaspoons vegetable oil
Ketchup or mustard
4 medium egg yolks

In a bowl, mix the sausagemeat with the bacon, mushroom, black pudding, spring onion and oil.

When you have rolled the dough out into a circle, smear it with ketchup or mustard, then apply a thin layer of sausage mixture – being careful to leave a good couple of centimetres of dough clean round the edge. Next, carefully scoop up the dough in one hand so that it forms a container.

Gently add an egg yolk into the basket of meat, and pinch the dough together to seal the bun. You have to watch that you leave enough dough around the edge to seal without squashing the yolk.

THE JAPANESE 'MORNING SET'

One of the most authentic breakfasts in Japan does not come strewn with cherry blossoms, served to the twang of a *koto* and carried in the folds of a silken kimono, but in a small brown café, served by an elderly lady who is probably smoking, to the sound of breakfast TV.

The 'morning set' is the staple of the Japanese backstreet café, generally consisting of a thick slice of white toast (and Japanese *shokupan* really does come sliced thick), a hard-boiled egg, cabbage salad and coffee. The rules of the morning set are loose, encompass endless variations, and are no doubt one of those peculiar post-war Western emulations that are only found in Japan.

Serves 2
2 hard-boiled eggs, unpeeled
Salt
½ small cabbage
1 medium tomato
2 thick slices soft white bread
Unsalted butter

Roll the egg in salt while still in its shell (surprising, perhaps, but authentic). Finely shred the cabbage, cut the tomato into wedges and combine them into a salad. Toast and butter the bread. On a square plate serve the egg in its shell, the side salad and hot toast with some weak black coffee.

GRAINS OF TRUTH

THE SAD TRUTH IS THAT for all the breakfasts we might enjoy, it's a bowl of commercial cereal that most of us go for, most of the time. It's convenient, quick and more or less nice-tasting. The producers of these basic processed grains and pulses – flaked corn, puffed rice, baked wheat – hook us in ruthlessly when we are children, their cartoon mascots beaming out irresistibly from the cereal aisle, that dazzling cardboard Manhattan that is the only place in the supermarket that feels as though it belongs to us rather than our parents. On average, a person in the UK, USA or Ireland gets through 193 bowls of the stuff in a year. It would be disingenuous to claim that there aren't times when most of us are struck with a craving for it, and that this should be resisted at all costs.

But porridge oats are better for you, and just better in general. Unlike cornflakes, they actually have a smell, a 'slow smell', as Jeanette Winterson once described it, 'thick like a blanket'. And while it's still simple to prepare, porridge is just complicated enough to inspire endlessly entertaining arguments about how to make it 'best' or, when it gets really heated, 'correctly'. If you prefer something cold in your cereal bowl, consider developing a taste for Birchermuesli, which is more like porridge than its name implies. Or invent your own trademark granola, a substance that can be a lot more addictive than is suggested by its wholesome image.

.... **PORRIDGE** ....

It's no coincidence that there are three bowls of porridge in the story of 'Goldilocks and the Three Bears', and *not one of them is the same*. That's just within one family. Forget Bruno Bettelheim and his silly psychoanalytical interpretations – that fairytale is blatantly a piece of government propaganda designed to teach children the versatility of porridge. From Goldilocks we learn patience and perseverance: that we may have to taste three bowls of porridge, or more, before we come across one that is 'just right'.

In its traditional Scottish form, porridge is made with just untreated oats, water and salt – nothing else. The Scots take their oats very seriously, and the national dish is cast in their own (albeit stereotypical) image. If porridge was a person, it would be Peter Capaldi: aggressive, yes, but also heartwarming.

It's the oats, of course, that play the leading role here, and boy, are there a lot of them auditioning. It's all to do with how they were treated in the grain. Purists favour untreated oatmeal, a category which includes steel-cut oats, which take longer to cook and, some would argue, require soaking overnight beforehand; and stone-ground coarse or medium oatmeal. Steel-cut are so-called because of the process by which they are made, the hulled grain of whole oats being cut into small pieces by a steel mill until the oats look like the heads of pins (they are also known as pinhead oats). Then there are rolled oats, which come either split or whole ('jumbo'); Scottish oats, which are steamed steel-cut oats; and finally, fearsomely, instant oats (like Ready Brek) – oats finely milled into dust. For smooth-textured porridge, split rolled oats or medium oatmeal (or – forgive us, traditionalists – instant) are preferable. Steel-cut oats, both the untreated and steamed varieties, produce porridge with bite and a more 'husky' flavour. Avoid using jumbo oats altogether, unless you're aiming for a consistency like that of an abandoned bowl of Sugar Puffs.

Once you've selected your oats, you need to decide on the liquid. The 2008 World Porridge-making Champion, Ian Bishop, claimed the secret to his prize-winning porridge was the water he used, drawn from a bore-hole near his home in the Highlands. If you're unlucky enough not to have access to a Scottish bore-hole, you might consider cooking your oats in bottled water – mineral water is said to enhance their sweetness. Tap water supporters, however, should stand firm. Let's be honest: the taste difference is negligible, it's more environmentally friendly than bottled water, and it is plainly more convenient.

For fence-sitters or reluctant dieters, a mixture of water and milk is perfectly viable; alternatively, to make more luxurious porridge, be brazen and use entirely milk. Select your preferred milk type, but note that the higher the fat content, the richer your porridge will taste. There are those who would argue that if you insist on using skimmed milk, you might as well stick to water. Semi-skimmed may be a good compromise; whole milk can sometimes be a little overbearing, even sickly. Especially if you go on to add cream...

At which stage you are far beyond the boundaries of traditional Scottish asceticism and may as well sweeten your porridge with sugar and all manner of additions. For sweet-tooth-tastic, truly podgy porridge, swathe your oats in golden syrup and double cream; or for more virtuous sweetness try a combination of chopped banana, raisins, brown sugar and cinnamon.

All you need to worry about now is your implement. In the absence of a traditional porridge-stirring stick such as a spurtle, theevil or gruel-tree, use a wooden spoon, stirring only in a clockwise direction with your right hand. Otherwise – according to folklore – the devil will get you. If he hasn't already. Oh, and be sure to always refer to your porridge in the third person plural. For absolute authenticity, eat them standing up with a bone spoon.

Per person
Using steel-cut (pinhead) oats
50g steel-cut oats
300ml water or milk (or a mixture of the two)
Salt to taste (optional)

Soak the oatmeal overnight in the fridge, covered, in 200ml of water/milk. In the morning add another 100ml water and/or milk, stir well and bring to the boil (if using milk turn down the heat just shy of boiling to avoid burning it). Add salt at this point. When the porridge begins to thicken, lower the heat and continue to simmer uncovered for about 15 minutes, stirring often. If you prefer sloppier porridge you can add more water or milk at any point (but you will need to extend the cooking time accordingly to allow the extra liquid to simmer down).

Note: If using unsoaked steel-cut oatmeal you will need to allow 30 minutes for cooking. The finished consistency will be grittier than with soaked oats.

Using medium-ground oatmeal or split-rolled oats

250ml water or milk (or a mixture of the two)
50g medium-ground oatmeal or split rolled oats
Salt to taste (optional)

Bring the water/milk to the boil (if using milk turn down the heat just shy of boiling to avoid burning it). Add the oatmeal and salt and stir well. When the porridge begins to thicken, lower the heat and continue to simmer uncovered for 4 minutes, or until the liquid has been absorbed, stirring all the time. If you prefer sloppier porridge you can add more water or milk at any point (but you will need to extend the cooking time accordingly to allow the extra liquid to simmer down).

Additions

Add any of the following to your porridge. Sugar and cinnamon can also be added at the beginning of cooking; dried fruits and sweeteners can be stirred in either shortly before the porridge is ready or afterwards; fresh fruits, milk and cream are best added once the porridge has been removed from the heat. Some people like to keep the milk or cream in a separate dish for dipping spoonfuls of porridge in as they eat, in order to preserve the warmth of the porridge.

For bite and flavour: Dried or fresh fruits, for example bananas, apples, raspberries, blueberries, raisins, dates, prunes or dried apricots
For sweetness: Golden syrup, maple syrup, honey, brown sugar, cinnamon or chocolate spread, or *äppelmos* (see opposite)
For richness: Milk, double or single cream, natural or thick Greek yoghurt, or buttermilk
For sheer decadence: Whisky or rum

Dream Porridge and Äppelmos

Porridge is also a popular breakfast in Sweden, where it is known as *havregrynsgröt*. In the province of Dalsland, there was once a version called 'dream porridge', traditionally eaten by girls wishing to know who they would marry. Teams of three would boil up some oatmeal in the evening. When it was ready, each would throw in a handful of salt and another of flour before eating it and drifting off into a thirsty sleep. The theory went that if the porridge worked then their future spouse, appalled by their thirst, would arrive in their dreams with a cup of water. It's unclear what happened if the unthinking boor turned up but was empty-handed; or if all three dreamt of the same man; or if the dream was of ascending a flight of mud stairs pursued by a creature halfway between a stag and a snowflake.

In the morning, whether or not one's spouse has been identified overnight, a favourite Swedish topping for porridge is *äppelmos* – apple sauce. Jarred versions of this sweet, autumnal condiment can be found on supermarket shelves across northern Europe, but it's easy to make a superior version at home: you simply stew some apples with a decent slug of sugar and spice, then blend. Halfway through this process you will possess a delicious-looking batch of stewed apples that it can be hard to bother mashing, so well do they complement a bowl of thick Greek yoghurt. The wise choice is to make loads so that you can do both.

Makes 4 servings
For the äppelmos
7 eating apples, cored and sliced
120g caster sugar
200ml water
3 cinnamon sticks
1 drop vanilla extract
½ lemon, sliced

Put all the ingredients in a large saucepan over a high heat. Bring to the boil, then turn down to a low simmer and leave alone, except for the occasional stir, for around half an hour. Turn off the heat and extract any apples that you want to eat right away. Leave it to rest for another half hour, then remove the lemon slices and cinnamon sticks. Blend the rest until smooth, and chill.

PORRIDGE AT SEA
by Blake Pudding

Porridge was the food of choice for most eighteenth-century navies, although during the revolutionary period much of the structure of the French navy broke down, so they didn't get any breakfast at all. The Dutch used to supplement it with a pickled herring.

Breakfast in Nelson's navy was a pint of oats every two days served with molasses or sugar. Oats were not popular with the English sailors, perhaps because of Johnson's dictionary definition of oats: 'A grain which in England is generally given to horses, but, in Scotland, appears to support the people'. Later two ounces of the oat ration were replaced with additional sugar, which was much more to the taste of the sailors. This was made into a sort of porridge called burgoo. When oats were out the term could equally refer to a grim substitute made using mashed, weevil-infested ship's biscuits.

SCOTTISH OATCAKES

Meeting a Scottish oatcake for the first time, you are struck by the way it has the appearance, texture and, in all honesty, flavour of cardboard. But still, having taken that first bite you find yourself hooked. Somewhere mid-mastication, the cardboard transforms into something more akin to wallpaper paste (in a good way, somehow), and a depth of flavour and texture emerges. Once that oaty monster is riding the oesophageal tidal wave to your stomach you're already munching a second...

Oatmeal is usually milled in three grades, fine, medium and coarse. Too fine and the oatcake is too smooth a proposition; too coarse and it's tough going. Health-food shops usually stock a range of good ground oatmeal; try medium first, and then mix it up a little with the other grades depending on your preference.

Oatcakes turn up at all times of day, often served with some cheese at the end of dinner, but a smart breakfaster will partner them with creamy scrambled eggs and strips of smoked salmon.

Per person
100g medium-ground oatmeal
Pinch of salt
½ teaspoon bicarbonate of soda
½ tablespoon melted bacon fat/lard or oil
¾ tablespoon hot water

Mix the oatmeal with the salt and the bicarb, and add the liquid fat. Stir briskly, adding the hot water until you have a tacky dough. Working quickly before the dough loses its heat and elasticity, on a board covered in oatmeal, roll it out into a circle 5mm thick, trim any untidy edges and cut into four.

Cook the four quarters (farls) in a medium-hot pan that has been lightly oiled, until the outsides turn brown and the insides have all but dried out; about 5 minutes per side. Alternatively, bake at 180°C/gas 4 for 20 minutes, until browned.

MUESLI

In 1900, a Swiss doctor called Maximilian Bircher-Benner devised a special dish to administer twice daily to the inmates of his sanatorium in Zurich. Bircher-Benner was a zealous vegetarian and advocate for raw food. His Birchermuesli consisted of oats (soaked overnight in water), fresh lemon juice and condensed milk, mixed with 200g grated apple and topped with ground nuts. It was completely disgusting.

Bircher-Benner was eventually barred from the Zurich medical association, condemned for his lack of scientific evidence. The writer Thomas Mann, who visited his sanatorium for constipation, described the place as a 'hygienic prison'. Nevertheless, nutritional science has since proved his speculations broadly correct, and humourless nutritionists see him as a sort of godfather. They have even made nice versions of Birchermuesli.

The combination of whole grains, fruit and nuts speaks to that part of us that would like to be at a sanatorium, surveying the Alps and recuperating in the care of a Swiss doctor. It is a breakfast of good intentions.

Dry Muesli

Prepared correctly, the modern version of muesli can be tasty too. Needless to say, it should be consumed only occasionally, as part of a balanced diet.

Makes 10 servings
200g rolled porridge oats (preferably jumbo)
50g rye*
50g bran*
50g whole almonds, skin on
25g flaked almonds
25g sunflower seeds
25g pumpkin seeds
50g plump sultanas
25g dried apricots, finely chopped
25g dried cranberries**

* These grains can be obtained from health-food stores; if visiting one is a drag, make up the quantities with more oats, or wheatgerm, barley or spelt.

** No one will die if you replace these with sultanas, raisins or whichever other dried fruit you can find.

First oven-toast the grains, nuts and seeds. Pre-heat the oven to 160°C/gas 3. Arrange all the ingredients except the fruit on one or two shallow baking trays, and leave in the oven for 5 minutes. Remove and allow to cool.

Combine the toasted grains and nuts with the fruit. Store in an airtight container until ready to use.

The best way to eat muesli is to spoon thick Greek yoghurt into a bowl, top it with muesli and fruit, and drizzle with honey. Almost any combination of flavoured yoghurt (without honey) or milk (goats' milk, soya milk, almond milk...) and fresh fruit (banana, berries, peach, nectarine, pear, plum, kiwi...) will do the trick.

Birchermuesli

Preparation for Birchermuesli begins the night before eating. Rolled oats are soaked in milk or apple juice, or a combination of both, stirred and then left in the fridge. The oats soften, expand and absorb flavour. In the morning you have a gooey cloud of porridge. The following, our favoured method, is for the divine version sold at Rosalind's Kitchen, the café above Rosalind's Cookery School in Fitzrovia.

Note: If you prefer a lighter, smoother texture, then try using oatmeal in place of rolled oats.

Serves 2
125g rolled porridge oats (preferably jumbo)
250ml apple juice
2 eating apples with skins on, cored
450g natural yoghurt
(thick Greek yoghurt, whole milk or – reluctantly – low-fat)

Place the oats and apple juice in a bowl. Mix well and cover. Leave in the fridge overnight. In the morning grate the apples using a coarse blade and mix into the oats and apple juice. Stir in the yoghurt. Serve topped with fruit salad, compote and/or granola (see pp.190 and 160).

FIRST BREAKFAST CEREALS
by Malcolm Eggs

Granula (1863)

Early in the nineteenth century, a Presbyterian minister named Sylvester Graham set about reforming America's eating habits. He sought to reverse the trend for ultra-white, nutrition-free bread by reinstating the bran, and furthermore felt the nation's meat-heavy diet was encouraging alcoholism and masturbatory urges. His followers, known as Grahamites, started showing up in all kinds of places across the land. It was one of their number, Dr James Caleb Jackson, who invented breakfast cereal.

Jackson owned a massive hydrotherapy institute in New York State where patients were relentlessly doused in water and fed a sparse diet of fruit, vegetables and grains. Seeking to improve the appeal of this 'scientific eating', he devised a new kind of breakfast, mixing bran-laced flour with water and baking it twice, forming a snack halfway between a modern Grape Nut and an old, broken brick. Granula needed to be soaked in milk overnight so as to be edible, and it retailed at ten times the cost of its ingredients.

Granola (1881)

Several decades after Granula's conception, a man named Dr John Harvey Kellogg took this idea of dry, cooked cereal and used it to change breakfast forever. Kellogg grew up in Michigan, in a town called Battle Creek, and was a devout member of the Seventh Day Adventists, a church founded in the town by the diet-obsessed Ellen White. After training in medicine in New York, he returned to his home town and took over his church's health farm, then called the Western Health Reform Institute. Renaming it The Sanitarium, he offered a programme of 'Nature's simple restorative methods', which included laughing classes, vibrating chairs and yoghurt enemas. Inpatients were fed a strictly monitored, strictly vegetarian diet. It was a huge success.

Granola (nothing like today's version) was the first cereal to emerge from the Kellogg experimental kitchens. It was similar to Granula, except these versions of the tooth-challenging biscuits were made from cornmeal and oatmeal as well as wholemeal flour. They joined 'Graham Gruel', 'Dyspeptic Wafers' and 'Vegetable Egg' on the Sanitarium's breakfast menus. Within a decade Kellogg was selling two tons per week.

Shredded Wheat (1893)

Henry Perky, a lawyer from Denver, turned to health food as a way of combating indigestion, then began experimenting with recipes of his own. Working with an engineer, he hit upon a process in which grains of wheat were steamed until soft, then rolled between two rollers – one grooved and one plain – forming strands that could be cut into biscuits. He called the invention Shredded Wheat.

Dr Kellogg soon caught wind of this innovation. He visited Perky in 1894 and offered him $100,000 for his patent. The lawyer accepted, only to be met at the last minute with cold feet, and the deal fell through. It was a move that Kellogg came to regret. By 1901, Perky had made enough money from Shredded Wheat to build a vainglorious factory in Niagara Falls, the so-called 'Conservatory of Food', a national tourist attraction powered by the energy of the waterfall itself.

Granose (1895)

Dr Kellogg's kitchen was supervised by his wife, Ella Kellogg, herself a noted author on 'healthful cookery'. The brief was to create dishes for guests that lived up to his principles but were also tasty and avoided monotony. The ideal was not always the reality: of their successful but foul Caramel Cereal Coffee Dr Kellogg reflected, 'it is a very poor replacement for a very poor thing'.

After witnessing an old lady destroying her dentures on tough Zweiback bread, Dr Kellogg decided it would be a good idea 'to have a ready cooked food which would not break people's teeth'. The solution his kitchen came up with was Granose, the first breakfast flake, made by boiling wheat, rolling it through a flattening device and baking the resulting thins. In the first year of production, customers bought more than 50,000 kilos.

Grape Nuts (1898)

Charles William Post was a former cowhand and a budding entrepreneur. In 1891, in an attempt to relieve his chronic indigestion, he and his family booked a stay at Dr Kellogg's Sanitarium. Months passed and he experienced no improvement. Even the Doctor saw him as a lost cause. Post left disheartened, only to experience a miraculous recovery hours after checking out. Experiencing an epiphany about the healing (and profitable) power of positive thinking, he opened his own medical institute, La Vita Inn. To Dr Kellogg's lasting annoyance it was located just down the road from The Sanitarium.

Post did very well out of emulating Dr Kellogg. Postum, his own version of Caramel Cereal Coffee, made inroads into the coffee substitute market, flooding the pages of newspapers across the US with cryptic but effective slogans ('There's a Reason') and outright lies (coffee makes you blind). Later came Grape Nuts, his first move into the cereal market, and another bestseller. The cereal took its name from Post's mistaken belief that grape sugar (the old name for dextrose) formed during the process of baking. By 1903, around a decade after La Vita Inn opened, Post's epiphany had made him a millionaire.

Corn Flakes (1898)

During the 1890s Dr Kellogg had given his business-minded brother, William Keith Kellogg, increased authority over his food interests, a role he fulfilled with considerable success. In 1898, the brothers applied the Granose flaking method to maize instead of wheat, thus inventing the corn flake. The original version turned rancid in the box, and did not sell well; it took several years to make an appropriately crispy corn flake. By this time, around 1902, Battle Creek was in the throes of a 'cereal rush'. The success of Granose and Grape Nuts had shown that you could get extremely rich merely by buying some grains or pulses (some of the cheapest and most basic foods available to man), baking them and putting them in a box. Businessmen, investors and con artists flooded into Battle Creek, which had gained the soubriquet 'Cereal City' –a kind of Silicon Valley for cereal start-ups.

In 1902 W. K. added cane sugar to corn flakes to improve the flavour. The Doctor prioritised health over profit (he had been known to prescribe corn flake enemas) – and was dismayed. A slow power struggle followed. W. K. bought up shares that Dr Kellogg had given Sanitarium staff in place of pay, covertly acquiring a controlling stake in the Kellogg's Toasted Corn Flake Company. With that move, the Doctor was sidelined and breakfast cereal's centre of gravity had effectively moved from the health farm to the industrial plant. The corn flake had become the icon of all this, and the most imitated of all cereals: by 1911 there were 107 other corn flake brands being produced in Battle Creek.

FORGOTTEN BREAKFAST CEREALS
OF THE 1980s

Pac-Man .... General Mills, 1983
C-3PO's cereal .... Kellogg's, 1984
E.T. Cereal .... General Mills, 1984
Ghostbusters .... Ralston, 1985
Breakfast with Barbie .... Ralston, 1989

BREAKFAST CEREAL

How to eat cereal? It seems a laughably simple meal. This sequence, from the back of a box of Cröonchy Stars (the cereal of the Swedish Chef from *The Muppets*, released in 1988) just about sums it up:

> Place cereal in bowl
> (remove from box first)
> Pour milk into bowl
> Place spoon in bowl
> Place cereal on spoon
> Place spoon in mouth
> Place teeth in cereal
> Repeat repeatedly

Anyone can make a bowl of cereal, but some bowls are better than others. A deep-seated fear is that an incorrect milk-cereal combination will result in a disappointing end-of-bowl experience. Too little milk and your final mouthfuls will be dry and scraping. Too much and the over-saturated solid will take on the texture and taste of papier-mâché.

The key is to focus on the ratio and distribution of milk: about half the volume of the cereal (less for skimmed milk; more for full-fat), poured around — not on top of! Never on top of! – the cereal. Eat at average speed. And enjoy the satisfaction, not just of (almost) sated hunger, but of the quiet smugness that comes with the knowledge of something executed properly.

GRANOLA

In the popular imagination, granola is to the world of mainstream breakfast cereals what folk music is to throwaway pop. The bright boxes of Corn Flakes, Froot Loops and Coco Pops are replaced by thick matt card and dull unshowy colours, or just unbranded plastic sacks. It's unprocessed and authentic, although in fact the word 'granola' was invented by Dr John Kellogg as a name for his first cereal (see p.156).

Making granola is as easy as 'Do Re Mi' and the results are addictive. Once you see how much honey goes in, you may stop seeing it as a health food. A splendid way to serve granola is with thick Greek yoghurt, fresh nectarines and an extra drizzling of honey – though with cold milk and banana is pretty good too.

Makes around 15 servings
300g rolled porridge oats (preferably jumbo)
(you can make up some of this with rye if you prefer)
50g shelled hazelnuts
50g whole almonds (feel free to substitute other nuts)
25g pumpkin seeds
25g sunflower seeds
3 tablespoons sunflower oil
3 tablespoons clear honey
Pinch of salt
50g raisins or sultanas

Pre-heat your oven to 150°C/gas 2. Line a baking tray with greaseproof paper.

Mix your dry ingredients – oats, nuts and seeds – together in a large bowl. Do not fret too much if you are lacking any one component, as long as you have oats. Haven't got hazelnuts? Use brazils! Short on pumpkin seeds? Top up with flax! Don't know what flax is? Don't worry, it's not that nice.

Heat the oil and honey in a small pan, adding a couple of tablespoons of water and a pinch of salt. The syrup should be warm but not boiling. This stage is pretty buskable too – feel free to substitute maple syrup for some of the honey, or add golden syrup. You can also add cinnamon or vanilla extract.

Combine the syrup and the oat mixture, making sure the grains are evenly covered. Spread the mixture thinly and evenly on to the lined baking tray and put in the oven for half an hour. Some bits of the oven are hotter than others, so open the oven door and jumble the mixture up with a wooden spoon every 10 minutes or so to prevent burning. The granola is ready when the oats have turned an appealing maple brown. Leave to cool (if the oats still seem soft, don't worry: they will be crisper at room temperature).

When cool, mix in your dried fruit. Play around with flavours and combinations: maple syrup, pecans and dried cranberries? Golden syrup, cashews and dried tropical fruit? Honey, almond and dried cherries?

Store in a sealed container in a cool, dry, cupboard. Oats and dried fruit will keep for months, but roast nuts will start to go bad after a week or two.

················· **TOASTED MUESLI OR CRUNCH** ················

Between muesli and granola there is a third way. Proof, in the form of this hitherto secret formula, was passed on to us by a New Zealander turned Londoner. It is her family recipe and the result – an indecently moreish and sweet cereal – is *never* described as 'granola', but as either 'toasted muesli' or, in everyday conversation, 'crunch'. Served in a simple bowl of natural yoghurt with a few slices of banana, it's so delicious you find yourself missing the sensation of eating it before it is finished.

Makes around 20 servings
340g rolled porridge oats (preferably jumbo)
40g dried coconut
40g wheatgerm
60g sesame seeds
60g pumpkin seeds
60g sunflower seeds
25g bran flakes
50g flaked almonds
55g toasted chopped hazelnuts
110ml sunflower oil
110ml maple syrup
1 teaspoon vanilla extract

Pre-heat the oven to 150°C/gas 2. Mix all the dry ingredients together in a large roasting tin.

Heat the oil and the syrup together in a saucepan. When they come to the boil, quickly remove from the heat and add the vanilla extract. Pour this liquid over the seeds, nuts and grains and mix it all around until everything is well coated.

Bake for 30 minutes, turning over every 10 minutes with a wide spatula. Allow to cool completely before storing (for up to two weeks) in an airtight container. Serve with natural yoghurt and/or fresh fruit.

PANCAKES & OVENBAKED

CAKE – STRAIGHTFORWARD, spongey, everyday cake – has no place at the breakfast table. Victoria sponge isn't acceptable. Nor is banoffee pie. Nor is Battenberg. These are for dessert, afternoon tea – birthday elevenses at a push. Yet strangely, food that is *sort of* cake is rife. Pancakes, for instance, are true breakfast fodder, as are Portuguese custard tarts. Admittedly there are rare exceptions (madeleines or madeiras turn up at dawn hotel buffets or Spanish coffee bars occasionally), but as a general rule it is a case of muffins, tarts, pastries, scones – things that flirt relentlessly with cake status but never make the leap.

PANCAKES

A tower of warm pancakes, dripping in maple syrup, has become the definitive icon of the American breakfast. It's like a culinary Empire State Building – a simple totem to success and gluttony, standing proud above the insubstantial Continental crêpe, freed from its Lenten associations of abstention and guilt.

But whichever side of the Atlantic you are on, pancakes are an age-old problem. For centuries, 'first pancake disorder' has tormented breakfasters. Why is the first pancake always the worst? Antonin Scalia, a Supreme Court Justice, once pointed out parallels with parenthood. 'In a big family the first child is kind of like the first pancake,' he said. 'If it's not perfect, that's kind of OK, there are a lot more coming along.'

The solution is actually simple. At the point of making the first pancake, the cook will have recently put the fat in the pan. Thus the initial one becomes misshapen as it absorbs the surplus. You can usually cure the problem by wiping the pan down a little before you introduce the batter (and if it doesn't work, Scalia would have said, give it to your firstborn).

All-American Buttermilk Pancakes

The classic. The trademark rising effect relies on the reaction of bicarbonate of soda with buttermilk to create a flurry of bubbles in the batter. The basic principle is to mix the dry ingredients, and combine with the wet, cook in batches and serve in stacks. Classic additions include fresh blueberries (stir 125g into the mix at the last minute) or a side of crisp fried streaky bacon.

Makes around 12 pancakes
225ml buttermilk (or milk plus fresh lemon juice – see method)
160g plain flour
20g caster sugar
1 teaspoon baking powder
1 teaspoon bicarbonate of soda
½ teaspoon salt
1 medium egg
40g unsalted butter, melted and cooled,
plus extra butter for frying

If you don't have any buttermilk, squeeze the juice of ½ lemon into a measuring jug, and top up with milk to 225ml. Leave to thicken into 'soured milk' for 10 minutes.

Mix all the dry ingredients in a bowl, and in a separate bowl whisk up the wet ingredients.

Add all the wet to the dry, and whisk until all the flour is incorporated. Do not over-mix, as it can over-develop the gluten, making the pancakes rubbery: the batter should be a little lumpy and quite thick. Let it sit for 10 minutes.

In a large, medium-hot frying pan melt a teaspoon of the butter. Very carefully give the pan a quick wipe with some kitchen paper to soak up any excess grease. Now add a tablespoon of the mixture – it should spread a little but hold its shape. Cook until the surface is covered in bubbles and the underside is browned; this should take a couple of minutes. If you're adding blueberries, now's the time: sprinkle over the just setting top side. Gently flip the pancake and cook until both sides are browned.

It's a good idea to cook a test pancake first. Check it doesn't brown too quickly and that the batter is not too thick or thin. If it's too thick add a little more milk; too thin, a dash more flour. Once you're happy with the mix, add a few tablespoons to the pan, but be careful not to overcrowd it. Between pancakes, carefully give the pan a quick wipe with your buttery kitchen paper. If the pancakes begin to stick, add another teaspoon of butter and repeat the wiping process.

Serve hot from the pan with a smear of butter and lashings of maple syrup. Fruit scattered over the pancakes, especially banana, is excellent.

Maple Syrup with Toasted Nuts

Because it already feels like a luxury (not least in terms of price) many will pour maple syrup directly from bottle to pancake. This is a mistake a little like watching the original version of *Blade Runner*, before Ridley Scott's re-edit transformed it into a darker, more complicated masterpiece. You can transform your maple syrup too. Toasted nuts add a *noir* new dimension. If you have no nuts, or an allergy, you could heat the syrup up in a saucepan with a little butter.

For 12–16 pancakes
70g shelled pecans, walnuts or both
250ml maple syrup
50g unsalted butter

Pre-heat your oven to 200°C/gas 6. Cut the nuts in half and place in the oven on a baking sheet for 5 minutes. When you open the oven door you should just be able to smell toasty nuttiness. Meanwhile, put the maple syrup in a saucepan and simmer on a lowish heat. When the walnuts are done, add them and the butter to the syrup and stir until the butter has melted. Transfer to a small jug.

Drop Scones

The drop scone is the old-world cousin of the American pancake. At teatime drop scones are taken toasted, but many of Britain's finest bed and breakfasts will serve them at sunrise, soft and fresh from the pan. Strictly speaking, a buttermilk pancake could be called a drop scone (after all, it is just the traditional British term for a small, tall pancake), while our drop scone recipe would not be unheard of in any roadside diner between Maine and New Mexico. Either way, this recipe is a good simple shortcut to something that is still round, still sweet and still beaming with that sense of occasion that only a pancake can bring.

Makes around 10 drop scones
250g flour, plain or wholemeal
1 ½ teaspoons baking powder
Pinch of salt
40g caster sugar
2 large eggs, beaten
240ml milk
40g unsalted butter, melted
Unsalted butter, for greasing

Sift the flour into a large bowl then stir in the baking powder, salt and sugar. Create a well in the centre, break in the eggs and lightly whisk the mixture. Keep whisking as you slowly pour in the milk and then the melted butter. Mix until you have a thick pancake batter.

Lightly rub a large heavy-based frying pan with butter, then place it over a medium to high heat. When it's hot, ladle a little more than a tablespoon's worth into the pan. Do this for as many drop scones as you have space for. When the tops of the drop scones are covered in bubbles, flip them over and cook the other side for around a minute. Serve or set aside in a warm place until serving time.

German Pancakes

'German pancakes' they call them – when to any Englishman they are quite patently Yorkshire puddings. Yorkshire puddings, however, are only eaten for breakfast in very limited circles. Not so German pancakes, because the Germans do not limit them to roast beef. They treat them as sweets – adding cinnamon, sugar and lemon, raisins and apples; and as savouries, sometimes adding bacon to the batter. Sausage could be added, too – then you would be eating toad-in-the-hole for breakfast, which is perhaps taking things a bit too far. The recipe here is adapted from Jane Grigson's *English Food*.

Makes around 6 pancakes
1 tablespoon unflavoured oil (sunflower, groundnut, grapeseed)
4 medium eggs
300ml milk
250g plain flour, sifted
Pinch of salt
Icing sugar

Pre-heat the oven to 250°C/the highest your oven will go. Coat a hardy metal roasting tin with a film of oil and put it into the oven to heat up.

Beat the eggs and the milk together vigorously – an electric whisk helps. Leave to stand for 15 minutes or so, then whisk in the sifted flour and the salt. You will have a thin batter. Pour this batter into the hot roasting tin and leave in the oven for 20 minutes. It will rise splendidly! And then gently collapse... As it is collapsing, sift over icing sugar.

Serve with maple syrup and perhaps some baked apple slices, or any of the suggestions mentioned above.

WAFFLES

A waffle is essentially a pancake in extraordinary circumstances. Hailing from medieval times when sellers used to flog them on saints' days, waffles crossed the Atlantic with Dutch settlers before becoming an American breakfast favourite. The principle has remained the same: extruded around a metal grid not dissimilar to Milton Keynes, a leavened batter ends up with a maximum surface area, crispy in all places at once. The Scandinavians use heart-shaped moulds (the Swedes even have a specific waffle day or Våffeldagen on 25 March). The Belgians' are square but with very dramatic peaks and canyons. Without a waffle iron, waffles just turn into fluffy pancakes, which are not undelicious, but slightly miss the point. We recommend serving with fresh fruit (bananas and/or berries are particularly sympathetic) and honey, although maple syrup would not be amiss; nor would peanut butter or any topping you might conceivably have with a pancake.

Serves 2 hungry waffle eaters
(number of waffles depends on size of waffle iron)
160g plain flour
1 teaspoon baking powder
Pinch of salt
25g unsalted butter
1 medium egg
½ teaspoon caster sugar
250ml milk

Sieve the flour, baking powder and salt into a large bowl. Melt the butter in a small pan and leave to one side.

Separate the egg into white and yolk. Save the yolk, and whisk the white (in a clean bowl) until it forms soft peaks. In a separate bowl combine half the melted butter with the sugar, egg yolk and milk, and whisk lightly. Make a well in the centre of the flour mixture, and slowly mix in the milky mixture, until you have a thick batter. Whisk a little to get rid of any large lumps. Fold in the egg white, but gently as you want to avoid losing any of those air bubbles.

Use the rest of the butter to grease your waffle iron, and ladle the batter in. Cook according to your machine's instructions.

That the French call it *pain perdu* and the English eggy bread speaks volumes of their respective culinary pretensions. This is the same combination of bread soaked in milk and eggs and fried in butter, but the French describe it as the hero of a romantic tragedy ('lost bread!') while the English go with an adjective commonly used for particularly sulphurous farts. It is best to stick to the American – French toast.

As is so often the case with breakfast foods, French toast can be made as either wholly savoury or wholly sweet. It almost goes without saying that it will act as a beautiful foil for streaky bacon or fried pancetta with a little maple syrup. A spoonful of vanilla yoghurt and a few slices of fresh mango make a romantic alternative (even if only a romance with yourself).

Serves 2
4 slices bread (white, please), crusts removed
2 medium eggs
25g caster sugar
50ml milk
1 teaspoon ground cinnamon
25g unsalted butter
4 rashers bacon (smoked streaky is best)
Maple syrup, to serve

Very lightly toast the bread to dry it out a little (if the bread is slightly stale already, so much the better).

Beat the eggs with the sugar, then whisk in the milk and the cinnamon. Dunk the bread in the egg mixture, leaving it to sponge up the liquid for approximately 30 seconds.

Place the butter in a frying pan on a medium heat and allow to melt. Put the bread in the frying pan and cook for 3 minutes on one side; flip and cook for 2 minutes on the other. Meanwhile, fry the bacon in a separate pan (see p.38). When the French toast is nicely browned on both sides, remove from the pan, sprinkle with a little extra cinnamon and serve with the bacon and the topping of your choice, honey or syrup at the very least.

STAFFORDSHIRE OATCAKES

One rumour has it that when the men of the North Staffordshire Regiment returned from India at the end of the nineteenth century they brought with them a taste for chapattis, and promptly set about creating their own – and so the 'Potteries chapatti' or Staffordshire oatcake was born. A likelier tale is that it simply evolved from rural cooks making the most of the local Pennines oats. When the Industrial Revolution arrived there was a boom in the number of hungry potters in the Stoke-on-Trent area. The sale of these flat oaten pancakes leavened with yeast became a thriving industry, with oatcakes being sold out of holes in the walls of city kitchens.

While Staffordshire devised a dinner-plate-sized oatcake, neighbouring Derbyshire developed a thicker, smaller version of its own. Either style makes a delicious accompaniment to a full English, or can be rolled up with whatever filling you desire – cheese and crispy bacon is very popular. Local makers guard their recipes fiercely, but it is possible to make a good approximation at home, using wholemeal flour, fine-ground oatmeal, yeast, water and milk. They are traditionally cooked on a hotplate called a baxton, and are moister and more pliable than their Scottish oatcake cousin. Some of the small Staffordshire producers even sell ready-mixed packets of dry ingredients, or mail-order ready-made oatcakes.

For a Derbyshire oatcake, reduce the amount of liquid slightly, and use to make two thick oatcakes.

Makes 6
110g fine-ground oatmeal
110g wholemeal flour
½ teaspoon salt
½ teaspoon caster sugar
3.5g (a half sachet) dried instant yeast
210ml warm milk
210ml warm water
Vegetable oil, for greasing

Mix all the dry ingredients in a large bowl, and add the milk and water. Whisk until you have a smooth batter the consistency of double cream. It will seem a little thin, but the oatmeal will swell, making it thicker. Leave covered with a clean tea towel in a warm place for 1 hour, until the batter is thick and frothy.

Heat a heavy-based frying pan over a medium heat, and coat the surface of the pan with oil, using a piece of kitchen paper to wipe off any excess. Add one ladle of mixture, and tilt the pan so that it is evenly spread. Cook for 2–3 minutes on a medium heat, until the surface is covered in bubbles and the underside is brown. Flip and cook for another 2–3 minutes. Keep an eye on the heat, as the oatcakes need to cook through without burning. Serve hot, rolled around the filling of your choice. If you have any spares they will reheat well between two plates over a pan of boiling water.

AMERICAN MUFFINS

The first rule of the American muffin club is: You do not talk about cupcakes. The recent popularity of oversized cupcakes and fun-size 'mini' muffins has led to widespread confusion over where the line between breakfast cake and party cake might be drawn. Make no mistake, the cupcake has no place on the breakfast table. It is too weak and sugar-dependent to carry you through the day. American muffins should be good and heavy, containing less sugar and more fruit. They can be identified by their bulky shoulders and trim waists: if you must imagine a cupcake, imagine a cupcake playing American football. As one blogger succinctly puts it: 'If you threw a cupcake against the wall, you would hear something of a "Poof!" If you threw a muffin, you would hear a "Thud!"'

A standard muffin has a diameter at the base of around 5.5 centimetres. For heavy-hitters, a larger muffin – sometimes known as a giant or Texas muffin – with a diameter of 9 *full centimetres*, is available in the US. The most portable of breakfasts, muffins are relatively straightforward to make. The key to a good texture is in the mixing. Muffin batter should be folded, not beaten; otherwise the end result will be tough. Introduce the ingredients to each other, but don't force them to get along. To bake muffins you will benefit from a muffin pan. Paper cases are optional, but will assist in transportation (of course, for many muffins, their experience of travel is limited to the short journey from oven to mouth).

Aesthetics are often the biggest problem. Achieving the all-important 'top' can be tricky. 'Flying saucer' tops – when the muffin top splurges sideways (like a deflated chef's hat) rather than rising upwards to form a satisfactory dome – are common. A surge of heat at the beginning of baking (increased by 20 degrees, or up a gas mark) for 2 minutes may help even rising. For the best chance of achieving nicely domed muffins, avoid over-filling the muffin cups (each cup should be no more than two-thirds full), and grease only the bottom and halfway up the side of each cup (this allows the muffin to cling to the side of the pan, which aids rising).

The three recipes below have been selected to appeal to the full gamut of American-muffin fans, from the healthy eaters to the 'Cake for breakfast? Hell, yeah!' thrill-seekers.

Breakfast Muffins

These are the kind of muffins Squirrel Nutkin might have had for breakfast. With a couple of these under your belt you'll soon be scrabbling up and down trees.

Makes 12
250g wholemeal flour
50g jumbo or split rolled oats (plus extra for sprinkling on top)
75g soft brown sugar
3 teaspoons baking powder
½ teaspoon grated fresh nutmeg
½ teaspoon ground cinnamon
100g sultanas
50g pumpkin seeds (plus extra for sprinkling on top)
50g shelled walnuts, chopped (plus extra for sprinkling on top)
100ml sunflower oil
6 tablespoons natural yoghurt
4 tablespoons milk
2 bananas, peeled and mashed
1 apple, peeled, cored and grated
1 carrot, peeled and grated
1 medium egg

Pre-heat the oven to 190°C/gas 5. Prepare a twelve-cup muffin tray by either greasing or lining with paper cases. (Since these muffins are on the sticky side, using paper cases *and* greasing them is probably the best option.) Combine the flour, oats, sugar, baking powder, spices, sultanas, seeds and nuts and set aside. Mix the remaining ingredients in a separate bowl and then fold into the dry mixture. Spoon the mixture into the prepared tray, dividing the mixture evenly between the muffin cups, filling each cup almost to the top (these are not particularly high-rising muffins). Sprinkle a small amount of chopped walnuts, pumpkin seeds and oats on top of each muffin.

Bake for 25 minutes or until a skewer inserted into the muffins shows they are done (because of the high fruit content in this recipe, the skewer will not come away 'clean', but any crumbs clinging to it should be moist rather than wet). These muffins freeze well and can be brought back to life by heating in the oven or microwave.

Blueberry Muffins

A design classic and an underrated icon, the blueberry muffin is as American as apple pie, but more breakfast-appropriate. The government tells us that four heaped tablespoons of blueberries equal one of your five a day, so if you eat four or more of these you 'know' you're on the right track.

Makes 9
125g blueberries
110g plain flour
110g unsalted butter
85g caster sugar
2 medium eggs
1 ½ teaspoons baking powder

Pre-heat the oven to 190°C/gas 5. Prepare a nine-cup muffin tray by either greasing or lining with paper cases. Dampen the blueberries, shake the water off and then mix with ½ tablespoon of the flour, and set to one side to dry out (this encourages the fruit not to sink to the bottom of the muffins).

Cream the butter and the sugar together. Slowly add the eggs. Add the rest of the flour and the baking powder and mix together carefully. Now add the blueberry and flour mixture and fold in gently, taking care not to crush the fruit. Spoon into the prepared tray, filling up each muffin cup a little over halfway. Bake for 20 minutes, until golden on top.

Chocolate Muffins

OK, we admit it. The chocolate muffin is a cake. We can't even pretend. It contains no fruit, no seeds, no whole grains... nothing remotely start-the-dayish. Its GI is *sky-high*, baby. And yet... what a way to start the day.

Makes 12 muffins
150g plain flour
50g cocoa powder
2 teaspoons baking powder
2 medium eggs
200g caster sugar
150ml whole milk
¼ teaspoon vanilla extract
150g unsalted butter, melted
125g plain chocolate, roughly chopped

Pre-heat the oven to 180°C/gas 4. Prepare a twelve-cup muffin tray – by either greasing or lining with paper cases.

Sieve the flour, cocoa and baking powder into a bowl. In a separate bowl beat together the eggs and the sugar until pale and fluffy. Gradually combine these two mixtures along with the milk and vanilla extract. Now gradually add the melted butter and mix in gently. Finally, fold in the chocolate.

Divide the mixture evenly between the muffin cups, taking care not to overfill. Bake for 20 minutes, until risen and firm to the touch.

CHURROS CON CHOCOLATE

Roaming the Spanish grasslands is a sheep, the Churra, that sports long curly horns. Legend has it that the shepherds of these flocks needed a portable snack, a need that inspired the invention of the *churro*. Extruded from a *churrera*, a special pump with a star-shaped nozzle, these long strips of dough are deep-fried and then dredged in sugar and ground cinnamon.

They are best when served with a cup of Spanish hot chocolate. The Spanish have a long history with the mighty cocoa bean, having been the first Europeans to import it from the New World. They make a lascivious cup of breakfast chocolate, which if done right should be thick enough to stand a *churro* in.

Making *churros con chocolate* at home is not a quick breakfast or for the ill-equipped. You'll need an icing bag with a star nozzle through which to extrude the dough into the oil.

Serves 2
225ml water
100g unsalted butter
¼ teaspoon salt
160g plain flour
3 medium eggs, beaten
Vegetable oil, for deep-frying
Icing sugar and ground cinnamon, to serve

For the chocolate
½ teaspoon cornflour
450ml milk
120g dark chocolate (more than 60% cocoa solids)

For the *churros,* bring the water, butter and salt to the boil, and then remove from the heat. Stir in the flour until well incorporated. Add the beaten eggs to the saucepan while continuing to stir the mixture until it forms a smooth dough. Allow it to cool before spooning into an icing bag with a large star-shaped nozzle.

Heat the oil in a saucepan to 180–190°C (or until a cube of day-old bread browns in 30 seconds). Squeeze the batter into the hot oil in a large circle or in short strips, being careful not to overcrowd the pan. Remove when golden brown and drain on a board covered in kitchen paper. Dust with icing sugar and cinnamon and serve.

For the *chocolate,* mix the cornflour in a glass with a little of the milk, until it is well dissolved. Add to the rest of the milk in a saucepan and bring to a gentle boil, stirring constantly.

Take the pan off the heat, break the chocolate into small pieces and add to the pan, stirring until all the chocolate has melted. Place back over a low heat and stir gently until the mixture thickens. Serve immediately in small cups with fresh *churros.*

PÃES DE QUEIJO

If you ever wondered what the girl from Ipanema ate for breakfast, your ship has just come in – and it's stuffed to the gunnels with *pães de queijo*! That's breads of cheese to non-Portuguese speakers, or more descriptively, cheese buns.

Pães de queijo are an appetiser-sized snack popular across South America's jagged elbow and are most likely to be spotted in the grip of a Brazilian at breakfast time, and not far from a cup of coffee. Made with tapioca flour and, typically, the Brazilian cheese *queijo minas* (from the Minas Gerais region where the buns themselves are said to hail from), *pães de queijo* look like streetwise profiteroles and taste like cheese on a motorbike taking bread for a ride in a sidecar. At their best they have an aerated, pleasantly gummy interior that contrasts with a crisp outer shell.

In the absence of *queijo minas*, which is scarce outside Brazil, this recipe uses a combination of Cheddar and Parmesan, but a variety of alternative cheeses (a sharp flavour is best) can be substituted. Tapioca flour can also be tricky to locate, but it should be available in major supermarkets, and a well-stocked health-food shop will certainly be able to oblige. *Do not* substitute regular flour. *Pães de queijo* are gluten-free, which is excellent news for coeliacs – though, since it's impossible to resist the cheesy devils, there's no guarantee you won't end up feeling rueful and bloated anyway…

Makes approximately 24
200ml whole milk
100ml rapeseed oil (or vegetable oil)
300g tapioca flour
2 medium eggs
150g Cheddar cheese, grated
50g Parmesan cheese, grated
1 teaspoon salt
Pepper to taste

Boil the milk and oil together in a pan until foaming. Remove from the heat and gradually mix in the flour as much as possible. Don't worry if it looks a little like roof insulation at this stage (but don't worry if it doesn't look like roof insulation). Leave the mixture to cool for 15 minutes. Meanwhile, pre-heat the oven to 180°C/gas 4 and prepare a medium-sized baking sheet, either greased or lined with baking parchment.

Once the mixture has cooled, add the eggs, cheeses, salt and pepper, mixing together thoroughly. Knead with your hands until relatively smooth.

When the dough is as smooth as you can get it, roll it into small balls (about the size of a golf ball) between your palms. It helps to grease your hands with oil or butter for this. Place the balls on the baking tray (not too close together, as they will puff up slightly) and bake for 15 minutes until golden.

These are best eaten straight from the oven. The balls can also be frozen prior to cooking for use later – freeze them on a baking tray first before decanting into a plastic bag or container; otherwise they will freeze stuck together. They do not need to be defrosted prior to cooking and take just slightly longer to cook, up to 20 minutes.

PASTÉIS DE NATA

Belém, a pleasant estuarine district of Lisbon, has very important tarts. They are *pastéis de Belém* – small puff pastry cups of sweet custard with scorched, caramelised tops that are the blueprint for Portugal's most famous food. We say 'blueprint' because *only* tarts made to a secret recipe at the Antiga Confeitaria de Belém patisserie are entitled to the name *pastéis de Belém*, with all others being *pastéis de nata*, mere 'tarts of custard'.

The secret *pastéis de Belém* recipe was devised early in the nineteenth century by a group of enterprising local monks, before being astutely snapped up by the patisserie when the monastery closed. To this day it remains the sole knowledge of four people, a manager and three trusted bakers, who always prepare the pastries in a locked room. Although legions of notebook-concealing, tastebud-flexing chancers have visited hoping to crack the code, the tarts of Antiga Confeitaria de Belém have remained uniquely fine for almost 200 years.

But even if *pastéis de nata* are something of a tart-world pirate DVD, they still taste excellent enough to have gained a place on countless of the world's café counters. Here's one way of making them, which kindly evades the need to make puff pastry from scratch.

Makes 12 tarts
(in a standard 12–hole muffin tray)
250g all-butter puff pastry
Unsalted butter, for greasing

For the custard
350ml milk
2 tablespoons plain flour
50ml double cream
4 large egg yolks
150g caster sugar
½ cinnamon stick
3 strips lemon peel
½ teaspoon vanilla extract

Pre-heat the oven to 220°C/gas 7.

Put around 2 tablespoons of the milk into a saucepan then sift in the flour, before tipping in the rest of the milk as well as the cream, egg yolks and sugar. Stir together until completely smooth before introducing the cinnamon, lemon peel and vanilla extract. Turn the heat on, but low, and stand there stirring the mixture until it all thickens into gloopy, wonderful custard. Taste a little. Mmm. Put it in a bowl and leave to one side.

Grease your muffin tray with butter. Roll out the puff pastry on a floured surface so it's around 3mm thick. Cut it into rounds slightly bigger than the muffin cups, and use them to line the muffin cups. Pour the custard into each one, but not quite to the top of the pastry.

Place the tray in the oven. After about 25 minutes the tarts will start to brown a little on top. Finish this process under the pre-heated grill, then cool the tarts on a wire rack. Best eaten while still a touch warm, and certainly the same day.

CROISSANTS AND PAINS AU CHOCOLAT

Nobody could deny that the French get a lot of meals right. But at breakfast you'd be forgiven for being sceptical. The term *petit déjeuner* speaks volumes – 'little lunch' indeed! And the flaky, effete croissant – that icon of French breakfast – stands in profound contrast to the reliable, robust Anglo-Saxon fry-up.

Try making croissants at home, however, and you will swear to never again disrespect this unfeasibly complex snack. Like climbing the Alps, croissant baking is drawn-out but life-affirming, requiring the scientific exactitude of bread-making, the forensic obsessiveness of puff pastry and the patience of a celebrity rehab nurse. You mix and then knead, then wait, then fold, then wait, then fold, then wait... all for a morsel an ungrateful child may eat in six bites. It is the kind of sophisticated culinary joke that only a prodigiously intellectual nation could make. The full English may be better but the croissant is a ridiculously elegant 'touché'.

A popular tale paints the pastry's origins as Austro-Hungarian rather than French. During the 1683 siege of Vienna, so the story goes, a vigilant baker raised the alarm, thus saving the city from a surprise breach. He celebrated by inventing a new baked good whose shape mimicked the crescents of Islam: 'There, we eat you for breakfast' being the witty subtext. Except this never happened. It was a false story that somehow snuck into the culinary bible *Larousse Gastronomique* as far back as 1938. It continues to ripple through breakfasting folklore, recently recounted in A. A. Gill's enjoyable *Breakfast at the Wolseley*, where it gave weight to the assertion that the siege of Vienna was the moment when Western breakfasting entered the modern age.

Makes around 10 croissants or pains au chocolat
310ml milk
500g strong white bread flour
40g caster sugar
1 ½ teaspoons salt
5g dried instant yeast
1 x 250g block unsalted butter
1 egg for glazing
240g dark chocolate (for pains au chocolat)

The first prove

Gently heat the milk until it feels just warm. Stir the flour, sugar and salt together into a large mixing bowl, then add the yeast followed quickly by the milk, stirring it all until combined into a single ominous mass. Tip out on to a work surface and leave alone for a few seconds (time, say, to clean your bowl) then knead briefly – no more than about fifteen shoves, or until the dough begins to feel a little elastic and consistent – before placing the dough back in the bowl and covering with plastic film or a damp tea towel. Leave to prove for 1–2 hours or overnight in the fridge.

The second prove

When the croissant dough has doubled in size, tip it on to a lightly floured work surface, then firmly pat, palm and roll it into a rectangle of more or less 25 x 60cm, roughly 4mm thick all over. Imagine it is split into three equal, smaller rectangles like the folds in a business letter. Fold the right-hand-side rectangle on top of the central one ('Dear Sir or Madam, thank you for your interest in making me into a croissant...'), then the left-hand one on top of it all. Put this on a lightly floured plate, cover and leave to rise.

Butter, folds one and two

This time, when the dough has doubled in size, put it in the fridge to cool down. Take the butter out. When it's warmed to the point where it's no longer brittle but hasn't yet turned greasy to the touch, dust the butter in a little flour, then place it between two large sheets of plastic film. With a rolling pin, bash firmly and carefully into a large, flat rectangle around 3mm thick.

Take the dough out of the fridge, flour it and roll it into a rectangle around 1cm wider than the butter and a third longer. Cut the butter in half widthwise and place one of these halves in the very centre of the dough, with its shorter sides at the edges of the dough (in other words it should almost fill the central section of the business letter). Fold the right-hand side of the dough over the top of this butter oblong. Now place the second half of your butter on top of that in the same way as before.

Fold the left-hand section of dough on top of all of it. Use your fingers and thumbs to seal the edges. Pat it down firmly with the heels of your hands.

Roll the pastry back out into a flat rectangle, then fold it in three again. Wrap it in plastic film and put it in the fridge for an hour.

Folds three and four

Remove the dough from the fridge and bash it gently all over with a heavy rolling pin to loosen up the butter. Leave it alone for 10 minutes. Roll it out, then fold it in three again. Repeat the roll and the three folds a final time before wrapping and returning to the fridge for another 2 hours.

Rolling and trimming

Remove the dough from the fridge, bash it gently with a rolling pin, then leave alone for 10 minutes. Lightly butter a baking sheet (preferably with raised edges to prevent butter trickling out into your oven, delicious though it will smell for the next week). Now roll the dough out until it's a little larger than 60 x 30cm and no more than 4mm thick. Use a knife to trim it so that all the lines are straight. The pastry is now ready to shape. Remember, a sheet of this pastry is a versatile thing and these are just guide measurements to get you started. It's likely, after the amount of work it took to get there, that you'll want to split each sheet between the different pastries, or experiment with different sizes.

Shaping and baking croissants

Remember the business letter? Cut the pastry into three rectangles along the lines where it'd be folded. You'll now have three pieces of pastry, each measuring 20 x 30cm. Put two of these pieces in the fridge. With the 30cm side of the third piece nearest you, cut two neat neighbouring triangles, each with a base of half the length of the pastry (so 15cm) and a peak that is centred over the base exactly. Use a ruler or a piece of card if you wish. You will now have three triangles with a 15cm base and 20cm tall, each of which can be shaped into a croissant. (At either end, you'll have a triangle half that size. You can form each of these into a slightly less neat croissant-ette).

To shape each croissant, hold the base with one hand and with the other gently stretch the tip away from you as far as it will comfortably go. Begin rolling the base towards the tip, continuing to stretch the tip away from you, until it's all completely rolled into a straight and yet unmistakably croissant-esque shape. Bend it inwards so that the tips of each end touch. When they spring back they'll retain something of a crescent shape. Place each croissant on the baking sheet with the seam facing down.

Repeat with each of your chilled sheets of pastry, then cover and leave to prove once more, until doubled in size. Pre-heat the oven to 190°C/gas 5. Beat the egg together with 1 teaspoon water and use this to lightly brush the croissants. Bake for 10–15 minutes or until golden brown.

Shaping and baking pains au chocolat

Cut the dark chocolate into 10g mini-bars.

Cut the pastry in half lengthwise. You'll now have two strips of pastry, each measuring 60 x 15cm. Put one of these pieces in the fridge to keep it cool while you work on the other. Cut the remaining strip into six rectangles, which will be 10 x 15cm each. For each rectangle, place a bar of chocolate at each end and roll it inwards, so that the two ends meet at the centre. Place on the baking sheet with the smooth side at the top.

Repeat with all your pastry then cover and leave to prove once more, until doubled in size. Pre-heat the oven to 190°C/gas 5. Beat the egg together with 1 teaspoon water and use this to lightly brush each pain au chocolat. Bake for 10–15 minutes or until golden brown.

YOGHURT
&
FRUIT

WHEN YOU QUIZ TOUGH-LOOKING, shaven-headed men about their breakfasting habits, it's surprising how many will quietly confess to enjoying a weekday bowl of fruit and yoghurt, just to balance out that weekend fry-up. This is surprising because, rightly or wrongly, the yoghurt-eating stereotype is someone who is liberal, urbane and good at knitting. Yoghurt's earliest written mention comes courtesy of the Roman philosopher Pliny the Elder, who described it as 'an acrid kind of milk with a pleasant flavour' that was eaten by 'barbarian nations'. Pliny was a middle-class intellectual, thus bearing out the stereotype, but he also fought in several wars and wrote an entire book about throwing spears from horses, so was probably quite tough-looking as well.

YOGHURT

Yoghurt began the journey from exotic otherworldly substance to multibillion-dollar consumer product when, early in the twentieth century, theories emerged linking the generous life expectancies of certain communities across the world with their predilection for thickened, fermented milk. Dr John Kellogg used to talk of its 'friendly bacilli', wowing lecture audiences by preserving the same piece of steak in a yoghurt bath for seventeen years.

The word comes to us from a Turkish root, meaning simply 'thick', but on the Western breakfast table it's the thinking person's milk; while milk is merely the vehicle of cereal, yoghurt offers something of a healthy parallel dimension into which we stir fruit, nuts, honey and all that's sweet yet natural and good for us. It's healthier than milk too, simply by virtue of being more digestible – within an hour of eating a bowl, you'll already have digested most of the protein, minerals and vitamins, whereas many will find whole milk more difficult to absorb.

Basically, it's hard to overdo it with yoghurt – but it is still probably best not to try.

How to Make It

In order to make yoghurt, you need a starter, which is to say something that will introduce the all-important bacteria or 'yoghurt cultures'. The handiest starter for most of us to get hold of is yoghurt itself. Many find this absurd. How many other foods contain themselves in the recipe? It starts making more sense when you consider that having used shop-bought yoghurt the first time round, you can keep using the final part of one batch to start off the next one.

Making it is simple. You heat the milk so as to destroy any unfriendly bacteria, add the starter and then let it thicken. Yoghurt makers, thermos flasks and thermometers will help maintain a good temperature as far as fermentation is concerned, but are unnecessary: at a lower temperature the yoghurting process will just take longer.

This method will get you the equivalent of a standard 500ml supermarket tub, but you can adjust the quantities to make as much or as little as you like.

500ml milk
2 tablespoons natural live yoghurt

Heat the milk in a saucepan until it begins to bubble and steam. Pour it into a jar or mixing bowl and leave to cool. You're looking for a temperature of around 46°C, which you can check with a thermometer or by dipping in a freshly clean finger and seeing if you can leave it for 20 seconds without it beginning to hurt.

Stir in the yoghurt with a fork and then put a lid on the jar or bowl. Wrap it tightly in a towel and leave it in a warm place such as an airing cupboard for 4–6 hours (or overnight). If you live somewhere without one of these culinary 'warm places', then create a temprorary one by turning on the oven for 2 minutes. Check it feels about as warm as an airing cupboard, leaving the door open for a little while to let heat out if you need to, and then place the jar or bowl inside with the heat off. (You can also maintain the temperature by letting the mix ferment in a Thermos flask.)

Once the yoghurt has thickened, transfer to your desired container before putting it in the fridge to cool.

What to Eat It With

Yoghurt is a substance as versatile as toast or porridge; many of the recipes in this book (including some of the savoury ones such as *shakshuka*) will not by any means be harmed by a strategically added glob of the stuff. For a quick bowl in the morning, try stirring in or sprinkling on any combination of the following:

Fresh Fruit: Blackberries, strawberries, raspberries and blueberries are particularly good if in season. Apples, bananas, figs and nectarine-type fruits work best when chopped into pieces around the same size as the aforementioned berries.

Sweet Liquids: Yoghurt and good honey are a match made on Olympia. Jams and compotes remind you why the ubiquitous supermarket 'fruit corner' pot is a laughable waste of time and money.

Nuts and Grains: Chopped or ground nuts are sublime. Granola (see p.160) is transcendental. Porridge oats (stir into the yoghurt, then leave for 10 minutes) add bulk and texture. Wheatgerm will add bulk, texture and unhinged quantities of vital nutrients.

Dried Fruit: Opt for fruits that retain some juice like raisins, sultanas or dried cranberries. The ripped flesh of Medjool dates makes a lavish, sweet and delectably chewy addition.

BREAKFAST ETIQUETTE
by Blake Pudding

Breakfast may seem like that most informal of meals but it is governed by a strict unspoken etiquette, whose rules you break at your peril.

Many people think that etiquette means which knife to use when, or whether you should say drawing room or lounge (it's a drawing room by the way, and use that little one there but don't put it in the butter). As fun as these little social indicators may be, they have less and less place in this increasingly egalitarian world. The rules of etiquette below are about getting the maximum enjoyment out of breakfast and making everyone as comfortable as possible. Stick to these rules and you cannot go wrong.

Rule 1: Leave Me Alone!

The first rule of breakfast has to be to respect the other people's right to silence. Some people, me included, like to breakfast in complete silence punctuated by occasional grunts about passing the marmalade etc. This is particularly relevant if you are staying at a hotel with work colleagues when breakfast is the only time when you can drop the pretence that you like each other or have anything in common. Which brings me on to the next rule.

Rule 2: No Talking about Work

Breakfast meetings should be used as an excuse to gossip and have eggs Benedict at a swanky hotel, not to talk about work. Only book them with people who are aware of this rule, as many people nowadays are not.

Rule 3: Just Grab It

Breakfast being traditionally the only meal in country houses at which guests would help themselves to things rather than being served by the staff has filtered down to the middle classes as it being the only meal where it is acceptable to reach across or get up and get things for yourself. This is really a continuation of the first rule.

Rule 4: Talk about the Night Before

The first rule must be completely ignored if you are breakfasting with friends who you have been out with the night before. In this case chatter must be high-spirited and slightly hysterical. This is a good time to explain away anything embarrassing that you may have done or deflect criticism away from yourself by speculating about what someone not present has done.

Rule 5: Let Me Read

Reading should be compulsory at breakfast unless rule 4 has been invoked. Occasionally piping up with crossword clues is just about acceptable but it should not turn into a round table quiz. And please don't read out whole articles that you find funny.

Rule 6: To Finish or Not to Finish?

As a well brought-up young man I was always taught to finish what was on my plate. Not so at breakfast. Such is the bounty of a traditional English breakfast that it is perfectly acceptable to bite off more than you can chew and then leave half of it.

FRUIT

Fruit at breakfast can go awkwardly off-piste. Not enough prep and it feels underwhelming, rushed. Too much and you can find yourself trespassing on dessert territory. Here are some ideas.

Figs with Ricotta

Following the world's most disastrous apple breakfast, Adam and Eve opted for fig leaves as the world's first underwear. In the Qur'an the Prophet Mohammed is quoted calling the fig the fruit from Paradise. It was under a kind of fig tree that the Buddha achieved enlightenment. Dare we guess that all of the above were inspired by breakfast – namely the delicious, simple kind that the fig offers? We probably don't. But it is a good breakfast.

In the UK figs arrive imported from the Continent each autumn, optimistically wrapped in tissue to protect their delicate skins. Look for ones with a deep colour, which are soft to the touch, as you probably want them ripe and ready to eat. Simply wipe and then trim any stem with a sharp knife. For a puddingy breakfast figs pair exceptionally well with cheese and honey. Baking them enhances their sweetness, but you could easily make this cold, with a white cheese of your choice, drizzled in the honey dressing.

Serves 1, in peace and bliss
2 fresh ripe figs
2 tablespoons ricotta cheese
½ teaspoon sesame seeds
2 teaspoons good-quality honey
1 teaspoon fresh lemon juice

Pre-heat the oven to 180°C/gas 4. Trim the stem from the figs, and wipe with a damp cloth, taking care not to bruise the fruit. With a sharp knife cut 2–3cm into the figs as if to quarter them, but don't cut all the way to the bottom. Place in an ovenproof dish and pack the cuts made in each fruit full of ricotta. Bake for 20–25 minutes.

Meanwhile, toast the sesame seeds gently in a dry frying pan, mix the honey and lemon juice, and add the sesame seeds. Remove the figs from the oven, transfer to a plate and drizzle with the honey dressing. Eat warm.

Roast Plums and Peaches

This recipe is probably what most British readers will think of as pudding and a very good pudding it would make too. But in the Antipodes they serve this sort of thing for breakfast, and with good reason: it's excellent when served with pancakes or eggy bread and mascarpone cheese or thick Greek yoghurt. This recipe calls for peaches and plums, but you could use nectarines or any stone fruits that are in season. If you have very fine peaches, then don't use them for this recipe as they are much too delicious raw; use merely good ones.

Serves 4
2 star anise
1 cinnamon stick
Zest and juice of 2 limes
4 tablespoons demerara sugar
4 ripe plums
4 ripe peaches

Pre-heat the oven to 200°C/gas 6. Put the star anise in a small pan with the cinnamon stick, lime zest and juice, and sugar. Gently bring to the boil, stirring until the sugar has dissolved. Simmer for 3 minutes.

Meanwhile, halve and stone the peaches and plums and arrange, cut sides up, in a shallow dish large enough to hold them all in one layer. Pour the syrup evenly over the fruit, then roast uncovered for 25–30 minutes, basting halfway though the cooking time, until the fruit is tender.

The Grapefruit

No one can produce a book on breakfast without mentioning the grapefruit. There's a family of paraphernalia to go with this retro globe of a fruit – saucers to hold the halves, curved knives for cutting into segments and runcible spoons to eat it with (from 'The Owl and the Pussycat' by Lewis Carroll: 'They dined on mince and slices of quince,/Which they ate with a runcible spoon.' No one knew quite what Carroll meant by a runcible spoon but it has since come to mean one of those spoon/fork hybrids used for eating grapefruit). In the 1930s it was thought that eating grapefruit before every meal miraculously reduced fat. Many actresses lived solely on cigarettes, cocaine and grapefruit. This has since been discredited but who doesn't think, when tucking into a fry-up in a hotel, that having half a grapefruit beforehand somehow makes everything healthier? Grapefruit is tastiest eaten with a sprinkling (often followed immediately by another sprinkling) of sugar. Healthy? Not really, but delicious.

COMPOTE

While more in the dessert camp than the breakfast one, compote has always had mixed allegiances. The roots of this centuries-old dish's name are shared with the less appetising 'compost' – in medieval times the French and the English used to talk of 'fruit compost', and mean the bringing together of fruit and sugar syrup by way of heat application (rather than abandonment in the back garden).

To avoid that nagging feeling of having pudding for breakfast, it's best eaten with an unambiguous fast-breaker such as natural yoghurt or porridge. It should be served cold, though some people, amid much controversy, say they like it while it's still warm.

Raspberry Compote

A very simple compote with a salaciously orangey backdrop. Would work with most dark berries, or a combination of several.

Makes enough for 2 or 3 breakfasts
80ml freshly squeezed orange juice
50g caster sugar
1 cinnamon stick
250g raspberries

Pour the orange juice into a saucepan. Stir in the sugar and cinnamon stick and turn the heat to high. When boiling, add the raspberries, bring back to the boil and then reduce the heat. Simmer for 2 minutes. Remove from the heat, take out the cinnamon stick and transfer to a bowl to cool.

A BREAKFAST PLAYLIST
by Hashley Brown

Cole Porter .... 'Sunday Morning Breakfast Time' (*Jubilee*)
Dusty Springfield .... 'Breakfast in Bed' (*Dusty in Memphis*)
Richard Strauss ...... '*Wie du warst! Wie du bist*' (*Der Rosenkavalier*)
Frank Zappa .... 'St Alphonso's Pancake Breakfast' (*Apostrophe*)
Pete Seeger .. 'Beans, Bacon and Gravy' (*American Industrial Ballads*)
Tom Waits .... 'Eggs and Sausage' (*Nighthawks at the Diner*)
Supertramp .... 'Breakfast in America' (*Breakfast in America*)
Max de Wardener .... 'Kettle Song' (*Teaism*)
Julie London .... 'Nice Girls Don't Stay for Breakfast'
(*Nice Girls Don't Stay for Breakfast*)
Lee Patterson .... 'Egg Fry #2' (*Cathnor Recording Vignettes Series*)

Apple and Blueberry Compote

This recipe combines the happy brekfellows of apple and blueberry with a beautifully spiced syrup. It's a good case study of a compote: you could adjust the quantities to taste, or experiment with different fruits.

Makes enough for 3 or 4 breakfasts
2 Bramley apples, peeled and cored (about 300g)
2 punnets blueberries (about 300g)
Juice of ½ lime
Juice of ½ lemon
50g caster sugar
1 teaspoon ground mixed spice
½ teaspoon ground cinnamon
½ teaspoon vanilla extract
2 tablespoons water

Combine all the ingredients in a saucepan on a medium heat, stirring regularly. After about 5 minutes the blueberries will slowly begin to pop; the juices will become a deep red and the apple pieces pink. Allow it all to bubble on this temperature for a few further minutes, then reduce to a low heat, stirring regularly, being very careful not to break the fruit up, for a few more minutes. Remove the saucepan from the heat – the apple chunks should be soft but not collapsing. Transfer to a different bowl or container to cool before eating.

FOUR MARMALADES & A JAM

WRITING ABOUT BRITISH COOKERY in 1946, George Orwell noted that breakfast 'is not a snack but a serious meal' – one that 'in principle consists of three courses'. Today, at a time when so many of us urgently snack on ephemeral breakfasts, claiming we are time-starved, it seems astounding that a three-course breakfast was then normal. Are we really busier now than we were in the year following the Second World War?

The courses Orwell described were porridge (or cereal), followed by either fish or meat (he specified bacon, kidneys, sausages or ham) and eggs, then finally toast, which, he stipulated, would be served with butter and orange marmalade. On this point he was unambiguously firm: 'It must be orange marmalade, though honey is a possible substitute. Other kinds of jam are seldom eaten at breakfast, and marmalade does not often appear at other times of day.'

Today, of course, those other kinds of jam are naturalised residents of the breakfast table, clustered around your hotel toast rack in those cute little jars they provide. Some claim this is a worrying symptom of a dumbing-down society, that the complexity of marmalade has become too much for the breakfasting mainstream. But the stats say otherwise: with just shy of 95 million jars being sold each year, marmalade is still the king of the breakfast spreads.

MARMALADE

Marmalade was originally a quince-based spread like the Spanish *membrillo* or indeed the Portugese *marmelada*. In the seventeenth century the British started to make something similar but from Seville oranges. It would have been eaten not at breakfast but often during evening meals to aid digestion. It was the Scots who were the first to have marmalade for breakfast, though claims made by the Dundee marmalade magnate James Keiller to have 'invented' orange marmalade in 1797 should be approached with scepticism. Where the Scots led the rest of Britain followed and the fashion spread across the United Kingdom and the Empire. Marmalade became dominant amongst breakfast preserves.

The Seville or bitter orange is pretty much inedible unless cooked because of its high acidity, bitterness and lack of sugar. But it is these strong, rather difficult characteristics that make it so good when cooked with lots of sugar as a counterbalance to make marmalade. The ugly duckling becomes a beautiful swan – its bitter oils transformed into something aromatic and magical after extensive cooking. These properties make it popular in southern Indian and some Caribbean cuisines. The Seville orange is only in season from January, for four weeks at most.

It is worth learning to make your own marmalade, as commercial varieties are always a bit disappointing. While there are hundreds of different recipes, all of them take a long time to make. In the words of the Supremes, you can't hurry marmalade. No, you'll just have to wait. It's probably best to take a day off to do it properly.

Some Hints before You Start

1) Chopping the rind by hand does take time but putting it in a food processer risks making the finished product cloudy. Use a very sharp knife. The ideal is to have a completely clear, just set jelly with the rind suspended equally throughout.

2) Pith and pips make the finished product cloudy. Make sure they are removed.

3) Clean the oranges and all your equipment thoroughly. You are preserving the fruit for long storage and any impurities transferred into the marmalade could make it go off. This is why you sterilise the jars.

4) If you find that your marmalade comes out syrupy, then next time gently heat the sugar in the oven before using. This helps it dissolve.

5) It's worth investing in a preserving pan – this is a very large saucepan with a handle on each side like a light cauldron. If you don't have one, then you could use two large, heavy-based saucepans. You will also need jam jars and waxed discs.

6) You will need preserving sugar – very finely granulated refined sugar – but don't get sugar with added pectin, as oranges have lots in already.

Testing Your Marmalade for a Set

This is to see whether your marmalade will solidify when it cools. Before you start cooking, you should put a saucer in the fridge. When the recipe tells you to, put a small quantity of the liquid on the cold saucer. Put it back in the fridge and leave for a couple of minutes, and then poke the liquid with your finger. If the skin wrinkles, then the marmalade is set. While testing, it is a good idea to remove the pan from the heat to prevent overcooking. If it does not set then boil for longer and test every 5 minutes. The drips from the stirring spoon will give an indication as to whether a set is near. If they become slightly viscous, then you are nearing a set. If, however, they remain very liquid, then you have some way to go.

Sterilising and Potting

To sterilise jars wash them in lots of hot soapy water and rinse thoroughly. Place them in an oven on at 100°C or its lowest setting until they are dry. Do this just before you start to make your marmalade so that the jars are hot when you are ready to pot. Fill the hot jars to the top and cover immediately with waxed discs and either lids or cellophane and elastic bands. Wipe the jars clean while still warm, and label.

Seville Marmalade

This recipe will make the archetypal British marmalade. When one thinks of a traditional breakfast, this is what you would have on the toast. It will make quite a tart, powerful marmalade.

Makes around 7 standard jars
2kg Seville oranges
2 litres water
Juice of 2 lemons
About 1.75kg preserving sugar
10g unsalted butter

Scrub the oranges and remove the stalks. Quarter and place them in your preserving pan, then cover with the water and boil until the rind is soft and edible – this will take between 1 ½ and 2 hours. Leave to cool. At this stage you could leave it overnight and start again the next day. Just keep the pan covered to avoid evaporation.

Drain the oranges, saving the liquid and keeping it to one side. Scoop out the pith, pulp and pips from inside the rind using a teaspoon and set the rind to one side too. Put the pith, pulp and pips into a pan and just cover with around 250ml more water. Boil rapidly for about 10–15 minutes, stirring occasionally to stop it sticking. Pour this into a strainer and keep the liquid: do not push the pulp through the strainer, let it drip through slowly. Discard the pulp.

Finely chop the rind into strips about 2mm thick (you can stack the rinds on top of each other to make this quicker). Now combine the chopped rind and the two lots of liquid plus the lemon juice and put them into a measuring jug. For every litre of rind and liquid you will need 700g preserving sugar, or slightly less if you want a tart marmalade.

Put this into the preserving pan and add the sugar. Every orange has a different ratio of rind to pulp, so you may feel that you have too much rind at this stage. It's really a matter of personal taste. You can discard some now, but don't throw it away, as it could be used to make a delicious orange ice-cream or added to your favourite cake recipe.

Gently heat without boiling until all the sugar has dissolved. Make sure of this by stirring thoroughly: if the mixture feels gritty then the sugar is not totally dissolved. Now bring the marmalade to a fast rolling boil. Boil it like this for about 15 minutes, stirring every couple of minutes to prevent the rind from sticking to the bottom of the pan. If you've not done so already, now's your last chance to put a saucer in the fridge to be used to test for a set, and your jars in the oven to sterilise (see p.195). If you do have sterilised jars but they are not still warm, then warm them up again at around 100°C/ the lowest your gas oven will go.

After 15 minutes' cooking, test for a set (see p.195). Once the setting point is reached remove the pan from the heat. Allow to cool for a minute or two and then stir in the knob of butter. This helps to disperse any scum and gives a clearer marmalade.

Let the marmalade stand for 10 minutes more, stirring occasionally to prevent a skin forming. This also stops all the rind from rising to the top of the jars once potted. You can now pot the marmalade (see p.195), cover and label.

Sweet Orange and Lemon Marmalade

This is a much gentler animal than the Seville orange variety. It's also quicker to make, as these oranges don't require as much cooking. If the traditional Seville is a gentleman's club with wood panelling and a moose's head on the wall, then this is a verandah on a summer's morning.

Makes around 6 or 7 standard jars
1.5kg Valencia oranges
1 lemon
750g preserving sugar
1.5 litres water

With a potato peeler remove the rind from the oranges in thin strips, leaving the pith attached to the flesh. Keep the naked whole oranges. Chop the strips of orange rind into thinner strips about 5mm thick. Now halve the naked oranges and use a citrus squeezer to extract the juice from the fruit, discarding the husks. Halve the lemon and extract the juice.

Add the orange and lemon juice, strips of rind, sugar and water to a preserving pan. Heat gently until all the sugar has dissolved. Now briefly bring to the boil and then bring back down to a gentle simmer for 1 hour, stirring occasionally. Also put the sterilised jars into the oven to warm at about 100°C/the lowest your gas oven will go. Now test for a set (see p.195). Let the marmalade stand for a further 10 minutes, stirring occasionally to prevent a skin forming. This also stops all the rind from rising to the top of the jars once potted. You can now pot the marmalade (see p.195), cover and label.

Whisky Marmalade

This one is a real beastie. It manages to combine two of Scotland's greatest inventions – breakfast marmalade and whisky – in one handy package. The bitterness of the oranges goes beautifully with the malty flavour of the whisky. Make sure you use a whisky with a bit of flavour. Famous Grouse is a good choice. Only Scotch will do. The strange varnish-like flavours of Bourbon will spoil the whole thing.

Makes around 7 standard jars
1.5kg Seville oranges
1.5 litres water
Juice of 2 lemons
1.5kg preserving sugar
500g muscovado sugar
200ml whisky
10g unsalted butter

Scrub the oranges and remove the stalks. Place the oranges whole in a preserving pan and cover with the water. Simmer gently until the rind is soft and edible – this will take about 2 hours. Leave to cool.

Drain the oranges, keeping the liquid to one side. Halve the oranges and remove the pulp and pith, then boil the pulp, pith and saved liquid for about 10 minutes. Strain in a fine sieve, keeping the liquid and discarding the solids. Do not push the pulp through the strainer, let it drip through slowly. Discard the pulp.

Thickly chop the rind and add to the preserving pan (as with the Seville recipe if you think you have far too much rind, leave some out and use for other things). Add the liquid and also the lemon juice plus the sugars, and gently heat until all the sugar has dissolved. Stir until there's no grittiness to ensure this. Once the sugar has dissolved bring the marmalade to a fast rolling boil. Boil it for about 15 minutes, stirring occasionally to prevent the rind from sticking to the bottom of the pan. Add the whisky. Put the sterilised jars into the oven to warm at about 100°C/the lowest your gas oven will go. Now test for a set (see p.195).

Once the setting point is reached remove the pan from the heat. Allow to cool for a minute or two and then stir in the knob of butter. This helps to disperse any scum and gives a clearer marmalade. Let the marmalade stand for a further 10 minutes or so, stirring occasionally to prevent a skin forming. Add the marmalade to the hot jars, cover and label.

Lime Marmalade

Limes have much less pith than oranges, so you don't need to spend time removing it from the rind. This recipe makes a deliciously zingy breakfast treat which is far removed from commercially made versions.

Makes 7 or 8 standard jars
15 limes
2 litres water
1.5kg preserving sugar

Cut the limes in half and squeeze the juice out of them. Keep the juice to one side. Cut the limes into quarters and spoon out the pith and flesh from the skins. Then cut the rind into thin shreds.

Now put the pith, pulp and pips into a pan and just cover with some of the water (about 250ml). Boil rapidly for 10 minutes. Pour this through a strainer and keep the liquid: do not push the pulp through the strainer, let it drip through slowly. Discard the pulp.

Now add this liquid to the preserving pan along with the rest of the water, the chopped rind and the lime juice. Simmer gently, uncovered, for 2 hours or until the rind is soft and edible.

Pour the sugar into the liquid and stir, making sure that it all dissolves completely. Once it has dissolved, turn up the heat and bring the liquid to a fast boil. Boil like this for 15 minutes. Put the sterilised jars into the oven to warm at about 100°C/the lowest your gas oven will go, and then test for a set (see p.195). If it has reached setting point, then transfer to warmed jars, seal and label.

STRAWBERRY JAM

The classic. Is there anyone who doesn't like strawberry jam? No? We thought not. This is delicious on toast, on croissants or stirred into porridge or natural yoghurt. Only make when strawberries are in season or you will end up with a jam of little flavour at great cost. It's better to use slightly under-ripe rather than over-ripe berries, as any rotten flavours will be amplified by the preserving process.

Makes around 6 standard jars
1kg strawberries, hulled
1kg preserving sugar
2 tablespoons fresh lemon juice
10g unsalted butter

Place a saucer in the fridge. Put 250g of the strawberries in the pan with 250g of the sugar. Over a gentle heat break up the strawberries with a wooden spoon. When they are warmed through add the rest of the strawberries and gently bring to a simmer, stirring occasionally to stop the strawberries sticking. Add the rest of the sugar and the lemon juice. When all the sugar has thoroughly dissolved, bring to a rapid boil for 9 minutes. Put the sterilised jars into the oven to warm at about 100°C/the lowest your gas oven will go.

Now remove the saucer from the fridge, place a spoonful of the jam on it, then return to the fridge. Remove the pan from the heat. After a couple of minutes, give the jam on the saucer a poke with your finger. If the skin wrinkles, the jam is at setting point. If not, return the pan to the boil and keep repeating this test every 5 minutes.

When setting point has been reached stir in the butter and skim off any foam on top of the jam. Leave to cool for 10 minutes to make sure the strawberries are evenly distributed.

Now it's time to pot the jam. Pour into the hot jars so that the jam almost reaches the top, then cover immediately with discs of waxed paper and lids or cellophane and elastic bands. Label.

CONTINENTAL

THE CONTINENTAL IS AN EXCUSE for budget hotels not to offer a proper cooked breakfast. 'How Continental,' you think, plucking a dry croissant from a rustic basket as the traffic roars past on the A44. 'Just like Paris in the spring.'

'The Continent' is of course also shorthand for meddling Europe, the one that is trying to destroy time-honoured British things like pints, flat caps and casual racism. Whether or not you object to the mass stereotyping of around fifty countries' eating habits, the key factor in distinguishing a *Continental* repast from an *English* one tends to be a lack of cooking. It seems that whilst we spend our mornings grilling, jugging or poaching anything that moves, once you cross the Channel no-one can be bothered to light a match.

It would be ungenerous to suggest that the Continental breakfast is inferior, but it is certainly simpler. Should you wish to attempt this harmless diversion at home, here are a few recipes, or more accurately *assemblages*, for a taste of the non-American Occident.

France: Spread out a red gingham tablecloth and arrange the following: fresh baked baguette, some farmhouse butter, local jam, and strong black coffee in a bowl.

Germany: Find the largest plate you can, pile on slices of smoked ham, salami, at least two varieties of cheese, grapes, slices of orange, a small bowl of natural yoghurt, a freshly boiled egg, a Kaiser roll, some jam, lots of butter and perhaps even a couple of salad leaves. Serve with coffee and fruit juice.

Austria: Soft-boil two eggs, peel them whilst still hot and drop them in a short drinking glass. Top with a little salt and some chopped chives, and you have the Viennese café speciality *Eier im Glas*. Serve with a spoon, a Kaiser roll and a cup of coffee.

Spain: Nibble a couple of *magdalenas* – little fluffy cupcakes with just a hint of lemon – accompanied by a cup of *café con leche* (espresso topped up with hot milk). Wait a few hours, then have an enormous lunch. If you're feeling a little Catalan rub some toast with olive oil, garlic and a ripe tomato for the delight that is *pa amb tomàquet*.

Italy: Many will smoke a strong cigarette in lieu of food, but if you must eat something then have a croissant, *cornetto* or some other buttery pastry. If it's summer and you're feeling lavish, follow it with an almond granita. Accompany with a *caffè e latte* – it's the only time of day you can justifiably order one without looking like a tourist.

Denmark: On a plate assemble an austere piece of rye bread topped with a few slices of a mild creamy Danish cheese such as Havarti. If it's your birthday, tradition dictates you let your hair down and have a shot of Gammel Dansk, a bitters-based spirit not unlike Fernet Branca.

Finland: In the depths of winter eat a bowl of steaming oatmeal porridge topped with a pat of butter or some berries. In warmer times have a *pulla*, a small sweet roll flavoured with cardamom, and several cups of coffee (Finns drink more per capita than any other nation).

Lithuania: Have a bowl of cottage cheese – not the sloppy matter of British supermarkets, but a thicker curd version straight from the farm. Traditionalists liven this up with sugar and cinnamon, while modern breakfasters deploy fruit.

Greece: Breakfast is mainly a time to start thinking – carefully considering the mid-morning snack you'll be picking up from the bakery. Interim sustenance is a hard biscuity rusk called a *paximathaki*, and honey-sweetened black tea.

Portugal: Try a *queijada*, an elegant little cake made with fresh cheese, accompanied by a glass of milky *galão* coffee.

'BREAKFAST'

Arabic . . . . فطور

Azerbaijani . . . . səhər yeməyi

Cantonese . . . . 早餐

Bengali . . . . shokaler nasta

Croatian . . . . doručak, zajutrak

Czech . . . . snidat

Danish . . . . morgenmad

Dutch . . . . ontbijt

Filipino . . . . almusal

Finnish . . . . aamiainen

French . . . . petit déjeuner

German . . . . Frühstück

Greek . . . . πρωινό

Haitian Creole . . . . manje maten

Hausa . . . . karìn kùmalloo

Hebrew . . . . ארוחת בוקר

Hindi . . . . nashta

Hungarian . . . . reggeli

Icelandic . . . . morgunmatur

Igbo . . . . nrï ütütü

Indonesian . . . . makan pagi

Irish . . . . bricfeasta

Italian . . . . prima colazione

Japanese . . . . 朝食

Korean . . . . 조반

Lithuanian . . . . pusryčiai

Mandarin . . . . 早餐

Norwegian . . . . frokost

Oromo . . . . ciree

Persian . . . . صبحانه

Polish . . . . śniadanie

Portuguese . . . . desjejum

Romanian . . . . mic dejun

Russian . . . . утренний завтрак

Serbian . . . . доручак

Spanish . . . . desayuno

Swahili . . . . kifungua kinywa

Swedish . . . . frukost, morgonmål

Tamil . . . . காலை உணவு

Thai . . . . อาหารเช้า

Turkish . . . . kahvaltı

Ukrainian . . . . перший сніданок

Vietnamese . . . . bữa sáng

Welsh . . . . brecwast

Yiddish . . . . פרישטיק

Yoruba . . . . onjẹ òwúrọ

BREAKFAST ON THE EDGE
by Malcolm Eggs and Blake Pudding

WAR

British Army: If a soldier on active service skips breakfast and suffers as a result of poor nutrition, he or she can be disciplined. A sample breakfast box contains:

Chicken sausage and beans in tomato sauce
Pork sausage with omelette and beans
Bacon with omelette and beans
Oatmeal block
Vegemite
Strawberry fruit spread
Freeze-dried tea granules
Instant coffee
Hot chocolate-flavoured drink
White sugar
Beverage whitener

US Army: The ration pack is called an MRE (meal ready to eat) and heated up with an FRH (flameless ration heater). A sample breakfast MRE contains:

Pork sausage patty
Hash browns with bacon
Toaster pastry
Wheat snack bread
Peanut butter
Orange beverage
Cocoa beverage and instant coffee

SPACE

On the Apollo spaceflights (including the first successful moon mission) breakfast was known as Meal A. One spread, for example, contained:

Fruit cocktail (R)
Sausage patties (SBP)
Cinnamon toasted bread cubes (4) (DB)
Cocoa (R)
Grapefruit drink (R)

R = rehydratable
DB = dry bite
SBP = spoon-bowl packet

ANTARCTIC

During his doomed race to the South Pole, Captain Scott recorded a particularly fine breakfast of fish: 'We are living extremely well. At dinner last night we had some excellent seal soup, very much like thick hare soup; this was followed by an equally tasty seal steak and kidney pie and a fruit jelly. The smell of frying greeted us on awakening this morning, and at breakfast each of us had two of our nutty little *Notothenia* fish after our bowl of porridge. These little fish have an extraordinarily sweet taste – bread and butter and marmalade finished the meal.' (26 May 1911)

DRINKS

BROKEN ORANGE PEKOE OR CORPSE REVIVER?

THE TRUE BREAK OF THE NIGHTLY FAST, you might argue, doesn't involve food at all. A sip of hot liquid, or at the very least water, will be the first your belly knows of the day. And when we wake up too late to do anything but rush to work, a hot drink becomes our sole, precious source of breakfasting solace. As Chinese tea scholar T'ien Yiheng observed, 'tea is drunk to forget the din of the world': a sip from a favourite mug – preferably a gift from a loved one – can shield us momentarily from the blandest, most open plan of workplaces. If this sounds overblown, imagine the response if tea and coffee were banned. The police would lose control of the streets.

Tea and coffee are the most ritualistic drinks we have. Wine, for example, has an air of ceremony, but once we have selected the bottle and brought it home, the quality of what we'll eventually drink is out of our hands. To do justice to a hot caffeinated brew, on the other hand, takes skill as well as knowledge. It's not difficult to make a passable cup – if it was it would hardly be popular – but we have all had the occasional gulp that makes us stop what we're doing out of pure, impossible-to-describe bliss. This is the goal, and among other things achieving it involves just the right mix of temperature, quantity and brewing time.

Juice, the other classic of the breakfast table, offers a different kind of pleasure. What we lose in poetry, we gain in health – and it's for each to decide which he or she values more. Sometimes, especially during hangover situations, a breakfaster in a café will order a hot drink *and* juice, perhaps with some tap water too. That's fine, but bear in mind that the rule is one of diminishing returns: the first breakfast drink will always live up to its potential more than the second, and that one in turn more than the third.

Also remember that in hangover situations there is a third way, namely more booze. It should not be a road taken lightly, but if you want to take it then you may prefer to leave the lager alone (we would certainly recommend this) and opt for something from the surprisingly well-established world of breakfast booze. The Bloody Mary is the one that reeks of civility, while the Corpse Reviver reeks of something else. Don't do the alcohol thing regularly. If you're choosing it more often than the other three drink categories in this chapter, there are other books you should read.

TEA
COFFEE
JUICES & SMOOTHIES
ALCOHOL

TEA

VYING FOR THE STARRING ROLE in our breakfast drama we have tea, that elegant leading lady with an iron constitution. A royal's drink that generously gave itself to the people, tea is the Princess Diana of beverages, powerful, vulnerable and iconic, and it is now fêted as the drink of English gent and brickie alike. Tea's most relentless consumers are actually the Irish, who drink more per capita than any other nationality. It is always shocking when a British or Irish person professes a dislike of tea. For many of us it's our desert island drink, even our religion. In the manner of Jehovah's Witnesses, we peddle the word of tea, pitying those who view it as just so much hot water. 'If man has no tea in him,' runs a Japanese proverb, 'he is incapable of understanding truth and beauty.' He is also incapable of understanding breakfast.

Tea became fashionable in English aristocratic circles under the guidance of Catherine of Braganza, the Portuguese wife of Charles II. Arriving in Portsmouth in 1662 after an arduous sea crossing she requested a brew, only to be met with bemusement and offered ale instead. But Catherine's taste for tea soon set a trend in high society. Tea was rare in Britain at this time and its high price – due to heavy taxation – meant that it remained for some time a drink of the upper classes, who kept their stashes in porcelain jars or locked tea-chests. They drank both green and black tea (without milk) as a treat from delicate bowls. In 1745 duty was slashed, and the drink was finally allowed to discover its proletariat sympathies. It was around then that black surpassed green in popularity. Green tea, let's face it, never stood a chance: black tea is more oxidised, giving it a stronger flavour and, very importantly, it contains more caffeine.

In the UK the average tea drinker is likely to drink the same tea at breakfast time as they do throughout the day, and probably won't know their Flowery Orange Pekoe from their Precious Eyebrows. With mass-market teas, brand has become synonymous with blend, and determining what specific varieties your tea of choice comprises can be tricky. What we think of as English tea (the full-blooded kind that persistently eludes one on holidays in mainland Europe, except in the weakest forms) is a blend of black teas from India, Africa and/or Sri Lanka. English Breakfast and its stronger cousin Irish Breakfast are similar blends, occasionally incorporating teas from China and Indonesia as well. Stronger teas (blends emphasising Kenyan and Assam teas) are best with cooked breakfasts, where they can take the upper hand with grease, while lighter teas (Ceylon or Darjeeling) are good companions for the more delicate breakfast – picture a petal falling on to a silk bedspread.

Tea is an exquisite storybook you can open at any page and plunge into for tales of far-off lands, apocryphal histories, sensory delights and curious terminology. When you bring tea to your breakfast table you bring so much more than a drink – you bring the whole world. Just be careful your cup doesn't runneth over.

TYPES OF BREAKFAST TEA

The following black teas are often used in breakfast blends but can of course be imbibed separately.

Assam (India): A wet dog of a tea, Assam has the potential to bite but is satisfied with a gentle growl. Its flavour is gruff and malty, sometimes with a hint of raspberry jam, and a final whisper of bitterness, as if someone very far away is reminding you of a wrong you did them. Assam adds power and body to breakfast teas but is arguably best when blended with a light and sparky element, such as Ceylon.

Ceylon (Sri Lanka): Imagine a lady in a yellow silk dress shading herself from the sun with a parasol. That is Ceylon. Her taste is distant and citrussy, with a silky touch and a faint assertiveness. Secretly, she knows what she wants, but you'll have to coax it out of her and she may leave you feeling slightly frustrated. A passive-aggressive but enchanting tea that smoothes out the rough edges of breakfast blends.

Darjeeling (India): The highly prized Darjeeling is known as the 'champagne' of teas for its flowery, 'muscatel' aroma. It has a delicate, leafy flavour with a subtle fragrance of wine like a debutante at the end of a ball. It is not commonly taken at breakfast but is occasionally included in blends, probably as an alternative to Ceylon.

Kenya BOP (Kenya): The most recognisable flavour to those weaned on mass-market UK teas, Kenya BOP (Broken Orange Pekoe – one of the numerous delightful terms used in the grading of teas) is robust and business-like with a lemony personality and lacks the soft core of some of the subtler teas. It slides powerfully down the gullet like a commuter down an escalator and, indeed, will prepare you well if you are taking such a journey yourself.

Keemun (China): This aromatic, slightly spicy tea tastes smoked and, sometimes, almost meaty. Without milk (and it is better thus), it is almost crimson in colour (indeed, in Chinese-influenced languages, black tea is known as crimson tea). A magician in a velvet cloak, it wafts away, leaving an oaky aftertaste. To any breakfast blend it visits, Keemun adds a signature piquancy.

Yunnan (China): This bristly tea has a rich malty character with subtle undertones of chocolate, infusing to a warm molasses colour. Gruff and sweet, like a toffee-flavoured Alsatian, it's a leaper-upper of a tea, friendly if not always discreet, and sometimes itchy. (If you struggle to imagine tea in canine terms, try harder.) Occasionally marketed as Chinese Breakfast Tea, Yunnan may be included in the stronger blends of breakfast tea, such as Irish Breakfast.

READING TEALEAVES
by Poppy Tartt

A widow's bonnet, a pig, a circle and the figure 100... What else could this combination predict but a legacy from a widow? Subject your breakfast cup to a tealeaf reading and predictions of this kind could be forthcoming.

Also known as tasseomancy, tasseography or teomancy, tealeaf reading is surely the most refined of fortune-telling methods. Theories as to its origins vary. Some suggest they date back to ancient China, where a monastic tradition of interpreting patterns formed on the insides of bells may have developed into the reading of leaves, since tea was drunk from bell-shaped cups. The practice had certainly reached the UK by the nineteenth century. A popular parlour game among the Victorians, it took quite a knock when the teabag was invented and these days it is considered a somewhat esoteric activity.

Rituals vary according to different traditions, but most cup readers insist on the importance of using a wide, shallow cup with sloping sides and a plain, unpatterned inside surface (preferably white). A satisfactory reading cup may be prepared by either brewing a pot of tea and pouring without the use of a strainer, or just making an individual cup. After drinking, a teaspoonful of tea should be left in the bottom. Concentrating the mind upon their Destiny, the drinker, or querent, should hold the cup by its rim with their non-dominant hand and swirl it three times in a clockwise direction, then tip it upside down on a saucer for a few moments until the liquid has drained off. Once the cup is turned the right way, the leaves still clinging to the sides will form the basis of the fortune.

The cup should be held by the reader so that the handle points towards the querent. The reader must first look out for clear signs, such as any remaining drops of tea, which signify tears; large clumps of tea, meaning trouble; and tea-stalks, which represent people. Generally tealeaf readers interpret the shapes made by the tea itself, though there are some who also take into account images formed in negative space (where the image is seen on the cup itself, framed by the tealeaves). Leaves are read according to their distance from the handle. Leaves nearest the rim stand for recent or imminent events (to the right of the handle, the future; to the left, the past), while those closer to the bottom signify more distant events. Beware the very bottom of the cup, which represents misfortune.

Some readers adhere to standard interpretations of traditional symbols, comprehensive lists of which are widely available. They can seem wildly outdated. One presumes, at least, that a 'native with tom-tom' does not mean an indigenous person holding a sat nav. Straightforward symbols and their meanings include:

ACORN .... Good health, or improvement in health
BIRDS .... A lucky sign. If flying, good news from that direction;
if at rest, a fortunate journey
CHAIR .... An addition to the family, or a guest
FORK .... A warning against false flattery
HAT .... Success in a new enterprise or, sometimes, the arrival
of a visitor; if at the bottom of the cup, a rival
HEART .... Love, friendship, romance
OWL .... A bad omen – sickness, poverty, a warning against a
new venture (if the querent is in love, he or she may be deceived)
PIG.................................... Material success, or possibly greed
SCISSORS .... Quarrels, or a separation
TELEPHONE .... Forgetfulness leads to trouble

How the symbols relate to each other is also of importance – for example, a lucky bird may be outweighed by the presence of a larger and unlucky owl. Some combinations of symbols have assigned meanings and are so unlikely that it's hard to imagine them coming up twice. Look out for a magnet and a meat cover, which warns that an infatuation will end abruptly following an unpleasant discovery. Or a rhinoceros, an overcoat, a steamer and a large letter 'I', indicating that a vaguely dangerous undertaking will require an journey to India, which will be very eventful and lead to you becoming famous. At least 30 per cent of symbols seem to predict voyages to India, or run-ins with untrustworthy widows.

Contemporary readers may prefer to use their instincts when interpreting symbols. As one website says reassuringly: 'If you are perfectly certain that the leaf clump you are staring at can be NONE OTHER than Bob Marley, don't fight it.'

········ # HOW TO MAKE THE PERFECT CUP OF TEA ········

Following years of extensive research, we have come to this sobering conclusion: the ratio of cups of tea drunk to perfect cups of tea drunk is not what it should be. In homes, offices, cafés and on street corners across Britain substandard cuppas are being consumed on a daily basis and it is our mission to right this dreadful wrong. Follow our seven-step guide for enlightenment.

1. The Tea

The *Sophie's Choice* of tea-making is whether to use tealeaves or teabags. Tealeaves are the connoisseur's choice, and not just because of their fortune-telling potential. Loose-leaf tea is generally of a higher quality and a greater variety of teas is available in this form. But it means also embracing a whole family of tea paraphernalia: teapots, tea caddies, tea cosies, tea strainers, tea infusers – all those quaint and potentially crazy items that add a touch of the shamanistic ceremony to the tea-drinking ritual and could, if you're not careful, turn you mad as a hatter. Tealeaves take longer to steep and if left in the pot will stew the tea, but they are without doubt the more refined and eccentric option. Teabags, on the other hand, are practical, easy to store and dispose of and easier to buy. Most of us are experienced at working with teabags and may feel entirely happy with their performance.

2. The Vessel

The choice of vessel is also key, though it may depend on your choice of tea and also, of course, the occasion. Teabags are well served by mugs or teapots, but teacups are too small for individual teabags and should only be used in conjunction with a teapot. Steer clear of metal teapots, which are useless for retaining heat and likely to burn your hands. Use one teabag per person, *never* less. Never re-use a teabag. The only excuse for doing so is if you are extremely poor. The perfect cup of tea is strong; as George Orwell tells us, 'All true tea lovers not only like their tea strong, but like it a little stronger with each year that passes.'

Tealeaves do better in a teapot containing an inbuilt infuser, which keeps the leaves out of the water once the tea is brewed. For one-cup brews use an infuser ball (a sort of refillable mechanical teabag made of metal or mesh – avoid aluminium, which taints the tea). Allow one heaped teaspoon of leaves per person. In contrast to teabags, certain tealeaves, being of a higher grade, can be re-used.

Warm a teapot in advance by swilling boiling water around in it. If using a mug, note that the teabag or infuser ball must be in the mug *awaiting* the boiling water. Always add water to tea; *never ever ever* add tea to water.

3. The Water

Of course the type of water used also affects the taste of the tea. The Chinese 'Sage of Tea' Lu Yu (733–804), who wrote the first known book on the subject, recommended spring water for high oxygen content, purity and freshness. The worst type of water to use is water that has become stale through standing still – for example, water from a tea urn, which makes terrible tea. Hard water makes an extracted, tannic tea prized by experts while tea made with soft water has a more pleasant, gentle taste. Whether you deliberately select your water, or simply use what comes out of the tap, use fresh water, not the stuff left over in the kettle. Re-boiled water tastes flatter. Whatever you do, the most important thing to remember is that the water must be boiling when it hits the tea.

4. The Brewing

Once tea and water have been united, you must be patient and allow the tea to brew (ensuring teapots are covered with a cosy during the process). Optimum steeping times vary, but a good guide is 3–6 minutes. For most teabags 3 minutes is easily enough and if you leave them much longer the water will take on that stewed, mirrory look. A teabag that has been steeped for long enough has no need of being 'induced', that is, being humiliated by being squished against the side of the cup.

5. The Milk

If you had thought about milk before now, you are wrong. The only scenario in which 'milk first' may be appropriate or acceptable is when serving tea from a pot into teacups, especially if you're playing a part in an Oscar Wilde play. There is something delightfully dainty about that preliminary pouring in of milk. However, it is often impractical. Listen, again, to Mr Orwell: 'The milk-first school can bring forward some fairly strong arguments, but I maintain that my own argument is unanswerable. This is that, by putting the tea in first and stirring as one pours, one can exactly regulate the amount of milk whereas one is liable to put in too much milk if one does it the other way round.'

When tea is made in a mug with a teabag, ideally the tea must be brewed and the bag removed before milk is added. Adding milk where a teabag is present is not only unsightly but actually hinders steeping because the milk clogs the perforations of the bag. This (unfortunately widespread) method requires a considerable outlay of energy on the part of the tea-drinker, who will need to spend precious moments bobbing the indignant teabag up and down until the required tone is met. Such actions are really only excusable when a cup of tea is urgently required, with no regard whatsoever as to how far towards perfection the resulting cup might tend (not very far, to be sure). Where milk is put into the mug before even the teabag and the hot water, we are absolutely beside ourselves.

When step 4 has been followed to the letter, the correct shade of tea – the colour of a Quality Street toffee, as Noel Gallagher has observed – will be ready and waiting to be revealed in a beautiful swirl of cream and tan as the milk is added. (At this point a teaspoon may be used, to aid integration.)

It ought to be needless to say that the milk should always be cold. If you have experienced the ignominy of receiving a small jug of hot milk to accompany your pale, pale tea in the wilds of mainland Europe, you will know why.

6. The Sugar

Let us not speak of sugar.

7. The Consumption

The perfect cup of tea is drunk as soon as it is ready, as hot as you can stand it. It takes practice and a hell of a lot of burnt tastebuds before you get there, but when you do – wow. You will tingle all over and slam your empty cup down and slap your thighs and say: 'My *God*! That was a good cup of tea.'

COFFEE

WRITERS, PHILOSOPHERS, prophets, politicians: all have been held, enthralled, by coffee's bitter baritone flavour, its real-estate-shifting aroma, its siren promise of instant vim. In Enlightenment France there was Voltaire, single-handedly spurring along the intellectual life of the nation, the tens of thousand of letters and books he flung out powered by a minimum daily ration of fifty cups. In eighteenth-century England Joseph Addison, founder of *The Spectator*, was master of a coffee-house scene that could make or break political careers. And in Germany Johann Sebastian Bach wrote a composition called *Kaffeekantate*, with subtly coffee-endorsing words such as 'Coffee, coffee I must have/and if someone wishes to give me a treat, /ah, then pour me out some coffee!'

The coffee bean originated in the wild in Ethiopia and was initially cultivated in the Arabian Peninsula in what is now Yemen. Sufi mystics were the first to harness its qualities as a stimulant, imbibing a drink called *qahwa* to help them stay awake during prayer (this begs a surprising question: were Sufi mystic prayers *boring*?). By 1510 it was part of the fabric of life in Mecca and Cairo. A debate flared up for a while about whether, like other intoxicants, it should be forbidden, but an attempt at a ban was overturned by a sultan and the drink was given the nod. When it drifted west along Venetian trade routes, Pope Clement VIII waved it through.

London's first coffee house opened in 1652. Within fifty years there were over five hundred, their signs painted with the heads of Turks, their interiors a nest of gossip and ideology. Around the same time, coffee toppled ale as America's breakfast drink of choice, a position later cemented when the Boston Tea Party turned drinking coffee, by virtue of its not being tea, into an act of anti-British patriotism. Later, in Italy, the invention of the espresso machine in 1905 inspired a widespread breakfasting routine of standing, smoking, quaffing and leaving. These machines (and with them a vocabulary including *cappuccino* and *latte*) spread around the world with the Italian diaspora. They became an indispensable item for *breakfasteurs*.

'Coffee or tea?' the British ones will ask. It can be hard to decide. While tea is the breakfast drink of the establishment, of the community, of a sort of laconic shared nostalgia, coffee offers something more rebellious, creative and perhaps a touch vain. Those who completely reject food for breakfast will brag, 'Oh, I just have a cup of coffee.' To say 'Oh, I only have tea' just doesn't have the same sado-masochistic drama.

Coffee is a drug and like all drugs it should be handled cautiously. Few want to go the route of nineteenth-century writer Honoré de Balzac, driven as his tolerance increased to invent ever more brutal ways to maintain the 'cerebral power' it gave him. In his essay 'The Pleasures and Pains of Coffee' he describes a last resort of 'finely pulverised, dense coffee, cold and anhydrous, consumed on an empty stomach'. The effects? 'A kind of animation that looks like anger: one's voice rises, one's gestures suggest unhealthy impatience: one wants everything to proceed with the speed of ideas; one becomes brusque, ill-tempered about nothing.'

Similarly, Henry Ward Beecher, an American preacher writing in the late nineteenth century, described the drink's appeal with the stuttering fervour of a true junkie: 'A cup of coffee – real coffee – home browned, home-ground, home made that comes to you dark as a hazel-eye but changes to a golden bronze as you temper it with cream that never cheated but was real cream from its birth, thick, tenderly yellow, perfectly sweet, neither lumpy nor frothing on the Java, such a cup of coffee is a match for twenty blue devils, and will exorcise them all.' Well said. This is what coffee aspires to but doesn't often deliver. The maddening thing about coffee is how good it smells but how hard it is to get this smell into a taste. When you do, you'll have what FBI agent Dale Cooper called 'a damn fine cup of coffee'.

THE BEAN

Coffee comes from certain species of a small berry-producing bush called a coffea. Each berry contains two seeds – these are the coffee beans, green when harvested, brown when roasted.

Simply speaking there are two types of bean: Arabica and Robusta. Arabica is more expensive to cultivate but produces much the better coffee. Robusta is easier to grow, more resistant to disease and produces a full-bodied drink, though one with less flavour. It also contains more caffeine so it is the primary component of instant, which will be mainly Robusta with perhaps a tiny bit of Arabica for flavour. Most quality coffee will be 100 per cent Arabica, though some espresso blends contain some Robusta as it produces a good *crema*, or foam on the top.

Wine experts will speak almost mystically of *terroir*, the way in which a wine expresses the characteristics – the soil, landscape and climate – of its vineyard of origin. The same applies to coffee: where a bean is grown has a profound effect on flavour. Commercial blends, in which coffees from different sources are combined to create a consistent product, can be very good, but they do remove the fun a little. Try a very rich, full-bodied Javan coffee and then a more refreshing Kenyan one, and the difference is startling. The Java tastes rich and dark, almost like a cliché of how coffee is supposed to taste. When you compare it to the Kenyan, the difference is as shocking as trying an Alsatian Gewürztraminer if you are used to Californian Chardonnay.

Coffee grows best near the equator, in the so-called 'bean belt' that lies between the tropics of Cancer and Capricorn and hosts the great coffee-growing nations such as Columbia, Nicaragua, Guatemala, Sumatra, Brazil, India and Rwanda. There's also Jamaica, whose most famous coffee, Blue Mountain, was immortalised by James Bond, who ordered it in the way he used to order Dom Pérignon – to show what exquisite taste he had. Perhaps because of this, it is now very expensive. Some sceptical tasters would go as far as to say that it is grossly overpriced and not as good as it used to be.

Although coffee is a 'cash crop', very little of the cash actually reaches those who grow it. Most of the money goes to the brokers who act as middlemen between producers and retailers. Concerned vendors in first-world countries have responded with a number of initiatives including Fairtrade, the Rainforest Alliance and Utz. Broadly speaking, all these labels guarantee farmers a fair price for their crops which, whatever their respective points of distinction, is a good thing. But you should also bear in mind that the bureaucracy involved in certifications like this will have discouraged many on either side of the supply chain. If in doubt, only buy from companies who deal directly with farmers.

Choosing a Roast: Of prime importance to the flavour of coffee is the degree of the roast. In the simplest of terms, a heavy roast (plainly put, a longer roasting time) will make the beans dark and rich tasting; a lighter roast will bring out coffee's fruitier side. Roast names are glorious: they include Cinnamon Roast (light), New England Roast (light), City Roast (medium), Viennese Roast (medium dark) and Italian Roast (dark). There is a Breakfast Roast – it's slightly sweet and belongs to the medium category. Starbucks is known for a very dark roast. Some have said, perhaps unfairly, that this is only so that the flavour can make it through all that milk.

After roasting, the beans should be consumed as soon as possible. How soon is a matter of debate. Industrial roasters will plump for longer, arguing that vacuum-packing will seal in the freshness, whereas smaller 'boutique' roasters tend to assert that however you package the beans, they will start to deteriorate after about two weeks. If you live near a good small roaster make the most of them. The roast may not always be as consistent as those of the big players, but the beans will tend to be fresher.

Grinding: Coffee beans start to lose their aroma as soon as they are ground, so for aficionados grinding your own is a must. Don't use your hands or a piece of brick; there are machines. Here are the two most common types:

Blade grinder: The cheaper kind. Works a bit like a little food blender. Quite effective for using with a cafetière but not suitable for grinding for espresso, as no matter how long you run it for it won't achieve a consistently fine ground. Produces a lot of heat, which can burn the beans.

Burr grinder: This crushes the beans between a spinning wheel and a stationary one, crushing the beans less violently and producing a more consistent ground than the blade grinder. Such grinders tend to be more expensive. The most costly is a conical burr grinder, which produces almost no heat at all, so the coffee will not be damaged in any way.

In general try to use coffee within two weeks of grinding, or if buying pre-ground beans then within two weeks of opening the packet.

Ground coffee should be stored in an airtight container. You can store it in the fridge, but try to avoid this if you are making espresso, as the cold temperature will prevent the oils from emulsifying properly (see p.225). If you're going to keep the beans for a few weeks before grinding, freezing them is a viable way of maintaining freshness, but avoid keeping them for longer than eight weeks.

MAKING COFFEE

Yes, the great, stupid dream of coffee-making is for the taste, just once, to be as good as the smell. This is impossible. Coffee never tastes as good as it smells, but thank goodness there are people out there trying.

The Coffee-maker or Automatic Drip Coffee-maker
(coffee ground: medium to coarse)

The most popular way of making coffee in the States. All those bottomless coffee cups in a proper diner will be made using such a machine, which extracts a lot of caffeine and acidity from the bean but not enough of the magical aroma or body. Very good beans are a little wasted here.

Use 4–5 tablespoons per 600ml water – less if you run a diner in Iowa and more if you want to hallucinate. Fill the water chamber with water, put a filter paper in the place to put filter papers, then add the ground coffee. Switch on the machine. Much gurgling will commence and soon large quantities of coffee will be yours. It is vital that you drink it within 15 minutes or so of brewing. Most coffee from such machines will have been sitting on the hot plate for hours and will consequently taste stewed.

The Cafetière
(coffee ground: medium to coarse)

Invented in France (and known as a French press in the States), the cafetière has become the British coffee-maker of choice. It consists of a glass pot, a lid and a plunger with a built-in mesh filter. When used correctly this method preserves the aroma very effectively though beware: it will be hard to get away with low-quality or stale coffee grounds.

Boil the kettle. Half-fill the empty pot with boiling water. Push the plunger through the water and then back up again: this will remove any old oils clinging to the filter, as well as warming up the pot. Now empty the water out (empty, refill and reboil the kettle if there isn't enough left for the main event). Add coffee to the pot: 4–5 tablespoons per 600ml water (if it's not your ideal strength, then adjust the amount the next time you use it). Fill the cafetière with very hot but not boiling water (too hot and the grounds may burn). About 90°C or 2 minutes off the boil should do. Stir vigorously with a teaspoon. Put the lid and plunger on. Wait 3 minutes and then push the plunger down. Pour.

Stove-top Espresso-maker
(coffee ground: fine)

The most popular option in Spanish and Italian homes. Water is forced through coffee grounds by way of steam pressure. Comes in three pieces: a base, which sits on the hob, a middle chamber, which holds the coffee, and a screw-on top, in which the brewed coffee gathers. The stove-top produces a very strong coffee with great body and smell, which has many of the characteristics of the espresso. Smells wonderful too.

Add boiling water to the bottom, screw the chamber on top of it (protect your hand with a tea towel if necessary) and fill with coffee. Tamp down gently, but not too tightly or the water will struggle to get through. Place on a medium flame. Coffee will start percolating into the top of the maker. As soon at the coffee flow starts to splutter (and no later) take off the heat, wait for the rest to come through, and serve.

Instant

Let us not speak of instant.

Domestic Espresso Machine
(coffee ground: fine)

Like a Gaggia from an Italian café: that is the ideal. Very few domestic machines live up to it. The main hurdle is that the machine needs to be at the right temperature, which it is never going to be if you are just making one or two espressos after dinner. Many will nowadays use pods of coffee so that you have the right amount and ground.

Instructions: have you got an hour for the machine to warm up? Probably not. Fill the machine with water. Switch on, wait to warm up. Put the pod in the scoop-shaped thing.

THE PERFECT ESPRESSO

The first thing to say is what an espresso is not. It is not just a very strong coffee. It is a somewhat magical creation in which the oils from the coffee become emulsified as in mayonnaise, with the water creating something thick and delicious. This is achieved by forcing hot, but not boiling, water at high pressure through the grounds.

The way to spot a good espresso is if the *crema*, the foam on the top, is thick enough to hold a spoonful of sugar for a couple of seconds. Each step has to be followed scrupulously or you'll end up with something bitter and nasty. No wonder that most chains, despite good intentions and sometimes even good-quality beans, fail miserably. Antipodeans seem to make very good ones – if your barista is a bit over familiar, then you're probably on to a good coffee.

Here are the rules: the beans must be freshly roasted and of top quality; the grind should be fine but not powder; the scoop should be filled and tamped down gently so that the surface is smooth and grounds evenly distributed; the machine, the grinder and the cups should be scrupulously clean; the water should be filtered; it should always remain between 92 and 96°C; and it should be forced through the coffee grounds for 30 seconds.

BREAKFAST'S ENEMY
by Poppy Tartt

In 1890 Dr Edward Hooker Dewey wrote a book called *The No-Breakfast Plan and the Fasting Cure*. A Pennsylvanian physician with an interest in diet, Dewey knew his adversary well: 'The breakfasts in my house', he writes, 'were of a character that, without ham, sausage, eggs, steaks, or chops, they would not have been considered worth spending time over.' After a conversation with an old friend about the comparatively light breakfasts taken in Europe he concluded that 'morning hunger is a disease under culture', and devised a plan to defeat it.

He proposed that eating results in 'power wasted' in the stomach. One of his supporters summarised that his 'great remedy is to leave out the breakfast, so as to give the stomach a long rest of sixteen hours or more, with the object of allowing it to recuperate'. 'The No-Breakfast Plan', Dewey claimed, 'means for your children the best possibilities for the conservation of all the higher instincts and powers that will tend to save them from the saloon, the prison, the electric chair.'

Dewey's scheme involved advising the ailing to omit food in favour of a mere cup of coffee. Of course in all the examples he gives, the subjects find that the plan works, alleviating them from a wide range of symptoms including 'nervous prostration', indigestion, headaches, catarrh, alcoholism and mental breakdown. Whether there was any connection between the introduction of caffeine into the system and the reported rise in 'forenoon' energy is not something he was troubled to explore.

The influence of the doctor can still be felt on esoteric 'intermittent fasting' and raw veganism blogs the internet over, but for the most part his ideas have failed to find a purchase. Those who are tempted to heed Dewey's teachings should note that his death came as a result of a paralytic seizure said to be the result of a poor diet. As for everybody else, we hope you will be guided by your stomachs to look upon Dr Edward Hooker Dewey not just as a dangerous man but also as a man who should be pitied, for everything that he foolishly gave up.

COFFEE-SHOP TERMINOLOGY

Ordering a coffee can be confusing. For a time, a latte was seen as the height of sophistication. Then recently, with the sudden prominence of Antipodean-style coffees, a flat white became the caffeine hit of choice for the cosmopolitan elite. Here's a field guide to the coffees you may find on offer (at least at the time of writing – in five years, who knows?).

Ristretto (It.): An ultra-short espresso.

Espresso (It.): As per p.223. Generally just known as a *caffè* in Italy and a *café solo* in Spain.

Short Black (ANZ): Antipodean synonym for espresso.

Corretto (It.): An espresso 'corrected' with a shot of alcohol, usually grappa or sambuca.

Macchiato (It.): Usually this is an espresso with a little hot milk but there is some debate. Some say the milk should be foamed, some say it shouldn't, some say that it should be half coffee and half milk and some say it should only be a splash of milk. Some Italians even deny that it is Italian at all.

Cortado (Spain and the Spanish-speaking world): An espresso style coffee diluted with more milk than a macchiato but much less than a latte. Sometimes made with condensed milk, especially in Latin America.

Flat White (ANZ): A bit like a latte only with less milk and served in a cappuccino-style cup. The milk is heated and air is added to it but it is not frothy. Your coffee-maker will often make an elaborate pattern in the top of the milk.

Long Black (ANZ): A stronger, more flavoursome version of an Americano. Made by adding espresso to water rather than vice versa, thus retaining the *crema*.

Americano (It.): Named in honour of the American tourists who wanted their coffee weaker: espresso diluted with lots of hot water to make it the strength of filter coffee.

Cappuccino (It.): Espresso with lots of steamed and foamed milk, garnished with chocolate powder.

Caffè Latte (It. – just 'latte' in the US or UK): Lots of hot milk with a shot of espresso in it.

Mocha (US): Like a latte but with chocolate in it. Coffee for those who don't particularly like coffee.

Soya Decaf Eggnog Latte (US): See last sentence of 'mocha'.

JUICES & SMOOTHIES

TO SAY JUICE GOES BACK a long way seems a little obvious. It is just the contents of fruit; even wasps drink it. Five-thousand-year-old Ayurvedic texts from India prescribe it as medicine – orange juice with salt for fatigue, for example, or pomegranate for anaemia. When Hippocrates famously said 'Let food be thy medicine,' he partly meant juice, literally *nectar*, a Latin word which translates as 'overcoming death'.

Yet despite its million-year heritage, the juice we drink in modern times somehow manages to feel *less* historic than either tea or coffee. A coffee or tea room with wood panels, clinking crockery and bleached aprons is a sacred chamber of ritual and tradition. A juice bar is more like a child's PowerPoint presentation: primary colours are everywhere; capital letters don't exist. Canvas prints can often be seen on the walls depicting the kinds of people who arrive at an 8 a.m. breakfast having been for an eight-mile swim. It's all designed to say 'juice is healthy'. And it is. Drink it freshly squeezed every day and you may find yourself digesting vitamin C, potassium, thiamin, niacin, riboflavin, magnesium, naringenin and naringin.

When it comes to making juice at home, it can be hard not to feel that you'll need expensive machinery. There is a lot of hokum-pokum around, making it all feel like an exact science, but it's always worth remembering that you're just extracting liquid from fruit, that this is a fundamentally primitive process, and that a juicer is often completely unnecessary, as well as a nightmare to clean. Oranges and grapefruits can be squeezed in a citrus press; a cheap blender will deal with berries and most soft fruits. Costly gadgets only become necessary for hard fruits such as apples and pears and vegetables such as carrots and lettuce. We'd argue that the latter have no more place in breakfast juice than they do on the breakfast plate.

Then there is the smoothie, juice's slightly more hedonistic cousin. The exact definition of 'smoothie' is disputed, but a general rule of thumb is that it will contain yoghurt or milk or both, giving it a creamier texture and making it something of a complete breakfast in a glass. Usually it will be sweetened with honey. It's not as healthy, but is very tasty.

ORANGE JUICE

Simple, sweet, healthy, boldly coloured: orange juice is – and always will be – the most famous juice in the world. It's also one of the most nutrient dense. A recipe is unnecessary, but a satisfyingly barbaric method if you don't have a juicer is to smash each orange down firmly on a table before cutting in half and squeezing directly into a glass with the force of your hand. Four medium oranges will yield a respectable dose of around 300ml. Using a citrus squeezer is more civilised (and easier) but less impressive.

BREAKFAST JUICE

'Breakfast juice' is how a blend of orange and grapefruit juice is often sold by the big brands. The two fruits, fans will argue, counter each other's more extreme tendencies, the sweetness of the orange balancing the bitterness of the grapefruit.

Serves 2
600ml freshly squeezed orange juice
(around 9 medium oranges)
Juice of 1 grapefruit

Combine the juices. Serve immediately.

ORANGE, PAPAYA & LIME JUICE

Serves 2
1 papaya
200ml freshly squeezed orange juice
Juice of ½ lime

Blitz the papaya flesh together with the orange and lime juice. Serve in a glass with a straw.

ORANGE, APPLE, CARROT & GINGER JUICE

Serves 2
1 large orange
2 eating apples
1 large carrot
1cm slice of fresh root ginger

Extract the juice from the orange, by hand or using a citrus press (or any other method you have). Run all the other ingredients through a juicer. Stir in the orange juice. Serve.

PINEAPPLE, RASPBERRY & ORANGE JUICE

Serves 2
1 pineapple
250g raspberries
½ lime
200ml freshly squeezed orange juice

Chop up the pineapple into small chunks and blend with the raspberries. Squeeze in the lime's juice and stir it in along with the orange juice. Serve or chill immediately.

ALL-PURPOSE BREAKFAST SMOOTHIE

This recipe is delicious by itself or a good base for any breakfast smoothie. Try swapping the banana for a punnet of berries and the honey for maple syrup. Or using a washed, cored and diced apple for the fruit part and switching the nutmeg to a teaspoon of cinnamon.

Serves 2
200ml natural yoghurt
250ml milk
2 tablespoons rolled porridge oats
2 bananas
1 tablespoon clear honey
A modicum of grated fresh nutmeg

Mix the yoghurt, milk and porridge oats together and leave alone for about 5–10 minutes. Add to the blender with all the other ingredients. Blend it all together until it's smooth and thick.

MANGO LASSI

The South Asian grandfather of the Western smoothie. Adding the cream lifts the drink into a moreish and sinful place that you may or may not feel is worth going to the Hindu hell of Narakam for.

Serves 2
1 mango (hoping for around 300ml of juice when pulped)
200ml natural yoghurt
100ml milk
50ml single cream (optional)
1 cardamom pod

Peel, stone and dice the mango and blend until it's a smooth, thick juice. Mix in the other liquid ingredients. Grind the contents of the cardamom pod into a powder and stir them in. Serve or chill immediately.

ALCOHOL

AT THE BEGINNING OF Jez Butterworth's play *Jerusalem*, Johnny 'Rooster' Byron wakes up, steps out of his caravan, performs a handstand, fills a pint glass with milk, a jimmy of vodka, a freshly laid egg and a wrap of speed, and downs it in one. There is a man, thinks the audience. There stands a hero!

How much of the hardiness of Slavs is down to the Balkan habit of starting the day with a glass of Slivovica plum brandy? To what extent can we ascribe Britain's victory in the Second World War to Winston Churchill's legendary breakfast of a brace of cold snipe and a pint of port? Still more impressive are the 'cocktails' in *Moscow Stations*, Venedikt Erofeev's account of alcohol culture in the Soviet Union. The author recommends a concoction he calls a Canaan Balsam: 100ml methylated spirits, 200ml milk stout and 100ml clear varnish. Consumed first thing, it leaves the recipient requiring no further sustenance for the rest of the day, possibly ever.

These are breakfasts of good intentions, breakfasts of character. Ante-meridiem alcohol is often consumed to mitigate the effects of post-meridiem alcohol imbibed the night before. This is why the wonderfully revivifying Bloody Mary remains the most widespread of the breakfast alcohols. In P. G. Wodehouse's Jeeves and Wooster books, the admirable butler Jeeves administers to his master a tincture consisting of 60ml Scotch, 30ml double cream and a teaspoon of honey. This is to be recommended without caveat.

THE BLOODY MARY

The origins of Bloody Mary are a little cloudy but all stories point to New York. An actor named George Jessel invented a primordial version consisting of just tomato juice and vodka. Finesse and kick in the form of Worcestershire sauce and cayenne pepper were introduced by Fernand Petiot, a barman at Harry's New York Bar.

Modern recipes range from the sublime to the ridiculous. At the core of them all lie Jessel's vodka and tomato juice, usually with a tot of lemon juice, and sometimes a dizzying array of spice configurations, many of which over-complicate the matter. This drink has been too often ruined by the mediocrity of the pub Bloody Mary, so we turned our gaze to legendary barman Harry Craddock's *Savoy Cocktail Book* (1930) for inspiration. What we've created is a breakfast sharpener worthy of its cocktail status that is lighter and less soup-like than its public-house comrades, but infinitely more electrifying. This will open the palate and burst through the clouds of a hangover.

The perfect recipe uses the sweetness of home-roasted tomatoes, but if this is too arduous then use shop-bought tomato juice.

Serves 2
1kg very ripe vine cherry tomatoes
(to roast and achieve 120ml tomato juice)
Salt and pepper
90ml vodka
30ml freshly squeezed lemon juice
1 dessertspoon dry sherry
Couple of drops of Worcestershire sauce

Halve the cherry tomatoes, season liberally and roast in a warm oven (200°C/gas 6) until on the verge of blackening; this will take approximately 20 minutes. Blend and push through a sieve. Chill the strained juice.

Combine all the remaining ingredients with the tomato juice in a cocktail shaker (if using pre-packaged tomato juice, then add a pinch of sugar, salt and pepper). Shake with ice and strain into stemmed glasses. Best enjoyed before breakfast is served.

HUNTER S. THOMPSON'S BREAKFAST

'Breakfast is the only meal of the day that I tend to view with the same kind of traditionalized reverence that most people associate with Lunch and Dinner. I like to eat breakfast alone, and almost never before noon; anybody with a terminally jangled lifestyle needs at least one psychic anchor every twenty-four hours, and mine is breakfast. In Hong Kong, Dallas or at home – and regardless of whether or not I have been to bed – breakfast is a personal ritual that can only be properly observed alone, and in a spirit of genuine excess. The food factor should always be massive: four Bloody Marys, two grapefruits, a pot of coffee, Rangoon crepes, a half-pound of either sausage, bacon, or corned beef hash with diced chiles, a Spanish omelette or eggs Benedict, a quart of milk, a chopped lemon for random seasoning, and something like a slice of Key lime pie, two margaritas, and six lines of the best cocaine for dessert... All of which should be dealt with outside, in the warmth of a hot sun, and preferably stone naked.'

The Great Shark Hunt: Strange Tales from a Strange Time (1979)

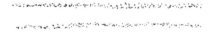

THE BLOOD TRANSFUSION

This is an excellent variation on the traditional Mary for when you are in serious trouble. It was devised by the barman Salvatore 'The Maestro' Calabrese, and makes use of the herbal liqueur Fernet Branca, which Italian mothers administer to their poorly *bambini*.

Serves 1
30ml vodka
30ml dry sherry
150ml tomato juice
30ml fresh lime juice
Pinch of celery salt
2 glugs Worcestershire sauce
30ml Fernet Branca

Fill a glass with ice cubes. Pour in the vodka and sherry, then the tomato and lime juice. Add the celery salt and Worcestershire sauce and stir. Gently pour in the Fernet Branca, allowing it to run off the back of a spoon so that it floats on top.

BUCK'S FIZZ

Buck's Fizz (note the apostrophe) was created in London in 1921 by a bartender, name of McGarry, to provide the members of the Buck's Club with an excuse for drinking in the a.m. As if they needed one. Buck's was the model for the Drones Club in P. G. Wodehouse's stories, which features prominently in the raucous short story collection *Eggs, Beans and Crumpets*. This recipe is simple enough to be made by one of the muddle-headed roustabouts who count themselves as members.

Serves 1
100ml orange juice (freshly squeezed if you can)
50ml champagne

Pour the OJ into a champagne flute. Top it up with champagne.

MIMOSA

Four years after McGarry invented Buck's Fizz, the Ritz in Paris came up with a strikingly similar recipe and called it the Mimosa, the name that is generally used outside the United Kingdom. The Mimosa has more champagne than orange juice and, correctly, a rakish ping of Grand Marnier.

Serves 1
50ml orange juice
100ml champagne
Dash of Grand Marnier

Pour the orange juice into a flute. Pour in the champagne and finish with a lick of Grand Marnier. Stir.

THE CORPSE REVIVER

In the nineteenth century, the term 'corpse reviver' seems to have referred to a whole family of cocktails, as we glean from the English journalist George Augustus Sala, who, in his *Notes and Sketches of the Paris Exhibition* (1868), observed 'cobblers', 'noggs', 'smashes', 'cocktails', 'eye openers', 'moustache twisters' and 'corpse revivers' at an American bar stand.

All but a handful are lost to posterity. However, two recipes were listed in Harry Craddock's 1930 *Savoy Cocktail Book*, and the second in particular is worth reviving. It is 'to be taken before 11 a.m., or whenever steam or energy are needed', though it comes with a warning: 'Four of these taken in swift succession will un-revive the corpse again.'

Serves 1
20ml gin
20ml Cointreau
20ml Lillet Blanc (substitute sweet white vermouth and a dash
of bitters if unavailable)
20ml fresh lemon juice
Dash of absinthe

Mix all the ingredients in a cocktail shaker over ice. Pour into a cocktail glass and consume immediately.

THE ZOMBIE REBOOTER

Joe Gilmore, one of Craddock's successors at the Savoy's American Bar, invented another corpse reviver. It is an excellent thing to drink when you are feeling completely trashed.

Serves 1
25ml cognac
25ml white crème de menthe
25ml Fernet Branca

Put the three liquids into a cocktail shaker, lob in some ice and shake. Pour the mixture into a chilled martini glass.

BREAKFAST OYSTERS

Many hangover remedies involve a raw egg suspended in a glass of alcohol. There is no generic name for such a construction. Having tossed about a few, we think 'oyster' describes the texture well. Use only the freshest and most reputable of eggs. Separate the yolk by cracking the eggshell into two equal halves over a bowl while keeping the egg in one of the halves and then slowly pouring the yolk from one half to the other, allowing the white to drip into the bowl below (you can use the white in a Whiskey Sour later).

The Russian Oyster . . . . 1 shot of vodka, 1 egg yolk
(garnish with a fresh chilli, deseeded and chopped)
The Thames Oyster . . . . 1 shot of gin, 1 egg yolk
The Glasgow Oyster . . . . 1 shot of Scotch, 1 egg yolk
The Kentucky Oyster . . . . 1 shot of bourbon, 1 egg yolk
The Baltimore Breakfast . . . . a raw egg in a glass of beer
(named after the preferred repast of the
stevedores in the television crime serial *The Wire*)

BREAKFAST QUIZ

Here are cryptic clues to 30 foodstuffs you might eat for breakfast. You might even have consumed several of them already this morning. How many can you identify? (For answers, see p.256).

11) pulp chambers

10) #sepia #beige

12) sounds regular

9) naked babes?

13) talks too much

8) small label 9

14) the Spice Girls?

7) raised glass

15) prison sentence

6) dread fibre?

16) sack the Spanish

5) can speak?

17) where golf begins?

4) Papal ova

18) America in wise herb

3) sleepers

19) hides in tall branches

2) Dutch energy

20) dark chocolate sorbet

1) gesg

21) policeman in henhouses

22) Kevin, Richard or Francis

23) limb dipped in French sick

24) evidence of peeling toes?

25) one invading angry insect

26) slime gunged all over you

27) made from geek and deer

28) price to pay for
throat-clearing

29)
something
gamekeepers
try to prevent

30) Anneka, Akabusi,
lemon meringue
and custard

Reprinted courtesy of London's finest blogger diamond geezer (diamondgeezer.blogspot.com)

BREKSTROLOGY
by La Soya Jackson

We asked an astrologer to prepare a guide to breakfast based on the ancient science of sun signs. Sceptical though we were, the results have proved frighteningly accurate.

The roots of Western astrology date back thousands of years before Christ, long before the invention of egg timers and bread machines. An astrological chart is complex and shows the precise location of the planets at the time of your birth. It is a map that is unique to you.

The readings below are based on the placement of the sun at the time of your birth. They talk of the breakfast quest we are on, not necessarily our breakfast beginnings but more the breakfasts we are born to pursue, those breakfasts which make us come alive.

ARIES
21 March–20 April

With vigour and courage you leap towards the unknown, driven forth by your ruler Mars, pursuing new ideas with fiery enthusiasm. Always needing to be first out the door, you've no time to fuss over food. A speedy kick to the adrenals is required, but a mere espresso proves too conventional. A macchiato (see p.227) is how you express your pioneering spirit.

TAURUS
21 April–21 May

Your ruler Venus imbues you with an appreciation of ceremony. You like to take it slowly, indulging in the sensual detail of every taste, preparing yourself leisurely for the day to come. Your ideal breakfast is in a garden with ingredients sourced from nature: yoghurt (see p.184) with granola (see p.160) and freshly picked peach, drizzled with local honey.

GEMINI
22 May–22 June

Ruled by changeable Mercury, you breakfast through brief encounters. When money is plentiful you are happiest hovering over a buffet at an expensive hotel, which should have a vast range of options and an omelette chef (see p.29). On frugal mornings, a variety pack containing various cereals (see p.160) may be your best way of satisfying your boundless curiosity.

CANCER

23 June–23 July

Influenced by both the emotional tides of the moon and an instinctive connection to baked goods, of course you are drawn to the croissant (see p.179). When abroad you indulge in the produce of local pâtisseries, from *pães de queijo* (see p.176) to *pastéis de nata* (see p.177). They will be served with a pot of coffee placed on a newly washed tablecloth.

LEO

24 July–23 August

Ruled by the sun, your heart is your centre, making you bold in love but easily wounded and sensitive to breakfasting slights. You feel best acknowledged when presented with an omelette Arnold Bennett (see p.122). If this isn't practical, you may be sated by truffle oil folded into buttery rich scrambled eggs (see p.24) and placed on a slice of freshly baked sourdough. Then you will shine with light and warmth and creative joy.

VIRGO

24 August–23 September

You will vary your choice of breakfast tea (see p.212) according to the region in which you find yourself; this isn't an act of regional solidarity but a meticulous sensitivity to the water quality and its effect on the quality of a brew. In your quest for perfect order you pursue precisely timed soft-boiled eggs (see p.27), or textbook eggs Benedict (see p.98) on a freshly baked English muffin (see p.75). It must be organised on an exquisitely laid breakfast table.

LIBRA

24 September–23 October

Your ruler Venus encourages you to seek self-knowledge in the reflection of another's soul. You're also never far from conflict, so it's fortunate that your charm and conciliation skills are second to none. So whether to 'make up' or to 'make out' an ideal breakfast will be one enjoyed with another. Take a bagel (see p.72) or piece of French toast (see p.169), slice it in half and share it with someone special.

SCORPIO
24 October–22 November

Ruled by controversial Pluto, you have the stamina and courage to unearth the things no one else wants to acknowledge, resulting in a life of profound transformation and deep contemplation. A solitary, existentially bracing breakfast like a fried egg taken directly from the pan (see p.21) is one you are partial to, or a Japanese 'morning set' (see p.144), eaten from behind a pair of dark glasses.

SAGITTARIUS
23 November–21 December

Ruled by abundant Jupiter, you are urged towards a lifelong quest for the higher meaning of breakfast. You may travel far abroad, deep inside or both to fulfil your first-meal potential. You seek to broaden your mind, and spirit, with kedgeree (see p.120), perhaps, or a Chinese century egg (see p.114). However you choose to take it, yours will be a journey of no return, even if you never leave the confines of your kitchen.

CAPRICORN
22 December–20 January

You are the builder of the Zodiac, ruled by Saturn, the keeper of time and the harvest of the seasons. Your purpose in life is one of hard work and your breakfast needs are of practical sustenance. You like to rise early to a very traditional breakfast of a fry-up, porridge (see p.148), or (if south of the Mason-Dixon Line) biscuits and gravy (see p.130). Such a breakfast equips you to meet the challenges you will overcome before retiring to bed only to rise, breakfast and work another day.

AQUARIUS
21 January–19 February

Ruled by revolutionary Uranus, you like to breakfast with the masses. Your radical inventive vision meanwhile draws you towards dishes that will transform breakfast as we know it: you seek an adventurous yet shareable breakfast of *baozi* (see p.141) or *shakshuka* (see p.106). Although you are fiercely independent your pursuit of freedom must be fair; you are on the side of truth and know that if a breakfast is good for one it is good for all.

PISCES
20 February–20 March
Like your ruler Neptune you are hard to pin down. You are imaginative, sensitive and elusive; letting go comes easily to you. You have transcended the boundaries of any breakfast: they are like water passing through fingers. You crack a raw egg into a large glass of vodka and merge with the essence of the day. Buck's fizz (see p.236), corpse reviver (see p.237), last night's pizza? It doesn't matter because to you there is no division. You know the magic of oneness and life just flows.

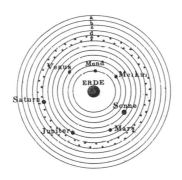

Seb Emina

For reasons of propriety and as proof of sanity I need to point out that when the book refers to 'we' it does not mean 'my pseudonym Malcolm Eggs and I' but 'I and the four others with whom I have collaborated'. Emily Berry, Richard Godwin, Henry Jeffreys and Peter Meanwell have been instrumental in compiling and writing the recipes, stories and oeuf-piste asides of which this book is made. Other much-valued contributors (of recipes, horoscopes, quizzes etc.) include Naomi Alderman, Rachel Anderson, Jean Hannah Edelstein, Rose Enright, Diamond Geezer, Helen Graves, Heather Kossow, Sanjana Modha, Tiffany Morris, Sarah-Jane Nelson and Rosalind Rathouse.

This book was only possible due to the vision and editorial fastidiousness of Bloomsbury Publishing. Thank you so much to my editors, Richard Atkinson and Natalie Hunt, who dished out valuable encouragement and criticism that turned it into something far better than it would otherwise have been. Will Webb deserves undying gratitude for the cover alone, let alone the amazing design inside. Thanks to Andy Sewell for the remarkable photographs, including that seminal portrayal of a baked bean militia. Also in the world of Bloomsbury (and its wider diaspora), thanks are due to Anne Askwith, Laura Brooke, Susan Fleming, Alexa von Hirschberg, Colin Midson, Anya Rosenberg, Xa Shaw Stewart, Tess Viljoen and everyone who has worked or will work on this book.

A huge collop of thanks to my agent Matthew Hamilton at Aitken Alexander for buying me breakfast one morning then choosing the right idea from the three I had brought along with me, and for shaping and advocating it so brilliantly; and to Jocasta Hamilton for talking to me about it all before I had even spoken to Matthew.

Others who have offered moral, material or breakfast-based support include Zoe Brauer, Jonathan Brown, Caravan Exmouth Market, Serge Cartwright, Miranda Cavanagh, Temra Costa, Matilda Culme-Seymour, Russell Davies, Hattie Ellis, Peter Emina, Laura Ford, Sue and Steve Fowler, Jess Gormley,

Amin Hasan, Laura Hassan, Tim Hayward, Keren Kossow, Alexis Mersel, Dean Moiler, Mandy Robinson and Andrew Samtoy. Thanks to Lauren Elkin for inspiring me (and editing me) as I made it through the final stretch. Thanks to my mother, Carole Wingett, for the breakfasts of my childhood, and to my grandmother, Greta Wingett.

Thanks to all those who have contributed to The London Review of Breakfasts, namely Damon Allbran, Koffee Annan, Maggie Arto, Flora Ashley, Des Ayuno, Chris P. Bacon, Megan Bacon, Herby Banger, Tina Beans, Salmon de Beauvoir, Ed Benedict, Georges Berecfast, Vita Bicks, Morcilla Black, Homefries Bogart, Gregg E. Bread, Reggie Brek, Farls Bronson, Hashley Brown, Dee Caff, Pam Cakes, Johnny Cep, Scott Cheigg, Pam au Chocolat, Eggatha Chrispie, Molly Coddle-Degg, Captain Cook, Armand Croissant, Henrietta Crumpet, Mariah Dairy, Holly N. Daise, Orva Easy, Duke Eggington, Phil English, Bob el Ensquique, Corin Flakes, Sian Flakes, Sebastian Forks, Dr Sigmund Fried, Sadie Frosties, Stephen Fry-Up, Cherie Funghi, Fidel Gastro, Muffin Gaye, Nelson Griddle, A. A. Grill, Brannie Hall, Paddy Hashbrown, Kiwi Herman, Eggmund Hillary, Billie Hollandaise, La Soya Jackson, Cher E. Jamm, Tommy Kay, Caff Kidston, Veggie Kray, Shreddie Kruger, Mama Lade, Grits Lang, Cathy Latte, Moose Lee, Bee Loobury, Eggy Mair, Pam de Mie, Bloody Mary, Typhoo Mary, Egg Miliband, Mack Muffin, Fleeter Noggins, Ronnie Oak, Haulin' Oats, Joyce Carol Oats, Yolko Ono, Anne O'Raisin, Bree Oshe, Hamish Pastry, Rhys Chris Peese, Al Penn, Sultan Pepper, Emmanuel Petit-Déjeuner, S. Presso, Blake Pudding, Goldie Quorn, Jane Rasher, Saul T. Rasher, Marge E. Reen, Emma Ricano, Dieggo Rivera, Séggolène Royal, Heidi Sausage, Mustapha Sausage, Brian Sauce, H. P. Seuss, Sunni Sidup, O. J. Simpson, Daw Aung San Mue Sli, Louie Slinger, Duncan Soldiers, Gracie Spoon, Juan Sugar, Kipper Sutherland, Mabel Syrup, Poppy Tartt, Fi Tatta, Terry Teagleton, Bernie Toast, Egon Toast, Fyodor Toastoevsky, T. N. Toost, Alotta Waffle, Evelyn Waughffle, Grease Witherspoon, Brad Wurst, Private Yolk and Thom Yolke.

Emily Berry

For inspiration, information, breakfast companionship and/or other forms of assistance, I would like to thank Peter Barry, Neil Berry, the incredibly well-stocked Bumblebee Natural Foods, Victoria Gray (winner of her primary school's My Favourite Meal of the Day art competition with her Hockney-esque painting of breakfast), Becky Hendry, Anna Jones, Lois Lee and the Loizos family. Thanks also to everyone who recommended literary breakfasts of note.

Richard Godwin

I would like to thank Johanna, my wife, the ideal breakfast partner – and Julian, James and Alex, my childhood friends, whose theories and fieldwork were a formative influence on my breakfasting.

Henry Jeffreys

I'd like to thank my wife Misti, my mother for her endless patience teaching me to make marmalade, Taylors of Harrogate and Tom Norrington-Davies, whose omelette Arnie Bennett I've shamelessly pinched/adapted from the recipe in *Cupboard Love*.

Peter Meanwell

I'd like to thank my vegetarian wife for her tolerance of all things bloody in the kitchen; all at Highbury Butchers for their meaty generosity; Tom for a night of science-grade Bloody Mary-making; Dean, Eleanor, Mark, Shasta, Sam & Kate Brown of Mt. Airy, North Carolina, for the crash course in the ways of the Southern breakfast; Tom and Eiko for their Japanese wisdom; David and Sylvia for the regular supplies of laverbread; Anna and Ben for the pre-nup poached eggs; and James and Seb for their breakfasting consistency over the years.

INDEX

First published in Great Britain 2013
This paperback edition published 2015

Text © 2013 by Seb Emina
Contributions from Emily Berry, Richard Godwin, Henry Jeffreys, Peter Meanwell
Photography © 2013 by Andy Sewell

The moral right of the author has been asserted

Bloomsbury Publishing Plc, 50 Bedford Square, London WC1B 3DP
Bloomsbury Publishing, London, New Delhi, New York and Sydney

Bloomsbury is a trademark of Bloomsbury Publishing Plc

A CIP catalogue record for this book is available from the British Library

ISBN 978 1 4088 4272 0

Designer: Will Webb
Photographer: Andy Sewell

10 9 8 7 6 5 4 3 2 1

Printed in China by C & C Offset Printing Co Ltd

All papers used by Bloomsbury Publishing are natural, recyclable products made from wood grown in well-managed forests. The manufacturing processes conform to the environmental regulations of the country of origin.

Excerpt on p.11 from *The House at Pooh Corner* by A. A. Milne. Text © The Trustees of the Pooh Properties WTP 1926. Published by Egmont UK Ltd London and used with permission. Excerpt on p.252 from *The Great Shark Hunt: Strange Tales from a Strange Time* © Hunter S. Thompson, 1979. Printed by permission of Pan Macmillan, London. Every reasonable effort has been made to trace copyright holders of material reproduced in this book, but if any have been inadvertently overlooked the publishers would be glad to hear from them.

www.bloomsbury.com/sebemina

Answers to quiz on p.239

1) Scrambled eggs • 2) Orange juice • 3) Kippers • 4) Eggs Benedict • 5) Pancakes •
6) Fried bread • 7) Toast • 8) Weetabix • 9) Baked beans • 10) Hash browns •
11) Mushrooms • 12) Cereal • 13) Waffles • 14) Pop Tarts • 15) Porridge • 16) Bagel •
17) Tea • 18) Sausage • 19) All Bran • 20) Black pudding • 21) Coco Pops • 22) Bacon •
23) Marmalade • 24) Corn Flakes • 25) Croissant • 26) Muesli • 27) Kedgeree •
28) Coffee • 29) Poached eggs • 30) Rice Krispies